WITHDRAWN

The Independent State of Croatia 1941–45

The Independent State of Croatia 1941–45 contains important new scholarship from a variety of perspectives on the structure, ideology and political history of the central fascist group in interwar and World War II Yugoslavia, the Croatian Ustaša.

This book represents the first study in English to closely explore the Ustaša's Independent State of Croatia between 1941 and 1945, a period when it was active collaborator with nazi Germany and Fascist Italy. By using the top scholars in the field to explore the nature of the NDH, this book contributes to scholarly understandings of Croatian nationalism, Balkan politics, European fascism, and genocide in World War II.

This book was previously published as a special issue of *Totalitarian Movements and Political Religions*

Sabrina P. Ramet is at the Department of Sociology and Political Science at the Norwegian University of Science and Technology.

Totalitarian Movements and Political Religions
Series Editors: (**Michael Burleigh**, Washington and Lee University, Virginia) and *Robert Mallett*, University of Birmingham.

This innovative new book series will scrutinise all attempts to totally refashion mankind and society, whether these hailed from the Left or the Right, which, unusually, will receive equal consideration. Although its primary focus will be on the authoritarian and totalitarian politics of the twentieth century, the series will also provide a forum for the wider discussion of the politics of faith and salvation in general, together with an examination of their inexorably catastrophic consequences. There are no chronological or geographical limitations to the books that may be included, and the series will include reprints of classic works and translations, as well as monographs and collections of essays.

International Fascism, 1919–45
Edited by **Gert Sorensen**, University of Copenhagen and **Robert Mallett**, University of Birmingham

Totalitarian Democracy and After
International Colloquium in memory of Jacob Talmon
Edited by Yehoshua Arieli and **Nathan Rotenstreich**

Religion, Politics and Ideology in the Third Reich
Selected Essays
Uriel Tal, with In Memoriam by Saul Friedländer

The Seizure of Power
Fascism in Italy 1919–1929
Adrian Lyttelton

The French and Italian Communist Parties
Comrades and Culture
Cyrille Guiat, Herriott-Watt University, Edinburgh
Foreword by **David Bell**

The Lesser Evil
Moral Approaches to Genocide Practices
Edited by **Helmut Dubiel** and **Gabriel Motzkin**

Fascism as a Totalitarian Movement
Roger Griffin

The Italian Road to Totalitarianism
Emilio Gentile
Translated by **Robert Mallett**

Religion, Politics and Ideology in the Third Reich
Selected Essays
Uriel Tal, with in *memoriam* by **Saul Friedländer**

Totalitarianism and Political Religions, Volume 1
Concepts for the Comparison of Dictatorships
Edited by **Hans Maier**

Stalinism at the Turn of the Milennium:
Russian and Western Views
John Keep and Alter Litvin

Totalitarianism and Political Religions, Volume II
Concepts for the Comparison of Dictatorships
Edited by **Hans Maier / Michael Schäfer**
Translated by **Jodi Bruhn**

Totalitarinism and Political Religions, Volume III
Concepts for the Comparison of Dictatorships - Theory and History of Interpretation
Edited by **Hans Maier**
Translated by **Jodi Bruhn**

The Independent State of Croatia 1941–45
Edited by **Sabrina P. Ramet**

The Independent State of Croatia 1941–45

Edited by Sabrina P. Ramet

LONDON AND NEW YORK

First published 2007 by Routledge
2 Park Square, Milton Park, Abingdon, Oxon, OX14 4RN

Simultaneously published in the USA and Canada
by Routledge
270 Madison Avenue, New York, NY 10016

Routledge is an imprint of the Taylor & Francis Group, an informa business

© 2007 Edited by Sabrina P Ramet

Typeset in Palatino by Genesis Typesetting Ltd, Rochester, Kent
Printed and bound in Great Britain by MPG Books Ltd, Bodmin, Cornwall

All rights reserved. No part of this book may be reprinted or reproduced or utilised in any form or by any electronic, mechanical, or other means, now known or hereafter invented, including photocopying and recording, or in any information storage or retrieval system, without permission in writing from the publishers.

British Library Cataloguing in Publication Data
A catalogue record for his book is available from the British Library

Library of Congress Cataloging in Publication Data

ISBN 10: 0-415-44055-6
ISBN 13: 978-0-415-44055-4 hbk

CONTENTS

List of Contributors	vi
1 The NDH – An Introduction SABRINA P. RAMET	1
2 The NDH State in Comparative Perspective STANLEY G. PAYNE	11
3 The Independent State of Croatia in 1941: On the Road to Catastrophe IVO GOLDSTEIN	19
4 Controversies surrounding the Catholic Church in Wartime Croatia, 1941–45 MARK BIONDICH	31
5 The NDH's relations with Italy and Germany MARIO JAREB	61
6 The NDH's relations with Southeast European Countries, Turkey and Japan, 1941–45 NADA KISIĆ KOLANOVIĆ	75
RESOURCES	
7 Personalities in the History of the NDH	95
Bibliography	101
Index	105

Notes on Contributors

Sabrina Petra Ramet is a Professor of Political Science at the Norwegian University of Science and Technology (NTNU), in Trondheim, Norway, and a Senior Associate of the Centre for the Study of Civil War, of the International Peace Research Institute in Oslo (PRIO). Her book, *Whose Democracy? Nationalism, Religion, and the Doctrine of Collective Rights in Post-1989 Eastern Europe*, was named an Outstanding Academic Book for 1997 by *Choice* magazine. Her latest book is *The Three Yugoslavias: State-building and Legitimation, 1918—2005*, co-published by the Wilson Center Press and Indiana University Press (2006).

Stanley G. Payne is Hilldale-Jaume Vicens Vives Professor of History Emeritus at the University of Wisconsin-Madison. His most recent book is *The Collapse of the Spanish Republic, 1933–1936: Origins of the Civil War* (Yale University Press, 2006).

Mark Biondich is Chief Historian (acting) of the Crimes Against Humanity and War Crimes Section of the Department of Justice, Canada. The views expressed in this article are those of the author and do not represent the opinions of the Department of Justice, Canada.

Ivo Goldstein is Professor of History at the University of Zagreb. Originally specialising in Byzantine and medieval history, he has focused more recently on 20th-century Croatian history. Among his books are *Croatia: A History* (McGill-Queen's University Press, 1999), *Holokaust u Zagrebu*, with Slavko Goldstein (Novi Liber, 2001), and *Židovi u Zagrebu, 1918—1941* (Novi Liber, 2004).

Mario Jareb was awarded a PhD in History at the Faculty of Philosophy of the University of Zagreb (Croatia) in 2003, and was a Fulbright Program Student at Indiana University, Bloomington, in 2001–2002. His research focuses on the history of the Independent State of Croatia, particularly the NDH media and propaganda. His book *Ustaško-domobranski pokret od nastanka do travnja 1941. godine* [*The Ustaša-Domobran Movement from its Emergence to April 1941*] was published in 2006 (Zagreb: Školska knjiga and Hrvatski institut za povijest, 2006).

Nada Kisić Kolanović is a historian working at the Croatian Institute for History (Zagreb). She is the author of *Andrija Hebrang. Iluzije i otrežnjenja* (Zagreb: Institut za suvremenu povijest, 1996), *NDH i Italija. Političke veze i diplomatski odnosi* (Zagreb: Ljevak, 2001), and *Zagreb-Sofija. Prijateljstvo po mjeri ratnog vremena 1941.—1945.* (Zagreb: Hrvatski državni arhivi & Dom i svijet, 2003). She also edited the memoirs of Slavko Kvaternik, under the title *Vojskovodja i politika. Sjećanja Slavka Kvaternika* (Zagreb: Golden Marketing, 1997).

James J. Sadkovich is a Research Associate at George Mason University. He is the author of numerous studies dealing with Yugoslavia and Italy, including *Italian Support for Croatian Separatism, 1927–1937* (Garland, 1987) and *The U.S. Media and Yugoslavia, 1991–1995* (Praeger, 1998). He is currently working on a biography of Franjo Tudjman.

The NDH – An Introduction

SABRINA P. RAMET
Norwegian University of Science and Technology

The Independent State of Croatia (Nezavisna Država Hrvatska, NDH) lasted barely four years, from its proclamation on 10 April 1941 to the entry of Partisan forces into Zagreb on 8 May 1945. During those four years, the Ustaša Party that ruled the NDH conducted a savage policy aimed at fashioning a largely homogeneous state out of a heterogeneous population. The method which was employed involved a combination of extermination and expulsion of Serbs, Jews, Roma,[1] and others deemed 'undesirable' by the ruling party. About 1,027,000 people of all nationality groups lost their lives as a result of unnatural causes in Yugoslavia during the Second World War, according to scholarly research conducted by the Croatian demographer, Vladimir Žerjavić; of this number about 623,000 lost their lives in the Independent State of Croatia.[2] Of the latter, some died in concentration camps operated by the Ustaše, others died as a result of exterminations, whether by the Ustaše,[3] the Chetniks, the Partisans, or by Axis occupation forces. Still others were combat casualties.

The NDH regime was the most brutal and most sanguinary satellite regime in the Axis sphere of influence during the Second World War.[4] From time to time there have been those wanting either to whitewash the NDH or to equate the Serbian collaborationist state of Milan Nedić with the NDH, whether in moral terms or in functional terms. Both of these theses must be rejected. Although the NDH was occupied by Axis troops, the Ustaše enjoyed tangibly more internal autonomy than Nedic's state; thus, while the NDH operated the concentration camps within its territory, the camps in occupied Serbia were operated by German occupation forces. Indeed, General Edmund Glaise von Horstenau, the General-Plenipotentiary representing the *Wehrmacht* in the NDH, met with Ante Pavelić, the *Poglavnik* [Leader] of the NDH, as early as July 1941, to express 'his grave concern over the excesses of the Ustaše'; and Herbert Troll-Oberfell, *chargé d'affaires* in Croatia, reported back to Berlin that same month that there had been 'acts of terror and excesses by the Ustaše committed against the Serbian population in many regions of the country', and characterised these acts as 'dangerous' for the war effort. He drew the logical conclusion and declared that it was 'necessary ... to limit these occurrences'.[5]

Nor would it be appropriate to suppose that wartime Croatia and Serbia were morally equivalent. The Ustaša movement was founded on the principles of racialism and intolerance and welcomed the break-up of the Yugoslav state, equating the Axis occupation with national freedom. By contrast, Milan Nedić, in a speech delivered on 2 September 1941, admitted more forthrightly that the German occupation signified a loss of freedom and warned that Serbs 'are facing

2 The Independent State of Croatia 1941–45

the danger of national extinction', claiming that he 'came into the government to save the people, to keep them from destroying each other'.[6] This by no means diminished the high esteem in which German authorities held Nedić, however.[7] (Some observers might also note that the NDH was ethnically more heterogeneous than Nedić's Serbia, although the relative heterogeneity of a country does not, in and of itself, say *anything* about the character of its regime.)

Nonetheless, it should be acknowledged, as already noted, that the NDH was an occupied country and that Ustaša rule was sustained for four years by the presence of German troops and, until 1943, Italian troops as well. Moreover, as early as May 1941, the German and Croatian governments agreed that German economic interests in Croatia would enjoy 'special consideration', that Germany might 'continue unrestricted exploitation of industrial raw materials, in particular minerals', that German companies would enjoy concessions in the oil sector in Croatia, and that 'the expenses of German military installations, in so far as these are expenses arising within the country itself, will be borne for the duration of the war by Croatia'.[8]

Even today, 60 years after the end of the Second World War, the NDH remains the subject of controversy. There are controversies about how many people were killed at the Jasenovac concentration camp,[9] about what happened to gold held by the Ustaša regime,[10] about the attitude of Zagreb's Archbishop Alojize Stepinac toward the NDH and the Church's response to the NDH's use of force to promote the conversion of Serbs to Catholicism;[11] even about whether the NDH should be seen as having been an embodiment of Croatian statehood, as suggested at one point by Franjo Tudjman, president of Croatia in 1990–99. Where Stepinac is concerned, one may distinguish among 'hard critics', 'soft critics', 'hard defenders', and 'soft defenders'. The 'hard critics' accuse the archbishop of various things, including treason, outright collaboration with the NDH, complicity in the forced conversions of Serbs, silence in the face of Ustaša atrocities, and sometimes even complicity in war crimes. At the other extreme, 'hard defenders' view Stepinac as a saint, whose every word and action stands as an inspiration for subsequent generations, a courageous critic of the NDH, the rescuer of Serbs and Jews, a man who refused to condone the regime's efforts to usurp the Church's authority in conversions, and an orator, the transcripts of whose sermons were read over the Partisan radio. While the 'hard critics' are typically motivated by Serb nationalism, old-style communism, hatred of Croats, or naïve ignorance, the 'hard defenders' are driven by wishful thinking and, usually, by Croatian nationalism as well. Between these extremes one may identify 'soft critics' and 'soft defenders', who share a mixed view of Stepinac, rejecting monochromatic representations of the archbishop. The chief difference between the two consists in the tendency of the 'soft critics' to downplay or ignore those sermons of Stepinac in which he criticised the NDH and its practices, and the tendency of the 'soft defenders' to emphasise precisely these sermons. Both groups admit that Stepinac's visit (*prior* to the capitulation of Yugoslavia) to Kvaternik in order to congratulate him on the establishment of the NDH was inappropriate – though Stepinac's critics are more likely to trace this to nationalism on Stepinac's part – while his defenders are more likely to suggest that the visit was due to a lapse of judgment on his part. Both groups further point out that *Katolički list*, the official organ of the archdiocese of Zagreb, repeatedly condemned racism, and that Stepinac repeatedly sought to defend and assist the victims of the NDH, as in May 1943, when the archbishop wrote to Andrija

Artuković to demand that he allow the Jewish religious district to continue to function freely.[12] But both 'soft critics' and 'soft defenders' also note that Stepinac was less resolute about defending non-Catholics than he was about defending Catholics, including recent converts to Catholicism. Moreover, 'soft defenders' have trouble explaining why, just two weeks after the proclamation of the NDH, Archbishop Stepinac contacted Artuković, Minister of the Interior, *not* to try to protest against the restrictions which were being imposed on the country's Jews, but to ask for an exemption for 'good Catholics of the Jewish race who have been converted to Catholicism', whom Stepinac characterised as 'good Croatian patriots'.[13]

As Nada Kisić Kolanović has pointed out,[14] there have been alternative schools of thought among Croats in approaching the NDH. She notes that, until 1990, two schools dominated scholarly approaches to the NDH: the Marxist school of critical analysis, which she identifies with Fikreta Jelić-Butić and Bogdan Krizman, whose works commanded the field in the 1970s and 1980s; and the nostalgic-apologetic school, which began among Croats in Buenos Aires and which she identifies with Vinko Nikolić and Antun Bonéfačić. She credits Jere Jareb, who occupied academic positions in the United States between 1966 and 1992 before returning to Croatia, with having made the first serious endeavour to write about Croatian history free of either Marxist methodology or nostalgic-apologetic assumptions.[15] Today one can also speak of a liberal school of analysis, which is critical of the NDH from a classical liberal point of view, rather than from a Marxist perspective.[16]

Because of its independence from Belgrade (though not from Berlin) and because of its association with anti-Serb and anti-Allied politics, the NDH would later serve as a rallying symbol for those wanting to declare their antipathy toward Serbia (during the War of Yugoslav Succession[17]) and the European Union (since 1995). Hence, in late 2004, as the EU turned up the heat on Zagreb to pressure the Croatian government to locate the fugitive General, Ante Gotovina, who had been indicted for war crimes in connection with the liberation of the Krajina from Serb occupation, graffiti appeared in Zadar for Gotovina and the NDH![18] In response to such expressions, Stjepan Mesić, president of Croatia since 2000, declared in April 2005: 'Those who think that by defending the NDH they are defending Croatia, are completely confused, because [the Independent State of Croatia] was not independent, was not a state, and was not Croatia'.[19]

Nearly a decade earlier, President Franjo Tudjman stirred controversy by suggesting that the body of Ante Pavelić be returned to Croatia from Spain and that the last remains of Yugoslavia's long-time president, Josip Broz Tito, be turned over to Croatia by Serbia, so that the bodies of the two sworn enemies might be buried side by side.[20] Tito's body remains in Belgrade and Pavelić's in Madrid. Ominously, at about the same time the New Croatian Right (*Nova Hrvatska Desnica*, or NHD)[21] registered its demand that Zagreb's Marshal Tito Square be renamed for Pavelić.[22] Tudjman, who had served in the ranks of the antii-fascist Partisans during the Second World War, continued to nurture respect for Tito,[23] but his endeavour to achieve a 'reconciliation' of antagonistic political currents in Croatia created a space in which strange things happened, such as the memorial mass conducted in Zagreb by Father Vjekoslav Lasić in December 1998 – the 39th anniversary of Pavelić's death – attended by several members of parliament. Following this mass, Archbishop Josip Bozanić asked the head of the Dominican Order to check into the allegation that Lasić had conducted such a mass, while a spokesperson for Tudjman's HDZ (Croatian Democratic Union) condemned the holding of a memorial mass for Pavelić as 'unacceptable and undemocratic'.[24] In spite of the government's efforts to stop such occurrences, there have also been reports of several similar incidents after the death of President Tudjman in December 1999. For example, the pop singer Marko Perković Thompson became popular with right-wing Croats, through his racist and xenophobic songs. After the performance of his song 'Jasenovac and Gradiška Stara' (named for concentration camps in the NDH) in 2004, Thompson was brought in for questioning by the police in Zagreb.[25] Later that same year, the HDZ expelled from its ranks Davor Aras, President of the city council of Zadar, after he attended a gathering of the Croatian Domobran association, where members wore Ustaša insignia and displayed photographs of Pavelić; President Mesić also condemned the rally.[26]

One of the *Poglavnik's* most ardent defenders has been his daughter, Višnja, who has claimed, against all evidence, that her father 'never liked fascism and certainly not Nazism', but that he 'had to accept certain things that he didn't like' for the sake of Croatia's own welfare.[27] Her selective interpretation remains a minority view; indeed, most of Pavelić's latter-day defenders are happy to defend fascism as well. In fact, the record of what happened in the NDH and who was responsible is both clear and well documented.

The population of the NDH as of April 1941 stood at about 6 million,[28] consisting of about 3 million Croats, almost 2 million Serbs, between 500,000 and 800,000 Bosnian Muslims, 140,000 *Volksdeutsche,* 70,000 Hungarians, 35–36,000 Jews, and about 150,000 members of other nationality groups (including Slovenes, Czechs, Slovaks, and Ukrainians).[29] About 307,000 Serbs are reported by Vladimir Žerjavić to have perished within the territory which would later comprise the socialist republics of Croatia and Bosnia-Herzegovina, alongside 255,000 Croats.[30] About 28,000 Jews either lost their lives at the hands of the NDH authorities or ended up in German concentration camps; another 4,000 or more managed to escape from the country, in many cases as a result of assistance from the Italian forces.[31]

Insofar as the extermination and expulsion of entire groups of people lay at the very core of NDH policy, that programme must be judged to have been genocidal in character. Indeed, the decree on the defence of the people and the state, already issued on 17 April 1941, laid the groundwork for the subsequent terror. The NDH authorities established the Office for Public Order and Security, as well as the *Ustaška nadzorna služba* [Ustaša Surveillance Service, or UNS, which would be renamed in January 1943 and placed under the jurisdiction of the Ministry of the Interior[32]]; the Third Division of the UNS was known as the Ustaša Defense and, together with the Office for Public Order and Security, was responsible for killing those who were judged to be 'undesirable'.[33] Although Jasenovac is the most notorious and best known of the NDH's concentration camps, it was not the only one. There were some 26 concentration camps in all, including installations at Drnje (the first such camp to be established),[34] Stara Gradiška, Jadovno, Slano, Metajna on the island of Pag, Kerestinec (in the vicinity of Zagreb), Lepoglava, Jastrebarsko (for the internment of children), Tenje (used for the internment of Jews), Djakovo, Loborgrad, and elsewhere. (The camps at Jadovno, Slano, and Metajna were closed in August 1941). According to recent scholarly research in Croatia, some 80,000–90,000 persons were liquidated at Jasenovac alone.[35]

The NDH endeavoured to represent itself as an organic part of Croatian culture and history, rather than as representing and effecting a dramatic rupture with the past. To this end, the Ustaše tried to lay claim to the legacy of Ante Starčević, Milan Šufflay, and even the Radić brothers.[36] In this connection, the Ustaše drew up plans to erect monuments to Starčević, the renowned Croatian liberal, in Zagreb and Banja Luka.[37] This was a falsifaction of Starčević's legacy, causing the nineteenth-century liberal's championing of human equality – including women's equality – to disappear from (their) sight.[38] Perhaps surprisingly, in spite of the regime's promotion of 'traditional' models of gender behaviour,[39] the regime was relatively tolerant in the cultural sphere.[40] Be that as it may, in spite of the Ustaša regime's professed Catholicism (a faith preaching centrality of Natural Law and Natural Right), citizens of the NDH were advised that they had no rights save those recognised by the state since, as the regime news organ *Hrvatski narod* (Croatian people) put it in 1942, 'Neither the individual nor the group is comprehensible outside the framework of the state'.[41] Within that framework, the regime issued two decrees at the end of April 1941, defining what it is to be Aryan and prohibiting marriage between Aryans and non-Aryans. The regime also paid attention to language issues, issuing a decree on 14 August 1941 regulating the orthography of the Croatian language and banning the use of foreign (i.e., Serbian) pronunciation and spelling, as well as foreign words 'borrowed from other, even similar languages' where they were not in conformity 'with the spirit of the Croatian language' and where Croatian equivalents were available.[42] The NDH banned the use of the Cyrillic alphabet as early as 25 April 1941, and undertook efforts to root out words that were viewed as Serbisms.[43] The regime also demanded that people think in an Ustaša way and talked of eradicating those thought to be behaving in an 'un-Croatian' way.[44]

Given their racial orientation, the Ustaše inevitably thought also of population exchange as a 'remedy' for ethnic heterogeneity. In practice, the NDH thought in terms of swapping 179,000 Serbs, whom they would expel to German-occupied Serbia, for 179,000 Slovenes who would be deported from German-occupied Slovenia (earmarked for incorporation into the Third Reich) and sent to Bosnia, with a somewhat smaller number to be settled in northern Croatia. But the resettlement of Serbs from the NDH was not carried out in an organised way, and was accompanied by a level of violence which even German authorities found shocking.[45]

During the War of Yugoslav Succession (1991–95), the Serbian propaganda machine made much of the atrocities committed in the NDH, and even managed to convince some naïve western journalists that the sins of the fathers somehow justified the sins of the sons. Yet, in spite of the long shadow cast by the NDH over socialist Yugoslavia (including the use made of the NDH by the communist regime to tarnish those advocating greater autonomy for Croatia); in spite of the way in which it figured in Serbian wartime propaganda more recently and, for that matter, in spite of the importance of analysing the NDH as a historical phenomenon, as a first step toward establishing what is common and what is not common to fascist regimes, there has been little published in English up to now. The collection of articles in this volume is an attempt to remedy this deficit.

This collection takes, as its focal points, the themes of ideology, genocide, and religion. As a renegade state surrounded by renegade states, the NDH's pursuit of genocidal policies and forced religious conversion was facilitated by the continent-wide war as well as by the Axis occupation of Croatia itself. But for the presence of German and Italian forces, the Partisans might – it may be speculated – have overthrown the NDH state much earlier. But genocide and forced religious conversion were justified by an ideology of racialism, in which the alleged 'Aryan' character of the Catholic and Muslim Croats was contrasted with the alleged 'non-Aryan' character of the Orthodox Serbs. As a specific incarnation of radical-right thinking, *Ustašism* rejected the heritage of the Enlightenment – rationalism and liberalism – substituting irrationalism and illiberalism in their stead. Thus, while classical liberalism touts the importance of the rule of law, individual rights, tolerance, respect for the harm principle, the equality of people, and the neutrality of the state in matters of religion, *Ustašism,* in a manner typical of radical-right formations, set the leader *above* the law, replaced individual rights with a notion of collective rights, declared the inequality of peoples, allowed for intolerance and violence toward those lower on the racial hierarchy, and gave preferential treatment to Catholicism, even while demeaning it by turning it into an instrument of state.

Stanley Payne sets the NDH in its political context, comparing and contrasting it with other radical right regimes in its day, including Monsignor Tiso's Slovak state and Marshal Petain's Vichy Republic. He notes that the Ustaša movement began without an elaborately developed ideology and that, in the beginning, it was more closely comparable to the Internal Macedonian Revolutionary Organization (IMRO) than to, let us say, Benito Mussolini's Fascists. In the course of the 1930s, however, the movement came under the influence of Nazi ideology in the first place, and Italian Fascism only secondarily. He traces the emergence of the Ustaše's racial ideology, at least in part, to the influence of the Third Reich. The claim that Croats were 'Goths' (whatever that might mean) rather than Slavs was one element in that ideology and provided an ideological groundwork for asserting that Croats (Goths) and Serbs (Slavs) were not related. Payne notes that the NDH introduced a number of features common among classical fascist states, including one-party rule, a racial policy, representation of professional and labour units in the assembly, a regime-sponsored youth organisation, and a regime-sponsored organisation for women, among others. In consequence, its institutional form was closer to that of Fascist Italy than to that of Nazi Germany, while its racial policy was closer to that exercised by the Third Reich.

In the next article, Ivo Goldstein offers an explanation of Ustaša violence against Serbs, Jews, and Roma, tracing this to the regime's ideological basis. For Goldstein, it is vital to understand *Ustašism* as 'a specific mixture of German Naziism and Italian Fascism'. He identifies the killing of 196 Serb men from Gudovac and its environs on 27–28 April 1941 as the first mass murder perpetrated by the Ustaše. He draws attention, too, to the importance of the Third Reich in setting the parameters for NDH policies as well as in providing an incentive for the persecution and extermination of Jews. Indeed, the Third Reich was a vital source of support for the renegade regime, as Goldstein notes. He describes how Croats generally greeted the German Army when it first entered Zagreb and other towns in Croatia, and welcomed the establishment of a supposedly independent Croatia. But, as he notes, 'disappointment soon set in and sympathy evaporated… [The] racial and ethnic persecution of Serbs, Jews, and Roma, and cruel terror over political opponents, antagonized most of the Croatian population and made them feel insecure'.

In the following article, Mark Biondich examines the controversies concerning the Catholic Church in the NDH – focusing especially on the allegation that the Catholic Church was in collusion with the NDH – the attitude of the Church toward the forced conversions, the participation of Catholic clergy in the Ustaša

Party and its functions, and the alleged 'refusal of the Church to condemn openly and unequivocally the genocidal policies of the Ustaša authorities'. Biondich suggests that Archbishop Stepinac was disenchanted with the NDH before the end of summer 1941, but speculates that 'it may not have been entirely clear to Stepinac' at that time that the atrocities being committed were part of a systematic plan rather than merely the excesses of fanatics. He therefore concludes, as Klaus Buchenau has elsewhere,[46] that Stepinac was innocent of the charge later brought against him by the communists that he had colluded with the NDH. On the other hand, he concedes that 'the Ustaša movement enjoyed the support of a substantial segment of the Catholic clergy in Croatia and Bosnia-Herzegovina'.

Much has been made of the forced conversions of Serbs to the Catholic faith, but Biondich points out that there were also a few conversions to the Lutheran Church as well as to Islam, with the latter justified in the eyes of the NDH leaders on the argument that the Muslims of Bosnia-Herzegovina were themselves Islamicised Croats. On the other hand, as Biondich points out, it was specifically the *Roman* Catholic faith to which conversions were encouraged; conversions to the Eastern-rite Catholic faith were considered a superficial ruse, even something 'detrimental'.

Biondich further stresses that the NDH's policy of forced conversions 'represented a direct challenge to the Church's authority in the spiritual realm'. Indeed, as he notes, Stepinac wrote to the Ministry of Justice and Religion to reject the regime's guidelines as 'unacceptable' (which is to say, uncanonical). Biondich finds that clergy over 35 tended, with some exceptions, to keep their distance from the Ustaše. On the other hand, there were individual clergymen who not only affiliated themselves with the Ustaša Party but even played a role in the atrocities. Finally, concerning the Church's alleged silence, Biondich concludes that, while opposed to many of the NDH authorities' policies, Stepinac 'could not bring himself to condemn their policies openly and unequivocally'.

Another two articles are devoted to the NDH's foreign relations: Mario Jareb's analysis of the NDH's relations with Italy and Germany, and Nada Kisić Kolanović's review of the NDH's relations with other southeast European countries as well as Turkey and Japan. Jareb emphasises developments in 1941, including the abortive efforts by Nazi Germany to persuade Vladko Maček to take the reins of the puppet regime and the cession to Italy of a long strip of Croatian territory. Indeed, Alfred Freundt, the German Consul-General in Zagreb, would report back to Berlin on 3 April 1941 that Maček gave an 'entirely negative' response to efforts by Walter Malletke of the Office of Reichsleiter Alfred Rosenberg to persuade him to assume the leadership post in the NDH.[47] Jareb notes that, at first, the German presence was not as evident as the Italian, although this changed after the Italian surrender in September 1943. Interestingly enough, after the Italian capitulation, Pavelić annulled the Rome agreements, under which Zagreb had surrendered coastal territories to Italy and declared his intention of reincorporating those lands.

As Jareb notes, the Chetniks – inspired by Serb nationalism and committed to a programme of creating a large Serbian state from which non-Serbs were to be 'cleansed' – saw the communist-led Partisans as their principal foe and were prepared to collaborate with Axis forces in joint operations against the Partisans. In this way, as Jareb notes, the Chetniks collaborated not only with the Italians but also with German forces and even with the NDH authorities.

Finally, Nada Kisić Kolanović breaks new ground with her article dealing with the NDH's relations with other countries in Southeast Europe as well as Turkey and Japan. Based on a careful study of documents preserved in the NDH embassy in Sofia, she points out that the NDH had quarrels not only with Italy (because of its annexation of most of the Dalmatian coastline and because of its view of the Balkans as its *Lebensraum*), but also with Hungary (because of its 1941 annexation of the Croatian Medjimurje region). The NDH's resentment of Hungary also led Zagreb to keep its distance from Bucharest, she notes, because the NDH authorities believed that any warmth in its relationship with Romania could sour relations with Hungary. Moreover, because of the loss of southern Dobrudža, Bulgaria was on unfriendly terms with Romania, and the NDH took Bulgaria's side in this dispute, looking to Sofia for support against Hungary. Meanwhile, Kisić Kolanović notes, Romanian authorities continued to hope that they could make a common front with their counterparts in Croatia.

Kisić Kolanović also charts the NDH's efforts to obtain diplomatic recognition from Turkey, and identifies the anti-communist stance of the Turkish government on this point as a reason for optimism in Zagreb. Interestingly enough, she reports that in April 1944, by which time the eventual defeat of the Axis was obvious to everyone, officials in Turkey were privately declaring their hope that Croatia remain independent of Belgrade after the war. In contrast with Turkey, Japan recognised the NDH as early as 7 June 1941, although Japanese relations with the NDH were guided by the Japanese embassy in Berlin, in deference to German authorities.

Ustashism was not a unique phenomenon, insofar as it reflected and embodied racist trends of its time. Its anti-Semitism, anti-Romaism and its attention to the alleged need to safeguard or restore the purity of the language are all features which the NDH shared with other radical right regimes in the 1930s and early 1940s, although Ivo and Slavko Goldstein point out that 'not all Ustaše participated in anti-Semitic propaganda or in anti-Semitic activities'.[48] Again the NDH's effort to exploit a selective recollection of national history to legitimate its rule is also a feature shared with other radical right regimes of the age. At the same time, the Independent State of Croatia had features that distinguished it from other radical right ideologies. The NDH placed more emphasis than the Nazis or the Italian Fascists on religion as a badge of national identity, for example, and, unlike its counterparts in Germany, Italy, and Spain, it never commanded the loyalty of the majority of its own nation.

ACKNOWLEDGEMENTS

The papers published in this issue were originally presented at a conference held in Trondheim, Norway in September 2004. The conference was made possible thanks to a generous grant from the Norwegian Research Council. I am also grateful to Christine M. Hassenstab for comments on the penultimate draft of this article.

Notes

1. On the Roma, see Narcisa Lengel-Krizman, 'Prilog proučavanju terora u tzv. NDH: Sudbina Roma 1941–1945', in *Časopis za suvremenu povijest* (Zagreb), Vol.18 (1986), No.1, pp.29–42; and Dennis Reinhartz, 'Unmarked graves: the destruction of the Yugoslav Roma in the Balkan Holocaust, 1941–1945', in *Journal of Genocide Research*, Vol.1 (1999), No.1, pp.81–9.

2. Vladimir Žerjavić, *Gubici stanovništva Jugoslavije u drugom svjetskom ratu* (Zagreb: Jugoslavensko Viktimološko Društvo, 1989), pp.61–6.
3. *Ustaše* is the plural of *Ustaša*, and refers to the members of the *Ustaša* party.
4. Portions of this paragraph and of the following paragraph are closely paraphrased from my book, *The Three Yugoslavias: State-building and Legitimation, 1918–2005* (Bloomington, Ind./Washington D.C.: Indiana University Press & The Wilson Center Press, 2006), pp.114–15.
5. Document No.90: D 708 (10 July 1941), Troll-Oberfell to Foreign Ministry (Berlin), in *Documents on German Foreign Policy 1918–1945*, Series D, Vol.13: The War Years – 1941 (Washington D.C.: U.S. Government Printing Office, 1964), pp.113–14.
6. Milan Dj. Nedić, *Reći Generala Milana Nedića Srpskom narodu i omladini* (Belgrade: Nacionalni spisi, 1941), pp.9–10 (speech of 2 September 1941). Even today, there are those who are inclined to give a positive assessment of Nedić's wartime role, sometimes representing him as having endeavored to 'save' the Serbian people. See, for example, Lazo M. Kostić, *Armijski General Milan Nedić. Njegova uloga i delovanje* (Novi Sad: Dobrica knjiga, 2000 [1976]), especially pp.10–16.
7. In December 1941, Gerhard Feine, stationed in Belgrade, wrote to Berlin to report, 'it can be said today after General Nedić has been Minister President for three months that so far he has justified the trust placed in him ...Today he is so much identified with Germany in the eyes of the Serbian people that it is hardly possible for him any more to abandon this line.' Document 538: Pol. S No.2 (3 December 1941), Feine to Foreign Ministry (Berlin), in *Documents on German Foreign Policy*, Vol.13, p.947.
8. Document No.526: Confidential protocol signed in Zagreb (16 May 1941), by Siegfried Kasche, Carl Clodius, Lovro Sušić, and Mladen Lorković, in *Documents on German Foreign Policy 1918–1945*, Series D, Vol.12: The War Years – 1941 (Washington D.C.: Government Printing Office, 1962), pp.831–2.
9. See, for example, Zorica Stipetić, 'Je li vrijeme da se ustaški logor Jasenovac, u ime istine, oslobodi i mitova i laži?', in *Globus* (Zagreb), 23 April 1999, p.87; and 'Uprava Spomen parka Jasenovac mora sačiniti pojedinačni popis stradalih', in *Novi list* (Rijaka), 3 May 2005, at www.novilist.hr (accessed on 1 September 2005).
10. Ladislav Tomičić, 'Tajna o ustaškom zlatu u arhivima Crkve', in *Novi list* (15 May 2005), at www.novilist.hr (accessed on 1 September 2005).
11. See, for example, 'Zagrebački nadbiskup fasciniran osnivanjem hrvatske države', in *Novi list* (5 March 2002), at www.novilist.hr (accessed on 19 June 2003); and Jure Krišto, 'Katolička crkva u Nezavisnoj Državi Hrvatskoj', in *Časopis za suvremenu povijest*, Vol.27 (1995), No.3: pp.461–74.
12. On these two points, see Ivo Goldstein with Slavko Goldstein, *Holokaust u Zagrebu* (Zagreb: Novi liber & Židovska općina Zagreb, 2001), pp.49, 540.
13. Letter from Archbishop Stepinac to Minister Artuković (23 April 1941), translated into English for *The Pavelic Papers: An Independent Project Researching the History of the Ustaša Movement*, at www.pavelicpapers.com/documents/stepinac/as0005.html (accessed on 10 June 2006). See also Goldstein, (note 12), pp.468–9.
14. Nada Kisić Kolanović, 'Povijest NDH kao predmet istraživanja', in *Časopis za suvremenu povijest* (Zagreb), Vol.34, No.3 (2002), pp.679–712.
15. Ibid., p.690.
16. Two recent examples are: Goldstein (note 12); and Ramet, (note 4), chap.4.
17. Anyone who still doubts that NDH mythology played a role for some Croats to express their defiance of Serbs need only look at Zdravko Tomac, *The Struggle for the Croatian State ... through hell to democracy*, trans. by Profikon (Zagreb: Profikon, 1993).
18. S. Klarica, 'Grafitima za Gotovinu i NDH', in *Novi list* (16 December 2004), at www.novilist.hr (accessed on 1 September 2005).
19. Z.C., 'NDH nije bila država', in *Novi list* (10 April 2005), at www.novilist.hr (accessed on 1 September 2005).
20. *Agence France Presse* (23 April 1996), in *Lexis-Nexis Academic Universe*.
21. The party's website is www.ultimatum.20m.com/nova_hrv_desnica.htm [accessed on 11 June 2006]. See also M. Bokulic, 'Schwartz: 'O meni je stvorena fama kao o nacisti i političkom monstrumu''', in *Vjesnik* (Zagreb), 3 April 2001, at www.vjesnik.hr (accessed on 11 June 2006).
22. Croatian Radio (Zagreb), 23 November 1996, trans. in *BBC Summary of World Broadcasts* (25 November 1996), via *Lexis-Nexis Academic Universe*.
23. Ivica Radoš, *Tudjman izbliža: Svjedočenja suradnika i protivnika* (Zagreb: Profil International, 2005), p.56.
24. Regarding the Mass itself, see *Agence France Presse* (29 December 1998), in *Lexis-Nexis Academic Universe*; regarding the archbishop, see HINA (Zagreb), 1 January 1999, in *NewsBank – Access*

World News, at infoweb.newsbank.com; and regarding the HDZ comment, see Beta news agency (Belgrade), 6 January 1999, translated in *BBC Worldwide Monitoring* (6 January 1999), via *Lexis-Nexis Academic Universe*.

25. HINA (12 February 2004), in *NewsBank – Access World News*, at infoweb.newsbank.com.
26. In connection with that incident, seven participants were later charged with having violated the law banning the display of symbols that could incite interethnic or racial hatred. See HINA (7 December 2004) and *Agence France Presse* (7 December 2004) – both in *NewsBank – Access World News*, at infoweb.newsbank.com.
27. *Agence France Presse* (21 August 2005), in *Lexis-Nexis Academic Universe*.
28. According to Ladislaus Hory and Martin Broszat, *Der kroatische Ustascha-Staat, 1941–1945* (Stuttgart: Deutsche Verlags-Anstalt, 1964), p.69. Sundhaussen estimates the NDH's population at 6.5 million. See Holm Sundhaussen, 'Der Ustasche-Staat: Anatomie eines Herrschaftssystems', in *Österreichische Osthefte*, Vol.37, No.2 (1995), p.500.
29. Hory and Broszat (note 28), p.69.
30. Vladimir Žerjavić, *Gubici stanovništva Jugoslavije u drugom svjetskom ratu* (Zagreb: Jugoslavensko Viktimološko Društvo, 1989), pp.61–6.
31. Toward the end of 1942, Mussolini personally took the decision to take Croatian Jews into protective custody in order to protect them from the Nazis and the Ustaše. See Fikreta Jelić-Butić, *Ustaše i NDH* (Zagreb: S.N. Liber and Školska knjiga, 1977), p.180; and Jonathan Steinberg, *All or Nothing: The Axis and the Holocaust 1941–1943* (London and New York: Routledge, 1990), p.133. See also Zvi Loker, 'The Testimony of Dr. Edo Neufeld: The Italians and the Jews of Croatia', in *Holocaust and Genocide Studies*, Vol.7, No.1 (Spring 1993), pp.67–76.
32. At that time, it was renamed the Directorate for Public Order and Security [*Ravnateljstvo za javni red i sigurnost*, or RAVSIGUR]. See 'Ustasha', at www.axishistory.com/index.php?id=7257 (accessed on 10 June 2006).
33. Ivo Goldstein, *Croatia: A History*, translated from Croatian by Nikolina Jovanović (McGill-Queen's University Press, 1999), p.137.
34. Holm Sundhaussen, 'Jugoslawien', in Wolfgang Benz (ed.), *Dimension des Völkermords. Die Zahl der jüdischen Opfer des Nationalsozialismus* (Munich: R. Oldenbourg Verlag, 1991), pp.321–2.
35. Goldstein (note 12), p.342. A history textbook for Croatian high schools published in 2003 gives 80,000 as the number of people (Serbs and non-Serbs alike) who lost their lives at Jasenovac. See Hrvoje Matković and Franko Mirošević, *Povijest 4, udžbenik za 4. razred gimnazije*, 2nd ed. (Zagreb: Školska knjiga, 2003), p.159. István Deák, in a review essay for *New York Review of Books*, accepts a figure of 60,000 persons killed at Jasenovac. See his essay, 'Jews and Catholics', in *New York Review of Books* (19 December 2002), p.42. Vladimir Zerjavic has offered a rough estimate of 'around 100,000' for the number of persons who lost their lives at Jasenovac. See Vladimir Zerjavic, *Population losses in Yugoslavia, 1941–1945* (Zagreb: Dom i svijet, 1997), p.89.
36. See, for example, *Hrvatski narod* (11 June 1942), p.1.
37. *Hrvatski narod* (13 January 1942), p.3, and (27 January 1942), p.7.
38. For more accurate accounts of Starčević, see V. Bogdanov, *Ante Starčević i Hrvatska politika* (Zagreb: Biblioteka Nezavisnih Pisaca, 1937); Vaso Bogdanov, *Starčević i Stranka prava prema Srbima i prema jedinstvu Južnoslavenskih naroda* (Zagreb: Naklaka 'Školska knjiga', 1951); and Mirjana Gross, *Izvorno pravaštvo. Ideologija, agitacija, pokret* (Zagreb: Golden Marketing, 2000).
39. *Hrvatski narod* (10 January 1942), p.3.
40. Dubravko Jelčić, 'Kulturni život u Nezavisnoj Državi Hrvatskoj', in *Časopis za suvremenu povijest*, Vol.27 (1995), No.3, p.522.
41. *Hrvatski narod* (26 March 1942), p.1.
42. 'Legal Decree on the Croatian language, its purity and spelling' (14 August 1941), trans. in *The Pavelic Papers*, at www.pavelicpapers.com/documents/budak/mbu0003.html (accessed on 10 June 2006).
43. *Hrvatski narod* (12 February 1942), p.7, and (1 January 1943), p.1.
44. Jelić-Butić (note 31), p.158.
45. Ibid., pp.168–72.
46. Klaus Buchenau, *Orthodoxie und Katholizismus in Jugoslawien 1945–1991. Ein serbisch-kroatischer Vergleich* (Wiesbaden: Harrassowitz Verlag, 2004), p.124.
47. Document No.262: Telegram 33 (4 April 1941), Consul Gen. Alfred Freundt/Zagreb to Foreign Ministry (Berlin), in *Documents on German Foreign Policy*, Vol.12, p.448.
48. Goldstein (note 12), p.628.

The NDH State in Comparative Perspective

STANLEY G. PAYNE
University of Wisconsin-Madison

The Independent State of Croatia's unique place in history was that of being the only new fascist state placed directly in power by Hitler with the opportunity to enjoy extensive autonomy and to develop its own system. The government of Vidkun Quisling only received power a year and a half after the conquest of Norway, but operated a puppet administration under occupation authority that was not allowed to construct its own state. The Arrow Cross state nominally placed in power in western Hungary in December 1944 was the nearest parallel, but the short-lived regime of Ferenc Szalasi administered only a portion of Hungary for three months under heavy military occupation and virtual battlefront conditions.

The Italian Social Republic was also placed in power by German arms, but differed from the status of the NDH in two ways. The first and most crucial was that it reorganised a pre-existing fascist regime, in fact the very originator of that ideological species. It governed proportionately less of Italy than the NDH did of Croatian-speaking territory, and under heavy military occupation enjoyed less autonomy. The Nedić government in occupied Serbia was also placed in power by Hitler, but enjoyed less autonomy and developed less of a state profile. The NDH was a puppet regime in the sense that it received power as a pure gift from a foreign conqueror, and throughout its life was under foreign occupation, first by German and Italian troops, and later, after the collapse of Fascism, by German forces alone.

It was never fully sovereign in its own house, yet it enjoyed more autonomy than any of the regimes cited above, so that for much of its brief history it might be considered something between a puppet and a satellite, with greater autonomy than any other regime in German-occupied Europe. (The Slovak Republic, by comparison, was a satellite, not a puppet. Though its opportunity for independence stemmed from the German destruction of Czechoslovakia, it was autonomously organised by the major Slovak political forces, and did not live under direct occupation. Thus its status was similar to that of Vichy France.)

This unique place in the history of fascism raises several questions about the character and place of the Ustaša regime. These include the degree of its fascistic identity, the comparative extent of its support, its place or role in the comparative politicisation of religion, its ranking in mass atrocities, and whether it has any comparative significance as an example of an autonomous fascist state. Two final considerations have to do with its unique status of being the only fascist-type regime to engage in a full-scale revolutionary civil war, and with the broader issue of fascism in the Balkans.

How 'fascist' were the Ustaše?

This is not a completely simple question to answer, since even the experts do not entirely agree on the exact definition of *fascistizzità*. It seems clear, however, that the movement began without any such elaborately defined doctrine, starting as a radical nationalist terrorist organisation, somewhat analogous to the Internal Macedonian Revolutionary Organisation (IMRO).

The early association with Fascist Italy was at first more a matter of geopolitics than of ideology. During the 1930s, however, the movement was increasingly influenced by fascist ideas, more from Germany than from Italy. The transformation became noticeable during 1936–37 amid Pavelic's confinement in Italy, and as the expansion of German power became significant. By the late 1930s the Ustaše were developing a Nazi-style racial ideology of the kind found in many – though not all – fascist movements, with their claim for a 'Gothic', non-Slavic identity for Croats, together with the assumption of a corresponding racial hierarchy. Other features, such as the idealisation of the peasantry, were reminiscent of fascism in Germany, Italy and Romania, though in turn the idealisation of the peasantry was characteristic of many different kinds of nationalist movements. This evolutionary, though also suddenly accelerated, path into fascism was not at all uncommon, but was noticeable among ideologues and movements in a number of different countries.

The categorical denunciation of capitalism and communism, in favour of a nationalist 'third way' in economic affairs, was typically fascist. Here the idealisation of the traditional peasant *zadruga* represented a specific south Slav idiosyncracy, though in fact it was in some respects directly reminiscent of late nineteenth-century Russian populism.

On the other hand, the Ustaša movement exhibited less theoretical sophistication and elaboration than did many fascist movements. Pavelić does not seem to have elaborated any very distinctive 'national fascist' ideology like those of Hitler, Mussolini, Codreanu, Szalasi and a number of others. This was all the more difficult because of the relatively recent conversion to fascism, and because the party never had any opportunity to consolidate and develop itself under anything approaching normal political conditions before it was actually given state power. Moreover, it was riven by factions that disagreed among themselves and had no strong intellectual leadership. In power, however, the Ustaše did subscribe to nearly all the basic points that would compose a 'fascist minimum', and their relations with the Catholic Church were more typical of those of a fascist than of a right-radical regime.

By the time that they were given power, the Ustaše seem to have become, in ideas and in practice, what could be called a 'mimetic' fascist movement. As with nearly all such movements, their extreme nationalism led them to emphasise a few points of singularity, but nothing either in theory or practice that was not consistent with generic fascism.

Did the NDH represent a mass movement or a fully mobilised state?

As a fascist-type movement, the Ustaše had been comparatively insignificant prior to the war, more a clandestine terrorist organisation than a mass movement. Indeed, their numerical and organisational weakness was a handicap when they were given power, and this may have been a factor in promoting instantaneous radicalisation as a mode of compensation.

Operating an autonomous state administration provided much more opportunity for mobilisation, and the regime endeavoured to develop the usual sets of organisations common to the period. It never conducted even controlled elections, however, and the growth of the party itself, though obviously considerable, cannot be separated from the obvious opportunism present in one-party regimes.

Moreover, the NDH eventually provoked much opposition among Croats, who in the long run joined the Partisans in disproportionate numbers. Whereas the Ustaše had the advantages of the state apparatus for their party membership and military groups, the Partisans probably elicited much more genuine volunteering. The NDH did not provide much evidence of being a significant mass mobilised system, even though it did manage to elicit a certain amount of popular support from a new basis of state power.

'Christian Fascism'?

In his 2003 study *The Holy Reich*, Richard Steigmann-Gall[1] raised the controversial issue of a 'Christian Nazism', which has provoked sharp criticism and debate. Somewhat different issues have been raised concerning the relationship between fascism and religion in such countries as Spain, Romania and Croatia. One of the most notorious and controversial aspects of the NDH was its relationship with the Catholic Church, this becoming in turn the target of great stigmatisation by the succeeding Communist regime. For present purposes, the issue is not only the nature of that relationship itself but whether it conforms to the general nature of such relations in fascist states and whether it gave evidence of producing a 'Christian fascism', as is sometimes charged.

The relationship of fascist regimes – meaning primarily those of Italy and Germany – with the Christian churches revealed a fundamentally different approach from that of classical Marxism-Leninism. The latter normally adopted a directly adverserial approach, facilitated by the violent military and revolutionary origins of Marxist-Leninist regimes. The original fascist regimes came to power, conversely, through political tactics rather than military overthrow, and proceeded much more by degrees, reversing the revolutionary priorities of Communist regimes.

The initial tactic of the fascist regimes was to seek peace with the churches and even attempt to gain the support of Christians. Both during their rise to power and in their consolidation, fascist leaders sought to emphasise points of apparent convergence, or at least parallels, with Christian belief, and did not discourage dual memberships in Party and Church, at least for the rank and file. This was facilitated by a certain evolutionary or pragmatic indeterminacy in aspects of fascist doctrine.

Beyond that, there were distinct differences of policy and doctrine on the part of the various fascist movements. The Romanian Legion of the Archangel Michael was the most religious, to the extent that, in this regard, it must be considered a distinct sub-type, even though some of its more sensitive or honest members recognised that aspects of its practice made it, to say the least, heterodox, if not worse.[2]

Nearly all nationalist movements in some form or another invoke the nation's religion(s), albeit in different ways and in distinct degrees. A basic difference, however, is that right-radical regimes (for example, those of Franco or Salazar, or the Slovak Republic) tend to evince genuine respect for the Church, its autonomy and even its political and spiritual recommendations. This was not the case with the fascist regimes, which were more purely pragmatic, and also increasingly willing to ignore or oppress the churches.

The Ustaša invocation of Croatia as a Catholic nation was unexceptional in this regard, but its relationship with the church was more that of a fascist than a right-radical regime. It systematically ignored rebukes and complaints, and in key respects simply followed its own religious policy, making concessions to 'Croatian Islam' on the one hand, while creating its own Orthodox church and its own secular programme of forced conversion to Catholicism. This was ultimately more like Germany than Spain, though in no other fascist state was a complete alternative church attempted as was briefly the case in Nazi Germany. Most of those points on which the regime enforced Catholic principles – such as elimination of abortion and pornography – were also fully consistent with contemporary fascist practice. Priests and monks who were the most full-fledged collaborators seem to have been borderline renegades who defied their church superiors. A smaller number of priests, conversely, collaborated with the Partisans.

In general, then, despite individual nuances, the NDH failed to achieve a genuine politico-religious symbiosis. It was never formally recognised by the Vatican, and in its brief history was unable to negotiate the kind of concordat that existed with Italy and Germany. A fairly close *de facto* relationship existed in some areas, but it was always partial and incomplete.

The NDH in the History of Mass Atrocity

Mass atrocity in the twentieth century obviously took many different forms. Though Communist regimes conducted mass executions, the greatest death toll which they exacted stemmed from the catastrophic conditions of famine and disease that they imposed. The atrocities carried out by fascistic regimes took primarily the form of widespread war and direct executions.

The sanguinary character of NDH policy has struck all observers and analysts, even provoking complaints from the German military. The direct execution of possibly as many as 150,000 victims in a country of no more than six million, even if in some cases the means were indirect, was an extraordinary mass crime, which at least in proportionate terms exceeded any other Balkan dictatorship and any other European regime save that of Hitler. The Antonescu regime was also lethal, but within Romania proper executed comparatively few Jews, concentrating its slaughter on the Jews of the northern borderlands and the Ukraine. It apparently massacred 200,000 or more Jews, but these were proportionately fewer victims in comparison to the state's own population than in the case of Croatia. The only positive note in the cases of these two Balkan regimes was a certain tendency to become less lethal with the passage of time (especially in the Romanian case), as contrasted with the escalation of genocide in the latter phases of the German regime. Outside of Europe, the NDH state was exceeded proportionately only by the Khmer Rouge in Cambodia and several of the extremely genocidal African regimes. There is little doubt that this programme did not stem from any purely Croatian or Yugoslav origins but was inspired by the example and patronage of the Third Reich, even though the immediate conception and entire execution of the extermination policy was the work of the Ustaše. In the gruesome history of mass atrocity, the NDH state has a secure and singular place.

The NDH as a 'Regime Type'

The Ustaše introduced most of the standard institutions of the fascist type of regime, even though these were often poorly developed: the one-party state, a racial policy, the beginning of a system of national labour syndicates, an outline of 'chambers of professional organisation' as the beginning of a corporative economic system (though the latter was never developed), a youth organisation, an organisation for women and a consultative assembly in preparation for a corporative parliament (though the latter was never introduced). This created a broad parallel with the Italian Fascist regime, though its racial policy was much more like Germany's. There is little doubt that German and Italian influence played important roles in ideological and institutional development.

A Revolutionary Civil War

The NDH regime was the only fascist-type state to become involved in a major revolutionary civil war. The First World War had produced conditions of breakdown that led to revolutionary civil war in eastern Europe, which also threatened central Europe as well. The Second World War produced this effect only in Greece and Yugoslavia, particularly because of the strength of the Communist resistance movement. For more than 15 years (prior to adopting of the Popular Front tactic in 1935), the Comintern had sought to create conditions in various countries in which a Communist insurrection might triumph, though the goal had been to limit the terms of any genuine civil war to those which could be managed successfully by the Communists.

Comintern theory did not necessarily propose a revolutionary civil war *per se* in Yugoslavia, the initial goal instead being a broad resistance movement that could undermine Germany's occupation and strategic position. Nationalist movements, particularly the Serbian Chetniks, refused to so associate themselves, however, so that the broader popular front-type resistance movement, more common in western Europe, was not possible. Though it enjoyed strong support abroad, the Partisan movement had no significant domestic allies and, partly due to the policy choices of its own leadership, pursued a more directly revolutionary policy (indeed, probably a more revolutionary policy than Stalin himself would have preferred).

Since the Ustaše, rather than the Axis powers, held responsibility for the domestic government, this struggle soon assumed the characteristics of a revolutionary civil war, though at the same time it was a war of liberation against foreign occupation. The scope of the conflict, however, stemmed particularly from the oppression and violence of NDH policy, which stimulated much greater support for the Partisans than might otherwise have existed. This was a case which might be termed that of fascism eliciting a civil war, which was to that extent the reverse, in terms of causation, of what happened in Russia in 1918 and

Spain in 1936. In the latter two cases, it was the presence of the revolutionary left in power which produced conditions of civil war. In those cases the opposition movement, counterrevolutionary, rather than revolutionary as in Yugoslavia, had, unlike the Yugoslav Communists, to fashion itself *ex nihilo*.

The counterrevolutionary movements began on comparatively moderate political terms but moved toward more radical forms, the radical authoritarian right in Russia and a semi-fascist state in Spain. In Croatia the political process was rather the reverse. Growth in support for the Partisans by 1944 may have been predicated on the assumption that theirs was the winning side, but it had become strong well before that. As suggested earlier, at some point it may have become as strong as or stronger than support for the independent Croatian fascist state. This presented the NDH with a growing domestic challenge, politically and militarily. Indeed, had the NDH been a geographically and militarily isolated entity, the revolutionary insurgency would soon have grown strong enough to have overthrown it directly.

This was nonetheless a novel situation for a fascist regime, which placed it increasingly in the situation of Mussolini's puppet Italian Social Republic of 1943–45, with very little in common with the classic Fascist regime of 1922–43. This merely emphasises the fact that the Ustaše were not a mass movement with an extensive social base, like their counterparts in Italy or Germany, or even in Hungary and Romania, but a small extremist movement only recently metamorphosed into something resembling a genuine fascist party. Rather than behaving like the Fascists in Italy before 1943, they behaved in their own country like German Nazis in Poland and Russia, progressively destabilising their own power even as they sought to establish it. Indeed, the Germans were so disgusted with the chaos being created in Croatia that Hitler was apparently willing after little more than six months to depose Ante Pavelić, but could find no equivalent collaborationist partner.

The Question of Balkan Fascism

The largest comparative question raised by the history of the NDH concerns the issue of fascism in the Balkans more generally. The only Balkan country with a strong fascist movement was Romania, but analysts have sometimes pointed out that any retrodictive theory of fascism might logically have posited the development of significant fascist movements in such countries as Bulgaria, Croatia and Greece. One of the main features of any retrodictive theory of fascism is that of international defeat or humiliation. Bulgaria and Greece were major losers in the First World War and its aftermath, while Croats soon became severely frustrated by the terms of the new Yugoslavia. In this perspective, the fact that a fascist movement did not emerge in Serbia until 1935, and then weakly, would not be surprising, because of Serbia's victor status and hegemonic role. Romania, ironically, was proportionately one of the greatest winners in the First World War, but otherwise suffered from just about every kind of problem imaginable.

The hypertrophy of the radical nationalist intelligentsia was probably proportionately greater in Romania than in any other Balkan country, and this alone was a major factor. Peasant agriculture seems to have been somewhat more stable and mesocratic in the other three countries, creating somewhat greater social and economic stability. Political energies were more effectively mobilised by peasant parties in Bulgaria and Croatia, and after the overthrow of Aleksandr Stamboliski

Bulgarian affairs were controlled by a reactionary nineteenth-century elitist parliamentary system. Peasant society was not the best breeding ground for fascist movements, though peasants were effectively mobilised by such movements in Hungary and Romania.

Quite distinct political conditions existed in Bulgaria, Croatia and Greece, so that no simple individual interpretation is likely to be able to encompass all three. Peasant politics thrived in Croatia, became dominant in Bulgaria and were then suppressed, and had to work through an established two-party system in Greece. In Croatia, the Peasant Party occupied a great deal of political space, while the duration of the regime of King Aleksandar and its sequel discouraged significant new mobilisation. This probably points up the fundamental irony that fascist parties required conditions of relative democracy in order to mobilise effectively. Such conditions more nearly existed in Greece than in the other two countries, but in Greece all significant political space continued to be virtually mobilised by the two traditional parties, after which the Metaxas regime closed off political life in 1936.

The foregoing observations may help to elucidate part of the problem, but the cases of the missing mobilisation of fascism in most of the Balkans prior to 1939 remain one of the notable problems in the comparative analysis of fascism.

Notes

1. Richard Steigmann-Gall, *The Holy Reich: Nazi Conceptions of Christianity, 1919–1945*. (Cambridge: Cambridge University Press, 2003).
2. See Constantin Iordachi, *Charisma, Politics and Violence: The Legion of the 'Archangel Michael' in Interwar Romania*. Trondheim Studies on East European Cultures and Societies No. 15 (Trondheim: PEECS Publications of NTNU, 2004).

The Independent State of Croatia in 1941: On the Road to Catastrophe

IVO GOLDSTEIN
University of Zagreb

The patterns of behaviour by the newly constituted Ustaša government stemmed from its ideological basis. Ustaša ideology was a specific mixture of German Nazism and Italian Fascism adapted to the specific Croatian environment. As everywhere in Europe, in Croatia and in Zagreb, the policies of the Third Reich set an example and served as an incentive for the persecution and killing of Jews, and it was this policy which generally played a decisive role in the NDH. Moreover, the NDH depended on National Socialism for its very existence. The Germans brought to power a group that they knew would be very similar to them in ideology and practice (had, for example, Maček and the Croatian Peasant Party [*Hrvatska seljačka stranka* – HSS] come to power, as some wanted and planned, there would have been no persecution of Jews and Serbs, and the Nazis would have had to organise the deportation of Jews by themselves, using violence). Indeed, the genocide against the Serbs stemmed from the Ustaša ideology and from the actual situation in the former Yugoslavia.

There is abundant evidence about how the Ustaše, with Ante Pavelić as their leader, planned to deal radically with the Serbs, Jews, as well as with all the real and potential political opponents of the Ustaše. The Roma were also included in this plan, but no mention at all was made of them in the media and in political life.[1] Nevertheless, doubts are now being voiced as to whether the Ustaša government deliberately committed crimes. There is an anecdote about how the above plan was viewed and how one member of government wanted to realise it. The Minister of Education, Mile Budak gave a well-known, rabble-rousing speech ('*Srbe na vrbe*') on 13 July 1941; he then spoke later to a closed circle at a party for about 50 chosen guests in a Franciscan monastery. He was:

> able to speak openly about something that is now more than topical ... about what will in fact happen to the Jews and the Serbs in our state ...

You are intelligent people and I need not spell it all out, it will be easiest to explain things with a story from our Ustaša emigration. It took place once when I was touring Ustaša camps. Conversation turned to the Serbs and the Jews, and to how they were behaving in our homeland, and how to solve this question when we returned home. One of our good Ustaše then said the following to me: 'When we return home, then you, Doctor, will certainly be a minister and represent the authority of the Croatian state. I will be a Croatian soldier and represent the Croatian fighting spirit. What shall we, Croatian soldiers, expect and demand from you, ministers and representatives of the Croatian government? Nothing but the following: when we soldiers are in the field somewhere, acting against the Serbs and the Jews, then you, as representatives of the state, will have to come and see what happened. All we expect is that you will always come *half an hour too late*.

'There: this is the secret and the answer to your question', concluded Budak, who was described by eyewitness Vladimir Židovec as 'unusually elated' at that moment, and 'obviously feeling at home in the mission meted out to him by Providence'. To make sure that the present Italian and German military representatives also understood him, so that 'none of his ideas are lost to future generations', Budak himself 'translated his speech first into Italian, and then into German'.[2]

Many facts show that the heads of the Ustaša regime endorsed the promulgation of anti-Serbian and anti-Jewish measures.[3] Nevertheless, it is also obvious that, after they came to power, differences appeared in their views on how to put such plans into practice, and how to make their actions comply with internal and external political developments. Although Pavelić usually wanted to give the measures of the Ustaša authorities a semblance of legitimacy, his frequent and extremely incendiary anti-Semitic public statements served as a basis for the increasing ruthlessness of his closest associates. Both the lower ranks of the Ustaša movement and police officials, on the other hand, took Pavelić's excesses as a good indicator that the regime at least tacitly supported activities against Serbs, Jews and political enemies, however cruel.

As soon as the NDH was created, anti-Semitic and anti-Serb propaganda in the media and at public engagements became the politically desirable behaviour. For example, Croats were described as having been traditionally endowed with 'those ancient Croatian virtues – patience, humility and intrepidness';[4] these qualities were contrasted with Serbs and Jews, who were systematically demonised. 'The Serbs spread everything that is bad among the Croats, and which is inborn to the Serbs, such as immorality, gambling, alcohol, fighting and stealing', reported an Ustaša *logornik* from Bjeljina (in north-eastern Bosnia).[5]

Furthermore, 'The Serbs are a people who always bring evil and misfortune – the entire life of the Serb people is filled with corruption and usury ... The Serbs left us a horrible, disgusting and unwanted heritage, which we must resolutely end'; whereas 'the Croatian people are one of the most courageous keepers of the Western heritage'.[6]

Nearly every day, texts threatening what would happen to the enemies of the Ustaše were published. On 20 April the leading newspaper in the new state, *Hrvatski narod*, under the title 'The strictest measures must be taken against the Jews' – reprinted the text of 17 April from *Deutsche Zeitung in Kroatien* [*The German*

Newspaper in Croatia] – ending in the words: 'Without solving the Jewish question there will be no final peace in the south-east area. And it is also certain that these measures can never be severe enough'.[7] At the end of April 1941, *Hrvatski radnik* (Croatian worker) added that 'the Croatian people must unite and together cast off the authority and influence of Serbs, Jews and Marxists'.[8] Only a day or two later, *Hrvatski narod*, (Croatian people) writing about Jews and 'Gypsies', claimed that 'the will for self-preservation demands that the people of every state precisely define their relations with foreign racial communities, and especially with those who came as guests and passers through, during short periods of time, and in many ways fatefully and negatively influenced the destiny of the people'.[9]

One of the basic goals of the Ustaša ideology was to create an 'ethnically pure Croatian territory'. The removal of foreign elements, primarily the Serbs, Jews, and Roma, was therefore an integral part of NDH policy. This genocidal 'cleansing of the area' of the Serbs had been prepared in advance, while the more systematic persecution of the Jews was added later, based on newly-passed laws. In the spring and summer of 1941, people were killed *en masse* in many Serb villages – often on their front doorsteps – usually without any effort to legally justify this in any way. However, the genocide of the Jews took place more gradually and rationally, in several stages. The Ustaša model had obviously been found in the Nazi method which foresaw a phase of excommunication, a phase of concentration; and finally, a phase of extermination. The Ustaša regime began to carry out this last phase, the phase of the extermination of the Serbs and the Jews, as early as the summer of 1941.

'Total elimination' (whatever that may mean) was planned for Jews and Roma, while the solution for the Serb 'problem' was seen in the slogan 'kill one third, deport one third, convert one third to Catholicism'. This was never put in writing, as some researchers have claimed, but was carried through literally in numerous places with only small differences. Documents from various parts of the NDH demonstrate that the implementation of the plan was burdened by much bad organisation, bad control, improvisation and excesses by local men in power. Nonetheless, the implementation of this plan was obviously being coordinated from Zagreb, despite the fact that its application in different parts of the NDH was supposed to differ. Primarily, it was to be adapted to local conditions; and in consequence, it was to be more ruthless in Bosnia-Herzegovina as well as in the mountain regions.

Yet what was the origin of this 3-stage plan? Perhaps we can find an answer in the memoirs of Hermann Neubacher, commissioner for southeast Belgrade, according to whom Pavelić's formula of thirds is reminiscent of exterminations carried out in the religious wars. The idea of 'thirds' was not originally Pavelić's, but was expressed in about 1881 – almost at the level of sarcasm – by Constantine Petrovich Pobedonostev, a theologian and conservative counsellor of the Russian Tsar Alexander III during the massive pogroms against the Jews. He is alleged to have said that the solution to the 'Jewish Question' in Russia would come about when 'a third (of Russia's Jews) will be converted, a third will emigrate, and a third will die of hunger'.[10]

As early as 4 April, Pavelić triumphantly stated in the paper *Ustaška pobjeda* (Ustaša victory): 'The free Independent State of Croatia is rising, and in it, Oh Croatian people of peasant origin, all the land and all the power shall be in your hands … and from which all the weeds sown by foreign enemy hands shall be uprooted'.[11] Although this statement may seem at first glance ambiguous and even unclear, when the events of the following several months are taken into account, it becomes evident what Pavelić meant.

It seems that by 19 April word was spreading, at least in some Serb villages, that the Serbs had been placed outside the law and were being persecuted alongside the Jews. On 23 April a new rumour started, alleging that the 'authorities had ordered the Serbs to move to Serbia within five days'.[12] A proclamation by Viktor Gutić, the Ustaša chief official [stožernik] for Banja Luka, in the regional paper *Hrvatska krajina* (Croatian frontier), shows that this rumour was not without foundation. Gutić ordered all Serbs and Montenegrins living in Bosanska krajina who had also been born in Serbia and Montenegro to move out within five days.[13] Although Gutić's proclamation had limited scope – and it is only some individuals who mention the spread of such rumours – word of this kind logically fit into the atmosphere of tension and fear being created in order to encourage Serbs to emigrate to Serbia of their own accord (or to revolt, giving the authorities an excuse to retaliate).

The Zagreb Police Directorate issued a decree (which was posted in streets as an announcement) on 8 May 1941, stating that 'all SERBS and JEWS' who live in the elite north parts of the city 'have 8 days to move to other parts of the city'. This decree specified that they were to move 'from the north side of Maksimirska cesta, Vlaška ulica, Jelačićev trg, Ilica as far as the Mitnica, and also from the city areas north of these streets'.[14] This was yet one more way of making some of the Zagreb Jews homeless, especially those who were wealthier, while simultaneously of robbing them of their property. The regulation, like all the rest, also included a threat: 'Anyone who does not comply with this decree shall be, after the expiry of the above deadline, FORCIBLY EVICTED at his own expense and PUNISHED in accordance with existing LEGAL PROVISIONS'. And this is what really took place. Anyone failing to move within the time limit was immediately evicted from his apartment and deprived of all property.[15] There were hardly any exceptions, although some Jews managed to go on living in smaller and more nondescript apartments and houses; the larger apartments and villas, however, were evacuated without exception. The authorities claimed that some of the apartments would be used to house 'unemployed private employees and workers',[16] but this did not happen.

In contrast, the mass deportation of Serbs was a much more complex plan that was more difficult to realise. At the beginning of June 1941, the NDH authorities readily fell in with the Nazi plans for the mass relocation of Slovenes, offering to deport Slovenes *en masse* to Croatia instead of to the *Generalcommissariate* of Serbia, and to deport Serbs from the NDH to Serbia. This agreement was to be put into practice very quickly, in the several following weeks in fact, because the Slovenes were meant to start arriving in the NDH on 11 July. Preparations for, and the implementation of, this extensive work coincided with the beginning of the German attack on the USSR, with the day of Vidovdan, and with the decision of the Communists – few in number but full of fighting spirit – to launch an attack on the NDH. In the meantime, the Ustaše continued to implement their plan for genocide.

On 27–28 April, the Ustaše committed their first mass crime in Gudovac, near Bjelovar (80 km east of Zagreb): in retaliation for the killing of a Croatian soldier by an unknown person, they killed 196 Serb men from Gudovac and its surroundings. This was followed on 9 May by the mass slaughter of 400 Serb peasants from the Kordun village of Veljun and its surroundings, and on 13 May by the murder of another 260 Serbs in Glina in Banija. A temporary stay in the genocidal activities then followed, in the first place because some members of the Ustaša hierarchy did not approve of such radical treatment of Serbs. Moreover, because of the massacre in Glina, Archbishop Stepinac wrote a letter to Pavelić protesting against Ustaša crimes for the first time. Finally, people had to be placated in the NDH because Pavelić was on the verge of signing the Rome Agreement with Italy; he knew that he would have to make enormous concessions to his Fascist allies, and that many people would object.

Thus, for a full six weeks – from 13 May to 1 July – there were no more mass slaughters of Serbs in Croatia, and in Herzegovina the killings did not start until the beginning of June. At the same time, the Ustaša authorities intensified other kinds of persecution: in May, measures against the Jews were stepped up almost every day; and in some places, their mass deportation to camps began. The arrest of prominent 'undesirables' in towns also continued, and the prisons were by now overflowing. Indeed, the Danica Camp near Koprivnica already had several thousand prisoners by the end of May, most of them Serbs. Summary courts also passed their first judgements. The threatening series of new laws announced a further worsening of the situation. In certain villages, especially in Lika, Ustaša and army patrols terrorised the population: sometimes they looted, and sometimes they took away prominent Serbs who were never heard of again. But for several weeks, there were no more mass murders of the kind that had taken place in Gudovac, Blagaj, and Glina.

In the shadow of the organised mass deportations of Serbs in Zagreb (already on 5 and 6 July) and its environs (starting on 10 July), mass murders began again (Suvaja, 1 July). All this time the Germans were advancing quickly on the eastern front against the Soviet Union. The deportations were part of state policy that was implemented by all the government institutions – ministries, state directorates, county districts, the armed forces. Two documents from different ends of the NDH, from Kostajnica and Stolac, give a good illustration of how the plan about thirds, never explicitly written down, was in fact being carried out. To be sure, there are many other documents of a similar nature.

On 8 July, the Ustaša *logornik* from Kostajnica wrote about a list, compiled by an unknown person, of 'dangerous and undesirable persons in the Kostajnica district' who were to be deported. He considered the list 'insufficient, superficial, [and] not serious' because it contained fewer persons than he wanted it to. It seems the list included only about 100–200 persons, and the *logornik* compared it to the 'work of a mower who takes blade by blade of grass from a large meadow'. He considered that if this number of people 'emigrated' the action would leave a 'very pale' impression. In his opinion, the Serbs – who he called a 'foreign pack' – in such a small action, such a pack 'itself would not be touched'. The *logornik* obviously wanted to instil fear among the Serbs, whom he suggested that 'a large bush should be taken out in one place, to shake the soul of the foreign pack by this exemplary amputation of the foreign element from the national Croatian body'.[17]

The Ustaša *logornik* in Kostajnica thought that the final goal of mass emigration – that 'shaking the soul' – was to 'force the process of spiritual excitement, so that they subject themselves to … the process of conversion to Catholicism'. He then proposed that 900 of the 2,213 inhabitants in the village of Slavinje should be deported, which would make room for 'poor Croats' and the 'appointed number of Slovene immigrants'. This would create a purely Croatian area, because emigration from that village would 'lead to an unbroken line of Croatian villages from Dvor na Uni to Jasenovac, and what this means from the strategic point of view ... it is unnecessary to say'.[18] The *logornik* therefore considered that emigration would speed up conversion to Catholicism; but it is clear that these two goals were interdependent, their final purpose being the creation of an ethnically pure area.

The head of the district office in Stolac had similar views: having reported on 11 July 1941 that there would be no emigration from the district, he then wrote that the family members of the Orthodox priests who had been killed by the Ustaše had 'applied for conversion to the Roman Catholic religion', adding 'that now about 250 Orthodox families from the more immediate territory of this district have applied for conversion' – obviously considering that this was a solution.[19] He mentioned the activities of Vice-Marshal Vladimir Laxa, who was to have stopped the 'wild Ustaše' and their crimes, asserting that there were no conditions for organising emigration; thus he thought that mass conversion to Catholicism offered the best solution. Government institutions were directly engaged in organising mass emigration, and in the process of conversion to Catholicism, although in the case of mass killings there was obviously a 'parallel line of command'.

From August 1941, both the Ustaša authorities and Pavelić himself – and later, as post-war émigrés other Ustaše as well – usually did not deny that some crimes against the Serbs had taken place. But they also claimed that these had been committed by the 'wild Ustaše', individuals and small groups who were beyond the control of the central authorities. This is not true, because the first crimes (those from April and May already discussed) as well as those committed during the summer, were perpetrated by groups under the direct command of Vjekoslav Maks Luburić. Luburić was a man in Eugen Dido Kvaternik's confidence. And Kvaternik was the main organiser and general administrator of all anti-Jewish and anti-Serbian persecution from May 1941 to September 1942. He was also the main director of the Public Order and Security Directorate NDH (Ravnateljstvo za javni red i sigurnost – RAVSIGUR), and commander of Ustaša Control (Ustaška nadzorna služba – UNS). As Ante Pavelić's closest associate, a man who enjoyed his greatest confidence between the days of Ustaša emigration until summer 1942, Kvaternik discussed and made all major decisions for Pavelić practically every day. Pavelić gave Dido Kvaternik his maximum authority and support for everything he did through the two police institutions the latter headed: he was looked on as the 'symbol of Ustaše terror in the NDH'.[20] Pavelić, Kvaternik and Luburić represented three levels of the genocidal crimes in the NDH: Pavelić as the main instigator, Kvaternik as the planner and organiser, with Luburić as the leading and cruellest executioner.

Nevertheless, scholars very rarely take into account the economic situation that largely contributed to the catastrophe. The NDH had to bear the expenses of all the German and part of the Italian troops on its territory. Italy took away the NDH's maritime economy and shipbuilding, and Hungary its most-developed agricultural areas. The Partisan uprising and Chetnik rebellion brought further insecurity. Consequently, by August many roads and railway lines were blocked. The destruction of the economy was so terrible that even in August – that is, at the time of the year when there should have been the most food – documents clearly show that 'much of Bosnia, i.e. the passive regions, depend on food imports', and that 'only the districts of Bosansko Grahovo, Bosanski Petrovac, Sanski Most, Prnjavor, Bijeljina, Derventa and Doboj [seven of a total 53] had enough of their own food, and even some surplus'.[21]

Malnutrition and hunger began to take lives in June – in Maglaj (in Bosnia and Herzegovina) at least three people died of hunger,[22] and as time passed conditions grew increasingly difficult. Prices rose fast but salaries remained the same: a report from Sarajevo at the start of 1942 showed that lower government officials could buy 25 to 30 kg of flour a month for their salaries on the black market, because there was none in the shops and the rationing system did not function.[23]

At the end of August there were estimates from Knin that 'nutrition everywhere suffers from the lack of food, high price rises, traffic disorders, the needs of the occupying army and Chetnik activities. There is a great lack of flour, lard and oil'.[24] 'Meat, if there is any' sold for astronomic prices.[25] On 5 September 1941, the local authorities requested a train from Zagreb by telegram 'bringing food for the Cetina Grand County at once, because of the hunger, which is having serious consequences'.[26] It seems that the situation was somewhat better in the villages. The report from Knin said that 'the peasant brings very little produce to the town [probably Knin], and what he does bring he wants to barter. If he sells it for money, then he demands much more than the normal price'.[27] For urban dwellers the 'normal price' would be the one that they, with their small incomes, could afford. By autumn, the urban population was rapidly growing poorer and many were on the verge of starvation.

The economic catastrophe was yet one more element that must be taken into account when talking about the ruthlessness and brutality of Ustaša crimes. The basic reason for the murders, there is no doubt, was ethnic and religious hatred. But the hysteria of the entire atmosphere – the desire to hurt others, to drive them from their houses, to steal their money and food – can be explained by fear for one's own existence and the existence of one's family.

How did the Croats react in these times? Judging from how they greeted the German army in Zagreb and other towns, as well as from various events at the time, most of the Croatian population was pleased about the defeat of Yugoslavia and the establishment of the NDH. The reasons for this attitude were certainly the extreme dissatisfaction with the Kingdom of Yugoslavia, the delusion that a period of peace would follow the short April war, and that Croatia, unlike most of Europe, had avoided the destruction and suffering of war. However, disappointment soon set in and sympathy evaporated. The first great blow to Croatian national sentiment was the Rome Agreement signed on 18 May 1941. This treaty ceded almost all of Dalmatia to Italy, in addition to much of Croatian Primorje and a small part of Gorski kotar, despite the fact that the population of these regions was about 90% Croatian and just under 10% Serbian. There were a negligible number of Italians. Gradually, but quite soon, other disappointments followed. Racial and ethnic persecution of Serbs, Jews and Roma, not to mention the terrorising of political opponents, antagonised most of the Croatian population and made them feel insecure. The sudden appearance and continuous growth of political and armed resistance to both the Ustaša regime and foreign occupation are the most convincing indicators of the political disposition of the Croatian and non-Croatian population within the NDH.

The relations among Ustaše, Croats, Jews and Serbs were by no means simple.[28] In the interwar years, there was a noisy minority in Zagreb that was clearly and outspokenly anti-Semitic. Due to the repressive political system in Yugoslavia, hatred of Serbs was difficult to express in public. Anti-Semitism was supported by a small part of the middle class, some workers and craftsmen, and in a few church circles. The majority of the middle class rejected anti-Semitism in both theory and practice, and from time to time they publicly expressed these views. Intellectual discussions about anti-Semitism obviously did not reach the population at large, but they were not indifferent to the problem. It seems that very diverse feelings emerged at the level of everyday practice: differences in religious and national identity, as well as opposition to Jewish merchants and to the repressive Belgrade government, often led to antagonism against Jews and Serbs. Yet on the other hand, the traditional Croatian multiculturality and multiethnicity, and the tolerance that this resulted in, simultaneously encouraged cooperation. Because of all this, and also because of traditional conformity and fear, many people in Zagreb kept to the maxim, 'I don't know anything, I haven't seen anything', even though the persecution and deportations of Jews and Serbs were taking place before their very eyes.[29]

As the years passed, the divergent elements influencing the prevailing attitude toward Jews increased or decreased, appeared or disappeared: anti-Semitism grew stronger or weaker depending on conditions in Croatia, in Yugoslavia, as well as in Europe and the world. When the Ustaša genocide of Jews and Serbs began in 1941, some Croats readily took part, but a large number actively or passively resisted this behaviour. 'Some Zagreb people ... greeted the Germans with bouquets of flowers and oranges', but 'Ljubo Majer, who always was and has remained a great Croat until the present, burst into tears', said Vlado Prašek, who then emphasised, 'This great popular enthusiasm quickly deflated when the first posters appeared about shootings and about opponents and innocent hostages who had been hung'.[30]

People who were considered leftists or who could be accused of cooperation with the hated Yugoslav regime were in great danger. They faced difficult dilemmas and reacted in different ways: for example, the distinguished lawyer and politician, Želimir Mažuranić, killed himself on 6 July, at the height of the deportations of Jews and Serbs; Oton Frangeš (1870–1945), Minister of Forestry in the royal government in 1929, wrote grovelling letters to the Minister of the Interior, Andrija Artuković ('I always worked for the good of the Croatian people'; 'I was always ready to defend the homeland') to have his telephone, which had been cut off in August, reinstalled.[31]

It is worth mentioning some illustrative reports showing how things were. On 12 June, the Brestovac-Sljeme Army Station (on the Zagrebačka gora mountain near Zagreb) reported to the Zagreb County District that three patients from the Brestovac Hospital on the mountain – Želimir Ivčić, Rudolf Puc and Tomo Berlek – 'criticised conditions in the State and said that the Jews were being treated cruelly, that the Germans would take away everything we have, and that the Italians have taken all of Dalmatia'.[32] After the anti-Semitic laws were proclaimed the German papers in Croatia defended them, with unhidden disgust, saying that 'slogans such as "The Jews are people, too", "Kindness is a Christian virtue" are appearing in Croatia, and there are protests in the whole country because of the anti-Jewish provisions'.[33] A number of reports by Captain Haeffner and Edmund Glaise von Horstenau, a German general serving in the NDH, show how Croats were reacting to news about Ustaša crimes against the Serbs. In a report dated 9 August, von Horstenau said: 'every Croat who is not an Ustaša is strongly against this ... In principle the Serbs have been placed outside the law, but there is great uncertainty among the Croats, too ... Eugen Dido Kvaternik is the most hated man in the land'. He continued to say that Orthodox families, after being maltreated, would not return to their villages and instead spent days in the forests. The terror carried out by the Ustaše induced the Orthodox population to join the Partisans, while many Croats became Communists, said the German general.[34]

Similarly, the abbot of the Franciscan Monastery in Knin said that the 'Croatian citizens were horrified' by the news about the murder of 24 Serbs from Knin and its surroundings, killed by the Ustaše in June.[35] Stjepan Vukovac, state secretary and Assistant Minister of the Interior in the NDH, realised that 'Dido Kvaternik and various other important "bigwigs" were preparing a real war of extermination against the Serbs and the Jews'. When the mass arrests and killing began, Vukovac 'was pensioned at his own request' on 28 June, as reported by *Hrvatski narod*.[36] But there were few such people in the state bureaucracy – it must also be taken into account that this was a time when it was not easy to get a job and make a living.

This negative reaction by many of the Croats resulted partially from the fact that very soon they themselves became victims of the Ustaša regime and its fascist allies. One could say that Croats were more sharply divided than citizens in most other occupied countries, or in countries allied with Nazi Germany: there were relatively more local participants to atrocities, and relatively more locals who resisted the criminals. Andrija Artuković and Eugen Dido Kvaternik were not alone in organising the killing: 'the deliberate and calculated planners of the slaughter were Pavelić himself and his closest circle (Budak, Lorković, Puk, Dido Kvaternik etc.), organisers in the field were people such as Gutić, Luburić, V. Tomić etc., while the many killers were themselves often unconscious tools in the hands of the real culprits, blinded by racial and other theories'.[37]

On the other hand, the prominent anti-Fascists Slavko Komar and Ivan Šibl were not alone in throwing bombs and joining the Partisans. In a speech in Glina in February 1944, the distinguished writer Vladimir Nazor (1873–1948) answered the question 'Why did I join the Partisans?' by saying that he had been moved to do so by the 'inhuman persecution and extermination of Jews, who are people just like we are, and – which is the main reason – I was moved to do so by the ill-treatment and slaughter of the Serbs, who are our brothers in blood and with whom we have been living together for so many centuries'.[38]

Although contemporary papers described conditions in the first months of the NDH in glowing tones, reports from the field gave a completely different picture. For example, at the end of August 1941 the army regiment command in Knin claimed that the 'disposition of the Croatian people to the state is good' but then contradicted itself by saying that 'among many people the faith in the government has been swayed, because it had not been capable of quelling the Chetnik activities at the beginning, or of preventing the lawlessness and tyranny of the Ustaše.[39] The following report from the beginning of September states that the disposition of the 'Croatian people to the State and the Leader is very good' and that the exceptions were 'individuals … Communist lovers or Greater Yugoslavs'. Yet the rather self-confident conclusion was that 'their influence can hardly be felt'. However, these positive assessments were immediately denied by the report itself: 'the military occupation of these areas by Italy has caused great consternation and confusion among the Croats', and people 'are convinced that this is only the first step … in the final annexation of these areas to Italy'.

Thus, it is not surprising that the Home Guard Assembly, in a report on conditions in Sarajevo and Bosnia in the second half of December 1941, found that because the great food crisis was not being solved, Croats (both Catholics and Muslims) 'are losing faith in the government... a state of expectation can be felt among all of them ... the word "how much longer?" is gaining in importance, and a kind of indifferenec to everything is spreading through all classes. Even the most fiery and most enthusiastic Croat from the early days of the takeover is beginning to cool, especially here in Bosnia'.[40]

Until the end of the year, Pavelić and his collaborators stubbornly continued to behave as they had earlier, using force, deliberately producing anarchy, and carrying out genocide. The economy collapsed; the Ustaše committed numerous crimes against Serbs and Jews; and the Partisan uprising started as well as the Chetnik movement. Soon the Chetniks showed the nature of their own ideology and practice by committing the first mass crimes against Muslim and Croatian civilians. By the autumn, the Italians and Germans started to interfere with the internal affairs of the NDH even more directly than previously. The NDH became a German-Italian protectorate in the true meaning of the word. In this way, all the more important processes that happened during the Second World War in Croatia had in fact started by the autumn of 1941. There was no way back.

Notes

1. In all, about 10,000 Roma were killed in the NDH but, contrary to the case of the Serbs and the Jews, this passed almost unnoticed; see N. Lengel-Krizman, *Genocid nad Romima – Jasenovac 1942* [*Genocide against the Roma – Jasenovac 1942*] (Jasenovac, Zagreb, 2003), pp.163–7.
2. See, HDA [Hrvatski Državni Arhiv – Croatian State Archives], fund MUP SRH, 013.0.56, V. Židovec, *Moje sudjelovanje u političkom životu*, p.38.
3. See, I. Goldstein, Holokaust u Zagrebu [*Holocaust in Zagreb*], Zagreb 2001,.
4. *Hrvatska mladost* 3/1941, p.55.
5. AHMBiH, VI/11, p.382.
6. *Hrvatska gruda* 65/1941.
7. *Deutsche Zeitung in Kroatien*, 17 April 1941; *Hrvatski narod*, no.67, 20 April 1941.
8. *Hrvatski radnik*, no.16, Zagreb 30 April 1941.
9. *Hrvatski narod*, 3 May 1941.
10. *Antisemitism: A Historical Encyclopedia of Prejudice and Persecution*, Santa Barbara – Denver – Oxford 2005, ed. R.S. Levy, t. II, p.551; H.H. Ben-Sasson, *A History of the Jewish People*, Harvard, 1976, p.884.
11. Ustaška pobjeda
12. S.D. Milošević, *Izbeglice i preseljenici na teritoriji okupirane Jugoslavije 1941–1945* [*Refugees and the Displaced in the Territory of occupied Yugoslavia 1941–1945*], Beograd 1981, p.113, quotes the manuscript of the doctoral thesis, inaccessible to me, of Đ. Stanisavljević, *Ustanak u Hrvatskoj 1941–1942*, Univerzitetska biblioteka, Belgrade 1965, p.79.
13. *Hrvatska krajina*, no.4, Banja Luka, 26 April 1941.
14. *Hrvatski narod*, 10 May 1941; *Ustaše, Dokumenti*, pp.172–3; HDA, fund ZKRZ GUZ, no. 306, box 10, p.322. The '*mitnica* [toll-house] in Ilica' or the 'Ilica *mitnica* [toll-house]' was located where the last tram stop in Črnomerec is today, in the northeast part of the city.
15. HDA, fund ZKRZ GUZ, no 306, box 10, p.147.
16. *Novi list*, Zagreb, 15 June 1941.
17. HDA, fond Ponova, br. 1076, Srpski odsjek, Opći spisi, box 441, 324/1941.
18. Ibid.
19. HDA, fond Ponova, br. 1076, Srpski odsjek, Opći spisi, box 442, 677/1941.
20. *Tko je tko u NDH* [*Who's Who in the ISC*], Zagreb 1995, 224–5; on the omnipotence of Dido Kvaternik and on Pavelić's support, see the testimony of Stjepan Vukovac, Assistant Minister of the Interior, in April and May 1941; HDA, fond MUP RH, 013.2.4, pp.70 ff.
21. HDA, fund MUP NDH, No. 223, box 27, Predsjednički ured, br. 30135, 30738, 1941.
22. HDA, D-2339–86.
23. AHM BiH [The Archives of the Museum of Bosnia and Herzegovina], p.421.
24. HDA, fond 1.1196, oružničke pukovnije NDH, box 3, j. s. 289/ taj. 1941.
25. HDA, fond 1.1196, oružničke pukovnije NDH, box 3, j. s. 321/ taj. 1941, pp.1–3.

26. HDA, Fund MUP NDH, No. 223, box 27, Predsjednički ured, No. 29304, 1941.
27. HDA, fond 1.1196, oružničke pukovnije NDH, kut. 3, j. s. 289/ taj. 1941.
28. See Goldstein (note 3), pp.626–35.
29. Testimony of Professor Stjepan Steiner (1915–2006), a doctor in Zagreb before 1941 who joined the Partisans and became a major general and Tito's personal doctor.
30. B. Prašek-Całczyńska, B., *Memoari jedne liječnice* [*The Memoirs of a Female Doctor*], Zagreb, 1997, p.144.
31. HDA, Fund MUP NDH, No. 223, box. 26, Predsjednički ured, No. 25132, 1941; on Frangeš: HBL 4, p.365.
32. HDA, Kotarska oblast Zagreb, box 71, pov. no. 334/41.
33. *Deutsche Zeitung in Kroatien*, No.37, 27 May 1941.
34. Gert Fricke, *Kroatien 1941–1944: Der 'Unabhängige Staat' in der Sicht des Deutschen Bevollmächtigten Generals in Agram Glaise von Horstenau*, 1972, pp.26–45.
35. *Ljetopis samostana sv. Ante u Kninu 1904–1963* [*The Annals of the Monastery of St. Anton in Knin 1904–1963*], ed. P. Bezina, Zagreb 1998, p.180.
36. HDA, Fund MUP SRH, 013.0.56, V. Židovec, *Moje sudjelovanje u političkom životu*, pp.31, 33; see also note 20, p.424; *Hrvatski narod*, 30 June 1941.
37. HDA, fund MUP SRH, 013.0.3, Dizdar, *Ustaštvo i NDH*, 55; see similarly, HDA, fund MUP SRH, 013.0.56, V. Židovec, *Moje sudjelovanje u političkom životu*, 138; Viktor Gutić was especially persistent in the persecution of Serbs, about which the Germans cautioned the authorities; see note 20, p.145.
38. *Jevrejski pregled*, Belgrade 1966, pp.7–8.
39. HDA, Fund 1.1196, oružničke pukovnije NDH, box 3, j. s. 289/ taj. 1941.
40. HDA, MHB, 12; the report is largely about the catastrophic conditions in the food supply, but it is clear that the apathy it also describes was caused not only by this but by the overall conditions in the country as well.

Controversies surrounding the Catholic Church in Wartime Croatia, 1941–45

MARK BIONDICH

Department of Justice, Canada

Few issues in the historiography of the Second World War arouse as much controversy as that of the wartime role of Pope Pius XII, the Vatican and the Catholic Church. One need only look to the contentious debate caused by two recent English-language publications, the first by John Cornwell and the second by Daniel Jonah Goldhagen, attempting to address the role of Pius XII and the Catholic Church during the war.[1] Among the many controversies surrounding the Catholic Church is its role in wartime Croatia from 1941 to 1945. During the war, Croatia's fascists, the Ustaša movement, collaborated with the Axis to achieve Croatian statehood.[2] Collaboration necessarily extended to several fronts, including complicity in the Final Solution; the Ustaše conducted their own murderous campaign against the Serb population, in addition to Jews and Roma. By most accounts, the Ustaša movement enjoyed the support of a substantial segment of the Catholic clergy in Croatia and Bosnia-Herzegovina. This support was not necessarily passive. Several priests and members of the Franciscan order joined the Ustaša movement and, in some cases, even participated in the implementation of its murderous policies. The Catholic hierarchy in Croatia, represented by the Archbishop of Zagreb, Alojzije Cardinal Stepinac, has been criticised for failing to distance itself publicly from that regime or to condemn its policies.

During his only state visit to Bosnia-Herzegovina, the late Pope John Paul II held a mass on 22 June 2003 in Banja Luka, in the *Republika srpska*, before a crowd reportedly numbering over 50,000. The Pope called for reconciliation and remarked that 'from this city, marked in the course of history by so much suffering and bloodshed, I ask almighty God to have mercy on the sins committed against humanity, human dignity, and freedom, also by the children of the Catholic Church, and to foster in all the desire for mutual forgiveness. Only in a climate of true reconciliation will the memory of so many innocent victims and their sacrifice not be in vain.'[3] These remarks implicitly alluded to the ethnic cleansing of Croats and Bosnian Muslims by Serbs during the war of the 1990s, but also to the killings of Orthodox Serbs by the Croatian government during the Second World War. Five years earlier, in October 1998, Pope John Paul II paid his second visit to Croatia, where he beatified, amid considerable controversy, Cardinal Stepinac.[4]

In October 1946, a Yugoslav people's court found Stepinac guilty of high treason and war crimes. Since then, he has been uniformly portrayed as a war criminal in Yugoslav historiography. According to this version of events, not only did Stepinac publicly welcome the Croatian state formed in the wake of the Axis invasion of Yugoslavia in April 1941, he actively supported some or all of its criminal policies. Moreover, it was alleged that the Ustaša movement had the backing of the majority of the Catholic clergy in wartime Croatia, who simply followed the lead of the hierarchy. In this way, the Catholic Church was held responsible, in whole or in part, for wartime atrocities.[5] On the other hand, Stepinac's defenders have insisted that the leadership of the Catholic Church in Croatia intervened for humanity whenever it could, and that it opposed the racist policies of both the Third Reich and Ustaša state. In the Church's view, Stepinac remained loyal to the tenets of the Catholic Church, tried to save Serbs, Jews and Roma from slaughter at the hands of the authorities whenever he could, and was critical of the atrocities perpetrated by both the Ustaše and the Communist Partisans. His defenders readily acknowledge that many individual priests behaved immorally during the war, but argue that they did so out of personal political conviction rather than general Church policy or directive, and that Stepinac was in no position to control the behaviour of all clergy in Croatia. Stepinac's post war conviction, they assert, was politically premised on his outspoken anti-Communist views.[6]

Outside former Yugoslavia, debate surrounding the wartime role of the papacy was unleashed in the 1960s. The German playwright, Rolf Hochhuth, initiated the debate with his 1963 play *The Deputy*, which portrayed Pope Pius XII as a Nazi sympathiser. In a 1964 interview with Hannah Arendt, Hochhuth remarked that Pope Pius XII 'is a symbol of all men who are passive when their brother is harmed.'[7] The play permanently transformed the image of Pius XII. Following the appearance of *The Deputy*, authors such as Guenther Lewy, Saul Friedlander, and Carlo Falconi began publishing studies that, to varying degrees, buttressed Hochhuth's portrait. Works sympathetic to Pius XII continued to appear, but the harm to his reputation had been done.[8] The work of Falconi in particular drew serious attention to the role of the Catholic Church in Croatia.[9] Since then, a number of studies have appeared generally addressing the role of Stepinac personally. Much of the recent scholarly literature has tried to mediate a critical position between the untenable extremes posited by Yugoslav historiography and Stepinac's faithful defenders.[10]

The controversies surrounding the wartime role of the Catholic Church in Croatia centre on four general issues, which I will identify as follows: (1) the alleged high treason of the Croatian Catholic hierarchy, headed by Stepinac, which welcomed the creation of the wartime Croatian state in April 1941 and allegedly lent its active support to the Ustaša regime from 1941 to 1945; (2) the Church's alleged role in forced and fear-induced conversions of Orthodox Serbs to Catholicism; (3) the participation of Catholic clergy in the Ustaša Party and/or various institutions affiliated with that party; and (4) the reluctance of the Church to openly and unequivocally condemn the genocidal policies of the Ustaša authorities, and to formally withhold its support from that regime. The article will try to address each of these points in turn.

The Context: Religion, the Catholic Church and Croat Nationalism, 1836–1918

Before turning to a discussion of these four issues, it may be useful for the sake of context to discuss the role of religion in Croat nationalism and the Catholic Church in the Croat national movement. Although it has often been argued that religion has been an important component of Croat nationalism – and that the Catholic Church has played a decisive role in preserving Croat identity – for the better part of the modern era, Croat national ideologues have refused to identify religion and nation. In actual fact, only after the Second World War did the Catholic Church become a significant factor in Croatian politics. After 1945, the most salient feature of Croatian political life was Communist dictatorship within a reconstituted Yugoslavia. Democratic institutions and interwar political parties were suppressed in Croatia as elsewhere, and the new system of federalism suffered at the hands of strict centralism within the League of Communists of Yugoslavia (1948–62). For Croat nationalists, whether exiled *émigrés* (such as the Ustaše, Croat Peasant Party) or former Communists like Franjo Tuđman, the Church became an important institution of national resistance, the only remaining autonomous establishment in Croatian society. Religion did not necessarily become a factor in Croat nationalism *per se*; but after 1945, Catholic confessional and Croat national interests were deemed by many nationalists to be, if not the same, then at least closely related. The failure of Yugoslavia's period of 'liberalisation' (1962–71), and the suppression of Croat nationalism in 1971 following its revival during the Croatian 'Spring' (1966–71), only strengthened the perceived bond between Church and nation, solidifying the importance of the Church in Croatian society. This was a major reversal of pre-1941 patterns.

Since the nineteenth century, Croat nationalism has been shaped by two important factors: (1) A state-oriented perception of nationalism rooted in the ideology of historic state right, according to which Croats as a nation are identified with the Croatian state. All of Croatia's nineteenth century national ideologues adopted a framework of historic state right, an ideology holding that the Croatian state, born in the medieval period, had never *de jure* lost its independence, despite the union first with Hungary (1102) and then the Habsburgs (1527). The bearer of this state right was originally the Croatian nobility (or 'political nation'), while in the modern era it was the Croat nation, which alone possessed a historic state right that the other nationalities of Croatia had to recognise and to which they had to submit. (2) Slavic reciprocity, the identification with other (South) Slavs; this factor was, as in the case of Czechs and Slovaks, a reflection of Croat numerical inferiority in relation to the dominant Magyars and Germans, also stemming from the fact that there was a numerically significant Serb minority in Croatia.

Religious affiliation simply was not a factor in the thinking of national ideologues, nor did they employ it as a criterion of nationality.[11] This was true of Ljudevit Gaj's Illyrianist movement (1836–48); Ante Starčević and his Party of (Croatian State) Right (1861–95);[12] and Josip Juraj Strossmayer and Canon Franjo Rački's National Party. The thinking of Croatia's nineteenth century national ideologues was conditioned by the legalistic traditions of the Habsburg monarchy; Habsburg rulers acknowledged ancient political entities and treaties, not popular or national will. Historical state right thus had a powerful sway over the thinking of all of Croatia's nineteenth century intellectuals, who generally refused to recognise the existence of a Serb (or any other) 'political nation' in Croatia. The thinking of the Croat political elites was similar to that of their Polish, Magyar, and Czech counterparts, who resorted to historical state right to legitimise their contemporary national rights and programmes.

Croatia's nineteenth century national ideologues resisted the association between religion and nation in favour of other criteria – political, cultural, historical, or a combination of these factors. This tradition persisted well into the twentieth century. For example, Stjepan Radić, who founded the Croat People's Peasant Party (HPSS) in 1904,[13] was anti-clerical by temperament and opposed the identification of religion and nationality, just as he repeatedly denounced the role of Catholic and Orthodox clergy in Croatia's political life. His colleagues from the so-called Progressive Youth, who founded the Progressive Party (1905–10), rejected religion as arcane and as an impediment to the unity of Croats and Serbs. Even as Ante Starčević's movement splintered after 1895, all the successor groups (including the so-called Frankists, Starčević's Party of Right, and Young Croats)[14] remained committed to the idea of a multi-religious Croat nation; they continued to refute the existence of Orthodox Serb, Bosnian Muslim, and Catholic Slovene nationalities in Greater Croatia.

Originating in the Habsburg period, Croatia's Catholic movement was associated most closely with the Bishop of Krk, the Slovenian Antun Mahnič (1850–1920). In Bosnia-Herzegovina, its main exponent was the Archbishop of Sarajevo, Josip Stadler (1843–1918). Like Catholic movements elsewhere in Europe, so too in Croatia and Bosnia-Herzegovina Catholics struggled against liberalism and all its supposedly negative implications, like the separation of Church and State, the individualist notion that each person should be the master of their own conscience, and the secularisation of education. But the Catholic political movement ('clericalist') was neither organisationally nor ideologically monolithic, especially on questions of nationality. Unlike the Catholic movements of Italy, France, and Austria, operating in predominantly Catholic societies, the Catholic movement of Croatia and Bosnia-Herzegovina operated in nationally and religiously heterogeneous lands. In Bosnia-Herzegovina, Catholics were the smallest of the three religious-national communities. In Croatia, there was a large Serb Orthodox population. Under the circumstances, the Croat Catholic movement was divided on the issue of national ideology. A conservative wing identified Catholicism with Croat nationality, but a moderate wing continued to operate in the liberal Strossmayerist tradition and downplayed the importance of religion in national identity. Archbishop Stadler, who emphasised the primacy of Catholic religious principles, represented the conservative strand. He tied Croat nationality to Catholicism, evidently hoped to convert Bosnia's Muslims to Catholicism and, like some other Croat (and Slovene) clericalists, even hoped to meld Catholic Croats and Slovenes into a hybrid South Slavic nationality.[15] When the first Croatian Catholic Congress was held in Zagreb in 1900, one of the participants, Baron Miroslav Kulmer, told the delegates that 'as a Croat in Croatia I identify Catholicism with Croat national identity.' The Church was 'the only institution capable of preserving our consciousness and nationality.'[16]

Many Catholic intellectuals and clergy continued to oppose the identification of Catholicism with Croat nationality, however. At the second Croatian Catholic Congress, held in 1913 in the Slovenian capital, Ljubljana, the Greek Catholic (Uniate) delegate, Janko Šimrak, explicitly opposed the identification of Catholicism and Croat nationality, and then urged the other delegates to do the same. He told the Congress that 'it is a great mistake when all Orthodox in the Croat lands are uniformly counted as Serbs, and only Catholics are counted as Croats. This separation of nationalities ... has done Croats, and does them today, great harm.'[17] In the event, in 1910 Croatia's Catholic clericalists merged with the so-called Frankists to form the Christian Social Party of Right. This was merely a marriage of convenience rather than a merger of ideologically kindred spirits, and the two would part company after 1918. Before this occurred, however, they made common cause with the clericalist Slovene People's Party. In 1912, Croat and Slovene clericalists jointly issued the 'Vienna Resolution', which asserted that Slovenes and Croats were one people. It showed, *inter alia*, that Catholic thinkers in Croatia and the region were on occasion amenable to supra-national formulas.

The Catholic Church, Croat nationalism and Yugoslavia, 1918–41

With the formation of the Kingdom of Serbs, Croats, and Slovenes (hereafter 'Yugoslavia') in December 1918, Croatian politics split along urban–rural lines even as it united in its opposition to Serbian centralism. Radić's Croat Peasant Party (hereafter HSS, *Hrvatska seljačka stranka*) represented the mainstream and moderate variant of Croat nationalism after 1918. Of his Croat opponents (for example, the Croat Union, the Croat Party of Right, the Croat People's Party) only the Croat People's Party (hereafter HPS, *Hrvatska pučka stranka*) could legitimately be classified as 'clericalist'. It never gained a substantial following among Croats, however. Opposed to Radić's politically and socially dominant (but anti-clericalist) HSS, it was dependent on and largely followed the autonomist national programme of the Slovene People's Party, a Catholic party with a mass following in Slovenia. In this regard, it could be counted as a member of the 'soft' opposition to state centralism. The Croat People's Party remained on the political fringe, a marginal factor in Croatian politics. Its main areas of support were those regions where religious affiliation was still more important than national sentiment as well as where Croat national awakening was still incomplete, as among the Catholics of Herzegovina and the Dalmatian hinterland and the Catholic Bunjevci of Bačka. It was also strong in areas where the Franciscans held considerable influence, such as Herzegovina and parts of Dalmatia, and probably had the support of most of Bosnia's Catholic clergy.[18]

Much has been made in Yugoslav historiography of the Catholic Church's distaste for, and even outright hostility toward, the formation of the Yugoslav state, and its subversive work against that state after 1918, allegedly in collusion with the Vatican. This view is far too simplistic. It is true that in some Church circles, the disappearance of the predominantly Catholic Dual Monarchy was bemoaned. Some clerics, like Archbishop Ivan Šarić of Sarajevo, were hardly sympathetic to the new Yugoslav state. At the same time, however, many Church leaders, like the Archbishop Anton Bauer of Zagreb, Bishop Antun Akšamović of Đakovo, and Bishop Mahnić of Krk, openly and sincerely welcomed the new state. In December 1918 and again in early 1919, Archbishop Bauer issued circulars to the clergy to that effect. The Church leadership's support for the new state mirrored, and may well have been influenced by, the enthusiasm prevalent at that time in Croat intellectual and middle class circles. It should also be remembered that some of the most important and politically active Catholic leaders in late nineteenth century Croatia, such as Bishop Josip Juraj Strossmayer of Đakovo and Canon Franjo Rački, were ecclesiastical 'liberals' and proponents of cultural Yugoslavism. And, as noted, neither the Slovene nor the Croat People's Party was opposed to Yugoslavia *per se*, although both wanted the centralist Vidovdan constitution of 1921 amended and the country decentralised along regional lines.

The support of Catholic Church leaders for the new state gradually waned, however. In part, this was due to the fact that many Yugoslav unitarists viewed the Church as alien and anti-Slavic, and thus *a priori* opposed to any Yugoslavia, whereas Orthodoxy was seen as native and 'national'. Some Yugoslav unitarists even encouraged a schism with Rome and the formation of a national Catholic Church, and welcomed the creation of the Croatian Old Catholic Church in 1923. In reality, the Old Catholic Church never posed as serious a challenge to the faith as some believed at the time. But the Catholic Church, accustomed to state protection in the Dual Monarchy, now encountered indifference and even hostility from the state authorities. The disenchantment of Church leaders with Yugoslavia also reflected the political evolution of the country as a whole. The imposition of the royal dictatorship in January 1929 moved the Croat Catholic movement generally into the ranks of the 'hard' opposition. But what did 'hard' opposition mean in practice? Croatia's Catholic movement now had to choose between a programme of liberal democracy and Yugoslav federalism (that is, the HSS line) on the one hand, and Croatian independence (that is, the Ustaše) on the other;[19] it had to decide whether it wanted reform within the country, which meant a return to some form of parliamentary democracy along the lines of the 1920s, or the destruction of Yugoslavia.

After 1929 the Catholic movement operated through a number of organisations, such as Catholic Action and the Crusader organisation, among others.[20] The movement's intellectuals voiced their views through periodicals such as *Hrvatska straža* [*Croatian Sentinel*, 1929–45] and *Hrvatska smotra* [*Croatian Review*, 1933–45].[21] These intellectuals and the Church hierarchy increasingly believed that Catholic (and Croat) interests were threatened, especially after the Yugoslav government failed to ratify the recently negotiated Concordat with the Vatican in 1937. The Croat Catholic political movement of the 1920s and 1930s was quite different from its progenitor of the late Habsburg era. By 'Catholic political movement' I mean those politically-oriented organisations in Croatia with an explicitly Catholic agenda. I would include in this 'movement' in addition to politically active Catholic clergy, Catholic-oriented intellectuals, Catholic student groups, and periodicals. It is difficult to attribute a coherent political ideology to the 'Catholic political movement', for its many periodicals were in the hands of the laity and expressed a range of political opinions. The Catholic 'front' in Croatia was so organisationally and politically fragmented that Stella Alexander has gone so far as to suggest that there was no such thing as a 'Catholic political (or clericalist) movement' in interwar Croatia.[22]

A generational shift was clearly evident in the movement; the cohort that rose to the forefront in the interwar period was raised in a milieu of dysfunctional democracy where the national question pervaded all aspects of political life. The assassination of the Croat leader Stjepan Radić in 1928, the royal dictatorship (1929–34) and Great Depression of the 1930s only heightened the nationalist radicalism of the younger members of the movement, especially those in nationally heterogeneous regions like Herzegovina, the Lika of Croatia and Dalmatia.

Unlike the Slovene People's Party, the Croat People's Party was never formally reactivated. Some of its moderate followers were prepared to yield to the HSS as the dominant political force in Croatia, while others looked to the more nationalistic political right, which eventually – by the late 1930s – coalesced around, or at least sympathised with, the Ustaša movement, which had committed itself to Croatian statehood.[23] As a generalisation, however, it is fair to say that by the late 1930s the Catholic political movement in Croatia expressed growing support for Croatian statehood. (Conversely, in Slovenia the clericalist People's Party continued to cooperate with the authorities in Belgrade in the late 1930s, which it believed was the best way to preserve Slovene political and national rights. This fact demonstrated that nationalist principles typically outweighed religious considerations when political interests were at issue.) The conclusion of the August 1939 *Sporazum* (Agreement), which created an autonomous Croatia within Yugoslavia, representing a final break of sorts between the political right and the HSS, was denounced for renouncing Croatian independence. What is more, the HSS leadership had remained largely silent during the acrimonious debates surrounding the failure of the Concordat in 1937, seen in many Church and Catholic clericalist circles as a neglect of Catholic interests.

In their treatment of the national question and the issue of nationality and identity, the Catholic intelligentsia's views were necessarily conditioned by their religious beliefs. Much like the Croat Party of Right (1918–29) and later the Ustaše, Croatia's Catholic intellectuals continued to deny the existence of both Serb and Bosnian Muslim identities in Greater Croatia. For the Croat Party of Right (and later the Ustaše), this denial was rooted in historicist thinking: the ideological legacy of Ante Starčević was evident in the continued insistence on one Croat nation in historic Greater Croatia.[24] In reality, however, throughout the 1930s Ustaše national ideology vacillated between exclusionist and assimilationist tendencies regarding the former, which accepted only the Catholic and Muslim populations of Greater Croatia as 'Croat' and excluded Orthodox Serbs entirely, being the stronger of the two.[25]

Many Catholic intellectuals in Croatia claimed that the Orthodox of Croatia and Bosnia-Herzegovina were not Serbs at all. Rather, they were for the most part regarded as 'Croats' who had adopted a Serb consciousness in the nineteenth century because of their religious affiliation and the 'nationalising' work of the Serbian Orthodox Church.[26] This theory of Serbs as Orthodox 'Croats' originated in the belief that the Orthodox of Greater Croatia were descended from the native, pre-Ottoman Catholic (and thus supposedly Croat) population. It was comprehensively articulated in the works of Ivo Pilar and especially in the numerous studies of the Church historian and Catholic priest, Krunoslav Draganović, among others.[27] For the Catholic intelligentsia, Orthodoxy in the western Balkans was the agency of a Greater Serbian ideology that had assimilated the Orthodox of Greater Croatia to a Serb identity. In 1918, when Pilar suggested that 'Serbdom' was an imperialist programme and ideology in which religion and nationality were inseparable, he became one of the first intellectuals in Croatia to suggest that the 'South Slav Question' was in essence a religious question.[28] For the Catholic intelligentsia, this conviction was based on religious precepts. In the case of the Ustaše, it is important not to confuse the utilisation of religion with what was essentially a secular worldview and programme.

Thus the Catholic movement in Croatia gradually moved away from its 'soft' opposition of the 1920s to the ranks of the 'hard' opposition in the 1930s. This trajectory was set during the dictatorship of King Aleksandar (1929–34). The Catholic intelligentsia came around to the view that Croat national rights could only be preserved in an independent, Catholic, Croatian state; as their commitment to statehood grew, so did their hostility to the HSS. They were also opposed to the HSS's social ideology, with its emphasis on the peasantry to the exclusion of other social groups in Croatia. They believed that the HSS's emphasis on peasants necessarily weakened the Croat national front of bourgeois, worker, and peasant. The Great Depression had encouraged the revival of Catholic criticism of liberal capitalism and its callous disregard for the poor across Europe. The Church and Catholic thinkers continued to support a hierarchical, organic view of social rights and obligations; each level of society (workers, peasants, bourgeois employers) enjoyed rights and exercised duties commensurate with its station. In short, capital and labour, both rural and urban, had to be subordinated to the good of the whole community, which should be guided by the tenets of the Catholic Church. Such views invariably led to confrontation with the HSS, with its emphasis on the primacy of the peasantry. In the 1930s, the Church and many Catholic thinkers adopted corporatism; the State should grant virtual monopoly status to 'syndical' or 'corporative' institutions that included representatives of both labour and management in the same profession or trade. These institutions would then direct all matters of common interest. The system supposedly ensured the harmonious collaboration of classes, the neutralisation of harmful socialist ideas, and insulated society from the destructive forces of revolution. The Catholic thinkers who adopted these views were usually quick to point out that they were quite distinct from Nazi ideology.[29]

Although the Catholic movement and the Ustaše shared some common views, they were hardly identical. The Catholic movement's alleged enthusiasm for Nazism and Italian Fascism has been exaggerated. The Catholic intelligentsia always stressed the unity of Catholicism, the Church and Croatdom, a view not necessarily shared by all, or even most, Ustaša thinkers. They were also prepared to grant the Church a far greater role in society than most secular Croat intellectuals on the political right. For these intellectuals, the most prominent of whom were Ivan Oršanić, Ivo Guberina, Mirko Kus-Nikolajev, Krsto Spalatin, Milivoj Magdić and Krunoslav Draganović, the Catholic Church was really the only bulwark against Communism. For example, Oršanić spoke of the Bolshevik Revolution as an assault against cultured Europe, which had been traditionally rooted in the Catholic Church. Since 1917, Communism had waged a war against all forms of traditional authority, the family, cultural institutions and religion; it sought the destruction of existing society. Europe's salvation, its first line of defence, he believed, lay in the tenets of Christianity and specifically the Catholic Church.[30]

Another prominent Catholic intellectual, Ivo Guberina, writing about the German invasion of Poland, saw the defeat of Catholic Poland as a tragedy. He believed Germany had a legitimate claim to parts of Poland, but added, 'By this we do not in the least want to remove responsibility from Germany and Hitler [for Poland's tragedy]. The responsibility for this lies in the very system of National Socialism, towards which we as Catholics have and must have our reservations.'[31] Indeed, the Ustaša weekly, *Hrvatski narod* [The Croat Nation, 1939–40], became involved in a polemic with the Catholic press over its allegedly racist and Nazi views.[32] Another Catholic intellectual and convinced Francophile, Krsto Spalatin, writing about the collapse of Catholic France in 1940, pondered the reasons for that collapse and whether a rebirth was possible. He asked whether democracy, moral bankruptcy, depopulation or 'unbridled individualism', or a combination of these factors, was to blame. It was difficult to determine:

> In the chaos of contemporary life, in the confusion and conflict of political interests, it was hitherto difficult, and remains difficult today, to discern the new order, the new world. Daily we listen to some sonorous declarations about the new order, about the new Europe. The certain collapse of capitalism and egotistical individualism is opined, but it is in no way clear how a new world will be built on these ruins. Both sides [fascism and communism] are destroying the old and promising something new. Both refer to the principles of justice, freedom and order. As if we are going at once to cross over from the chaotic present to a better, to an ordered future. As if a new political arrangement of the world will bring also a new man. This is, regrettably, a facile illusion.

Where Spalatin saw salvation, both for France and Europe, was in the Catholic Church and through moral rejuvenation. The French under Marshal Henri-Philippe Pétain, Pierre Laval and Maxime Weygand, he believed, were now seeking something that was spiritually new. 'Out of this search, out of this internal disquiet and out of the great war catastrophe, there will spring up a new order, a new French order'. As he saw the situation, France 'is seeking new paths to Christianity. Besides materialism, which has found its perfected form in Marxism, there is no other platform on which a new world could be built ... we have only Christ and Marx'. The family, fatherland and God were the only viable principles of any new order.[33] Spalatin's and Guberina's words reveal an unease, shared by many Catholic intellectuals in Croatia, with the New Order taking shape under the Third Reich.

That having been said, and as already noted, the younger, nationalist and more politically radical students, clergy and intellectuals in Catholic organisations – especially the generation that came to maturity during the late 1920s and 1930s – looked to Pavelić's movement because of his uncompromising struggle for independence. In fact, by 1939 he was the only logical choice for those nationalist groups in Croatia seeking independence. Although uneasy about aspects of Nazi and Fascist ideologies, and Fascist Italy's territorial aspirations in Dalmatia, they were disillusioned with Yugoslavia; and increasingly, with the HSS. They believed that only with the assistance of the Axis could an independent Catholic

Croatian state be formed, as had been the case with Slovakia in 1939. Croat Catholic thinkers would continue to insist that their political and socio-economic views were distinct from Nazi ideology. They rejected Nazism's atheism, its cult of action for its own sake, and cult of the racially pure *Übermensch*. But whatever their concerns about Nazi ideology, Communism was the greater evil and the errors of Nazism could be overlooked for the sake of statehood and the realisation of their nationalist aspirations.

It is no wonder, then, that during the Second World War, a considerable segment of Catholic clergy and intellectuals in Croatia sided, with varying degrees of enthusiasm, with the Ustaša state. Ivan Oršanić would become head of the Ustaše Youth, while Ivo Guberina and Milivoj Magdić became propagandists for the Ustaše regime. Krunoslav Draganović would hold several government posts in 1941–42. Despite their reservations, Catholic intellectuals preferred a Catholic Croatian State to a multi-religious and polyglot Yugoslavia, which they regarded merely as a Greater Serbian state interested only in strengthening Serbian Orthodoxy to the detriment of Catholicism and Croats. That is why, from 1941 to 1945, Catholic intellectuals committed themselves to the preservation of Croatian statehood.

For its part, the Church hierarchy attempted throughout the 1930s to remain outside the political arena. In February 1935, Archbishop Bauer issued a circular to the clergy forbidding their participation in the May 1935 elections, the first elections since the imposition of the royal dictatorship. Following Bauer's death in December 1937, Stepinac attempted to stay the course and to impose unity on Catholic organisations in Croatia in addition to subordinating them directly under his own authority. He never succeeded, however. As his biographer has pointed out, that Stepinac failed is probably due in large part to the fact that, as a young and relatively inexperienced cleric, he did not yet command the level of authority one would expect from someone in his position.[34]

There is little doubt that Stepinac harboured fears of Nazi Germany and Fascist Italy. It is equally true, however, that he was distrustful of the western democracies. For example, the 5 November 1940 entry in his 'diary' states, among other things: 'If Germany wins [the war], there will be an appalling terror and the destruction of little nations. If England wins, the masons, [and] Jews will remain in power ... If the USSR wins, then the devil will have authority over both the world and hell.'[35] If both Nazism and the western democracies represented dangers, admittedly of a very different kind, Communism was, at least to his mind, by far the greater threat. Indeed, after Pope Pius XI had issued his encyclical in March 1937, *Mit brennender Sorge* [*With Burning Concern*], criticising Nazi ideology, the Yugoslav Catholic Bishops' Conference followed suit by warning against both Nazism and Communism.[36]

One of the central themes in the articles of the semi-official diocesan weekly, *Katolički list* [*Catholic Paper*] – whose editor the Archbishop appointed and whose views were close to Stepinac's – was anti-Communism. The 24 April 1937 issue declared, for example, that communism 'is in its very essence evil'. Those who valued 'Christian culture' could never 'cooperate with [Communists] in a single thing'.[37] Some of these articles had an anti-Semitic tone, although of a traditional, pre-Hitlerian variety.[38] Freemasonry was a particular obsession of Stepinac's. He evidently believed that Yugoslavia was run by freemasons. The 30 May 1934 entry in his diary, made just after his appointment to the position of Archbishop-coadjutor, states: 'Today freemasonry rules in Yugoslavia. Unfortunately even the bosom of the Croat people in Zagreb this infernal society has insinuated itself, the offspring of immorality, corruption and everything dishonourable, sworn enemy of the Catholic Church'.[39] If Yugoslavia was run by anti-Catholic freemasons, it followed that Yugoslavia must be anti-Catholic. This particular obsession undoubtedly heightened his opposition to that state and his support for Croatian independence, especially after the Yugoslav government failed to ratify its Concordat with the Vatican. There is little doubt that Stepinac believed that the Catholic Church was unequal before the law in relation to other recognised faiths, especially the Serbian Orthodox Church.[40] When, on 27 March 1941, demonstrations broke out in Belgrade and elsewhere against Yugoslavia's accession to the Axis and Yugoslav officers staged a coup, Stepinac was embittered. His diary entry noted: 'All in all, Croats and Serbs are two worlds ... that will never move closer to one another without an act of God'. He would add: 'The schism [that is, Orthodoxy] is the greatest curse of Europe, almost greater than Protestantism. There is no morality, no principle, there is no truth, no justice, no honesty [in Orthodoxy]'. That same day, however, he issued a circular to the Archbishopric's clergy, calling upon them 'to turn in prayer to the Lord, to give His blessing and assistance to the young King and his rule, so that our Croatia and entire State will be spared the horrors of war'.[41] These sentiments may appear contradictory, as Ivo Goldstein has noted, but they merely expressed a longstanding principle whereby the Catholic Church expressed its traditional loyalty to the State, whatever its form and whoever stood as its leader.

How does this admittedly cursory background help us to understand the wartime policies of both the Catholic episcopacy and the Catholic political movement generally? First, it is important to emphasise that the Church was historically on the margins of Croatian political life and mass politics, the role of some prominent Catholic intellectuals notwithstanding. That Church leaders and intellectuals wished to exert more influence over Croatian society and politics seems evident, but they found themselves in a rather precarious position devoid of significant influence. Second, the political experiences of the 1920s and 1930s heightened this traditional sense of marginality; in light of the royal dictatorship; the ongoing political dominance in Croatia of the anticlerical HSS; and the threat seemingly posed by Communism in the era of the Great Depression. In light of this reality, the formation of the Independent State of Croatia (NDH) in April 1941 appeared to offer the Church episcopacy and the Catholic movement an opportunity. The new Croatian state possessed a Catholic majority, albeit a slight one; its new authorities were Croats who, if for no other reason than their own political interests, appeared inclined to work with Church leaders. The creation of the Croatian state seemingly and at first glance afforded the Church a significant improvement over its marginal status in the previous decades.

The Croatian State and the Catholic Church, 1941–45

High Treason: Recognising the Croatian State

Under these circumstances and viewed in this light, Stepinac's enthusiastic response to the formation of the Croatian state in April 1941, following the Axis invasion of Yugoslavia, is unsurprising. Stepinac may well have been unhappy about the association with the Third Reich and worried about Italian territorial pretensions in Croatia, but that did not diminish his enthusiasm for independence.

On 12 April 1941, Stepinac called on Slavko Kvaternik, a former Habsburg officer and one of the domestic leaders of the Ustaša movement, to congratulate him on proclaiming the Croatian state two days earlier. Kvaternik was received by Pavelić on 16 April, the day after his arrival in Zagreb. Stepinac's visits to Kvaternik and Pavelić could be interpreted simply as formal gestures from the chief representative of the Church to the leaders of the new state, but the tone of the circular issued to the clergy on 28 April, welcoming the creation of the 'young Croatian state', was certainly rapturous. In that circular he spoke of the Croat nation finally coming 'face to face with its age-old and ardently desired dream. The times are such that it is no longer the tongue which speaks but the blood with its mysterious links with the country ... Who can reproach us if we also, as spiritual pastors, add our contribution to the pride and rejoicing of the people, when full of devotion and warm thanks we turn to Almighty God?'[42] This was the typical sentiment running through Croat nationalist and many Church circles in the aftermath of the proclamation of Croatian 'independence'. The Catholic priest Dragutin Kamber, who joined the Ustaša movement in 1941, later wrote on the creation of a Croatian state in 1941 – and probably summing up the attitude of many nationalist lower clergy – that Pavelić 'was the hero of the day, the new and only programme ... the avenger of a martyred past.'[43]

Stepinac also undoubtedly assumed that the Church would have considerably more freedom in the new Croatian state, given its recent experiences in Yugoslavia. He had said in his circular: 'We believe and expect that the Church in our resurrected Croatian State will be able in full freedom to proclaim the indisputable principle of eternal truth and justice.' The entry in Stepinac's diary for 27 April 1941 reads, 'The Archbishop had the impression that he [Pavelić] was a sincere Catholic and that the Church would enjoy freedom to carry out its work, though the Archbishop had no illusions that it would all take place without difficulty.'[44]

In 1941 the Croatian episcopacy consisted of two Archbishops and 11 Bishops.[45] The territories of seven of the bishoprics (Dubrovnik, Hvar, Kotor, Krk, Senj, Split and Šibenik) were either annexed to or occupied by Italy in May and September 1941. Since the Zagreb Archbishopric was the largest in former Yugoslavia, and indeed one of the largest anywhere in East, Central or Southeastern Europe, it was also the most influential; the Archbishop was regarded as first among equals. This did not mean, however, that he was in a position to dictate the policies or behaviour of the episcopacy in wartime Croatia.

Yet Stepinac's enthusiasm for statehood did not translate into overt support for the new regime. Indeed, within weeks he began privately to distance himself from the Ustaša regime. Behind the scenes, differences emerged and tensions set in between Pavelić and Stepinac, primarily over the Race Laws – directed against the Jews and Roma – and the sweeping anti-Serb legislation of late April and May 1941.[46] The legislation was soon followed by arrests and subsequent massacres of the Serb population. On 22 May 1941, Stepinac wrote to the Interior Minister, Andrija Artuković, protesting against the Race Laws and their application to converted Jews. He implicitly raised the issue of non-converted Jews by admonishing the Minister that members of other races should not be discriminated against 'through no fault of their own'.[47] Weeks earlier, on 14 May, Stepinac received a letter from the parish priest of Glina, who reported a massacre of Serb villagers by an Ustaša unit. That same day, Stepinac wrote to Pavelić

Just now I received news that the Ustaše in Glina executed without trial and investigation 260 Serbs. I know that the Serbs committed some major crimes in our homeland in these last twenty years. But I consider it my bishop's responsibility to raise my voice and to say that this is not permitted according to Catholic teaching, which is why I ask that you undertake the most urgent measures on the entire territory of the Independent State of Croatia, so that not a single Serb is killed unless it is shown that he committed a crime warranting death. Otherwise, we will not be able to count on the blessing of heaven, without which we must perish.[48]

These private protests had no impact, for the Ustaša regime was determined to 'cleanse' the country, through murder or deportation, and later through forced conversion, of Serbs. On 4 June 1941, a Croat-German agreement was signed in Zagreb, regulating the deportation of Slovenes from German-occupied Slovenia to Croatia, along with a corresponding number of Serbs from Croatia to Serbia. When these deportations were initiated in early July 1941, they were accompanied by large-scale massacres against the Serb population. On 21 July 1941, Stepinac again wrote to Pavelić that he was sure 'that these things have been happening without your knowledge and that others may not dare to tell you about them'. He felt 'all the more obliged to do so myself'. Stepinac had heard from many sides 'that there are instances of inhumane and brutal treatment … during the deportations and at the camps, and even worse, that neither children, old people nor the sick are spared'. He had even heard that some of the deportees were recent 'converts to Catholicism, so that it is even more my duty to concern myself with them … humane and Christian consideration should be shown especially to weak old people, young and innocent children, and the sick.'[49] There is little doubt that Stepinac shared these observations with the Vatican, which noted his personal reservations about the regime. Already in mid-May 1941, Cardinal Luigi Maglione, the Vatican's Secretary of State, observed that Archbishop Stepinac and the other bishops were behaving 'cautiously' and 'avoiding compromising themselves' with the new leaders of the Croatian state.[50]

In the first weeks and even months of Ustaša rule, it may not have been entirely clear to Stepinac that the unfolding atrocities were part of a central plan. Certainly there is no evidence to suggest that he knew of any plan of mass murder. He may have believed, at least in these first months, that the violence was either spontaneous or the result of 'irresponsible' Ustaša elements, which would eventually be called to account by the central government. In any event, letters to Pavelić from this period suggest that he could not bring himself to believe that the leader of the Croatian state would sanction outright mass violence. His disappointment with the new regime appears genuine, however. In fact, Ante Pavelić mentioned Stepinac and the Catholic Church in passing in his first meeting with Hitler on 7 June 1941. According to the German version of their meeting, toward the end of their conversation, Pavelić mentioned 'a few personal experiences with the Catholic Church.' He said that many young clerics supported the Ustaša regime, but that 'the Bishop of Croatia [Alojzije Stepinac] had given him the advice that one could rule only if one were as forbearing as possible'; Stepinac was evidently displeased at that fact that many young priests had openly sided with his movement.[51] The Italian foreign minister, Count Galeazzo Ciano, upon meeting with Pavelić in December 1941, wrote in his diary that Pavelić had told him: 'The Catholic clergy … maintains a very favourable attitude [toward the Ustaša government] in its lower ranks and less so in the higher grades of the hierarchy. Some of the bishops are openly hostile'.[52] Indeed, some of the lower clergy, like Dragutin Kamber, a Bosnian Catholic parish priest who joined the Ustaša movement in 1941, were critical of the bishops for their refusal to support the Croatian government openly. Writing many years after the fact, Kamber, like many lower clergy who collaborated with the regime, remained unapologetic about his role during the war; he was critical of the Church's bishops for not offering, to his mind, sufficient support to the authorities in the Croatian state's formative months.[53]

The chief allegation made against Stepinac – that he was a sympathiser and even the spiritual leader of the Ustaša regime – is thus ill-founded. It is apparent through available documentation that Stepinac, despite his support for independence, began privately to distance himself from the Ustaša regime within weeks, and certainly within months of the Croatian state's formation. He continued to attend to ceremonial duties at official functions, but serious concerns were being raised privately with the Ustaša leadership. But was his behaviour in the spring of 1941 treasonable, as the post-war Communist authorities and others have alleged? At his trial, Stepinac directly posed this question to the court:

> You accuse me of being an enemy of the state and of the people's government. I beg you, tell me which government was mine in 1941? Was it that of the putschist [General Dušan] Simović in Belgrade, or the traitorous one, as you call it, in London or the one in Jerusalem, or yours in the forest, or the one in Zagreb? Even in 1943 and 1944, was it the government in London or in the forest? You are for me the government since 8 May 1945. Could I listen to you in the forest and those here in Zagreb? Is it possible at all to serve two masters? This does not exist according to Catholic morals or international or humanitarian law. We could not ignore the authorities here; though they were Ustaše, they were here.[54]

Ultimately, the issue of his alleged high treason was a political question. There is little doubt that, in 1946, Communist authorities had a vested political interest in convicting Stepinac; it is this fact more than any other which, in the end, explains his fate.

Forced Conversions

Perhaps the most serious allegation made against Stepinac by the post war authorities – and the key part of the indictment against him at his September and October 1946 trial – was his alleged collaboration with the Croatian government in helping to convert tens and even hundreds of thousands of Orthodox Serbs to Catholicism. In actual fact, the policy of Catholicising Serbs was the most serious issue plaguing relations between the Church and Croatian authorities in 1941–42. There seems little doubt that the Catholic Church welcomed the prospect of a large number of converts to Catholicism. Its main concern was that, as Stella Alexander has noted, 'these should be voluntary and under the control of the church'.[55] Yet it was the Ustaša authorities and not the Church who took the initiative in converting Orthodox Serbs in 1941. The government was determined from the outset to keep the policy of conversion under its control. It alone wished to decide which Serbs could convert and which ones were to be 'eliminated'.

Between May and July 1941, the Ustaša authorities issued several decrees on religious conversion, and on 14 July 1941 the Ministry of Justice and Religion informed the Croatian bishops about its conversion guidelines: no Orthodox Serbs would be permitted to join the Greek Catholic faith (Uniate church); the Serb intelligentsia was in principle barred from conversion; and Orthodox with Catholic spouses could convert only with the prior permission of the Ministry. Otherwise, the lowest sections of Orthodox society could be received with few reservations in principle.[56]

The Ustaša government likely assumed that the Catholic Church would merely consent to its policy directives on this matter, but the policy represented a direct challenge to the Church's authority in the spiritual realm. On 16 July 1941, Stepinac's office issued a letter to the Ministry of Justice and Religion that dismissed the government's guidelines as unacceptable. They correctly deemed this to be purely a religious issue, and their position was that the Church could receive anyone it wished. The Ustaša authorities ignored the Church's concerns and issued a circular on 30 July restating their earlier conversion guidelines to the bishops. The regime proceeded on its own, and enlisted a number of parish priests and especially Franciscan 'missionaries' for the purpose of conversion, without the express permission of their ecclesiastical superiors. Forced conversions were initiated on a large scale in September 1941.

That summer, Stepinac began receiving reports from the bishops, especially Bishop Mišić of Mostar, about atrocities committed by the Ustaše. There is a great deal of evidence that some Franciscans and priests, especially in Herzegovina, were implicated in forced conversions and possibly some killings.[57] Many were military chaplains. On 30 June 1941, Bishop Mišić issued a circular to his priests ordering them to abstain from politics, and to inform their parishioners that all who murdered or took the possessions of others would not be given absolution. On 18 August 1941, he reported to Stepinac that many local Ustaša officials were using various forms of intimidation and violence against Serbs; even those Serbs who converted were being arrested and killed.[58] He wrote to Stepinac that 'this can serve neither the holy Catholic cause nor the Croatian cause'. He added that 'in the interests of Croatia and the Church I say to His Excellency that we must do all in our power to prevent these disastrous consequences'.[59] On 7 November 1941, Bishop Mišić again wrote to Stepinac that 'a reign of terror has come to pass ... Men are captured like animals, they are slaughtered, murdered.'[60]

With the number of such reports mounting, the bishops met in conference on 17–18 November 1941 in Zagreb. Afterwards, Stepinac sent a diplomatically worded letter to Pavelić in the name of the episcopacy. The Catholic bishops called on Pavelić 'to protect personal and civil rights', particularly of Jewish converts to Catholicism.[61] On conversions in general, the position of the Catholic episcopacy was that this was purely a matter of the Church and not the state. Only bishops had the right to appoint missionaries to conduct conversions, who would be responsible to them alone and not to the government; conversions were valid only if they had been carried out according to canonical principles, and could not be forced. Nor did the civil authorities have a right to annul Church-ordained conversions; this was contrary to dogma and to canonical regulations. Stepinac referred to stories of atrocious violence in the country, though [it seems that] he could not bring himself to believe that the Ustaša leadership approved of such policies: 'No one can deny that these terrible acts of violence and cruelty have been taking place, for you yourself, Poglavnik, have publicly condemned those which the Ustaše have committed and you have ordered executions because of their crimes'. He would add: 'All men are the children of God and Christ died for all ... we are sure, Poglavnik, that you hold the same position and that you will do all in your power to restrain the violence of certain individuals'.[62] The letter was tactfully worded to be sure, and was probably deliberately crafted that way for greater effect. Pavelić ignored the bishops, although he remarked shortly thereafter, in December 1941, to Italian foreign minister Ciano that 'some of the bishops are openly hostile [to his government]'.[63] Whether Pavelić ignored them because they never threatened to withdraw publicly the Church's blessing from the new state – there is no evidence suggesting that the bishops even considered this option or had the endorsement of the Vatican to consider it in the first place – remains a contentious question.

In an earlier article, which is based on a reading of the Ustaša regime's Religious Section [*Vjerski odsjek*, hereafter VO], I attempted to explain the genesis and course of the policy underpinning forced conversions in 1941–42.[64] In the VO's extant archival collection there is hardly any correspondence with Church officials or lower clergy which suggests, among other things, that the conversion policy was driven by the state with generally little input from the Church. Indeed, the state authorities issued their directives and asked both local state and Party officials to report who, if anyone, was performing the conversions (most of which appear to have been performed by a small number of Franciscans). It appears that the state authorities simply assumed that the Church would readily comply with, and conform to, their directives. The Croatian authorities gave serious attention to forced conversions only in September 1941 and then abandoned it, for a number of reasons, by January/February 1942. At least 97,447–99,333 conversions occurred in 1941–42, with possibly an additional 1,500 conversions to the Lutheran Church. The standard figure cited in Yugoslav and western historiography of the number of conversions from Serbian Orthodoxy to Roman Catholicism is 240,000, which is derived from a report allegedly submitted by Stepinac to Pope Pius XII in May 1943.[65] Even if the report is authentic, the figure it mentions was merely an estimate as the whole policy was driven by the state authorities, who themselves never seemed to possess a firm grasp of the actual number of conversions.

The VO's archival material indicates that all but a very few of the registered conversions were to the Roman Catholic faith, although conversions were also permitted to the Lutheran Church and to Islam, as the Bosnian Muslims were regarded as Muslim 'Croats'. That almost all conversions were to the Catholic faith is hardly surprising. In a revealing letter to Pavelić of December 1941, in which he pleaded that conversions to the Uniate church be banned, the VO's chief, Dionizije Juričev – who was himself a member of the Ustaša Party and also a Franciscan friar – argued that conversions to the Uniate (or Greek Catholic) Church were detrimental, in his words 'a fatal matter' to Croatian state interests, because over half the Uniate clergy, and two-thirds of its faithful, were of non-Croat nationality. It would appear that Juričev's letter was prompted by the decisions reached at the Croatian Catholic Bishops' Conference of 17–18 November, where the bishops held that conversion to Greek Catholicism was preferable for Orthodox Serbs rather than direct conversion to Roman Catholicism, and that the Church alone, rather than the secular authorities, should solemnise conversions. In his letter to Pavelić, Juričev argued that conversions to the Uniate faith should be banned outright, for if they were permitted 'the number of foreign national minorities, who will only eat away at the bones of our national organism, will be multiplied'. The assimilationist intent of the conversion campaign would thus be muted, which is why he forcefully urged that 'either directly or through this Religious Section, *you issue notice according to which those who convert to the Greek Catholic rite will not be protected by the State* [emphasis added]'.[66] Pavelić's reply to this letter, if there was one, is unknown. Conversions to the Uniate Church were not banned, but the VO's figures reveal few conversions to that rite (or for that matter to Lutheranism or Islam), and Juričev's letter explains why this was the case. Conversion to Catholicism remained the goal not for purely religious reasons but, as Juričev's letter demonstrates, because it was seen as the best and really the only way of assimilating those Serbs deemed fit for assimilation.

What can be said with some certainty, however, is that Ustaša motives and policy had little to do with Catholic piety, fanaticism, or Catholic proselytism as ends in themselves. Nor did religious sentiment influence their genocidal policy in any significant way. The Ustaša regime's forced conversion campaign was an attempt at forced assimilation and was 'legitimised' in the Ustaša press by the theory that, from the time of Ottoman presence, many Catholics had supposedly converted to Orthodoxy, and that they were now simply returning to their 'true' Church. As Aleksa Djilas has quite correctly pointed out, Catholicism for the Ustaše 'was primarily an instrument for strengthening the state rather than a goal in itself', which distinguished the Ustaše markedly from the Hlinka movement in Slovakia, which was genuinely Catholic and led by priests.[67] It would appear that forced conversions were not implemented in tandem or in coordination with, let alone at the instigation of, the Catholic Church – as has been argued in Yugoslav historiography – but were undertaken independently of the Church. Juričev's letter to Pavelić thus reveals a major division of opinion between the VO, which was responsible for conversion policy, and the Church hierarchy. The Church episcopacy was not to blame for the policy of forced conversion, but its narrow defence of prerogatives, understandable enough under most circumstances, appears somewhat perplexing given the extreme nature of the Croatian government's policy. Its tactic of diplomatic dialogue is even less understandable if one remembers that many converts to Catholicism, whatever their background, were still being persecuted by the secular authorities and that these same authorities repeatedly flouted Church prerogatives.

Clergy in Ustaše Ranks

How extensive was support for the Ustaša regime among the lower Catholic clergy? Catholic sources certainly speak to this support and its nature. A June 1942 report – compiled by the Catholic priest and former Croat People's Party activist, Augustin Juretić, and submitted to the Croat members of the Yugoslav government-in-exile – spoke to the role of the clergy in independent Croatia. His report noted the many fissures within the episcopacy, the clergy in general, and the various Catholic orders. Based on the available information at his disposal at the time, Juretić concluded that the older generation of clergy, generally those over 35, were with few exceptions 'following the correct line', in the Zagreb Archbishopric, almost 'all are behaving properly'. He noted, however, that 'the younger clergy raised in the so-called Crusader organisations are, with few exceptions, completely Ustaša. The majority does not condone the killings – one small part has in general lost all *sensum moralem*'. In this assessment, the Franciscans of the Zagreb province and Bosnia were for the most part acting 'correctly', maintaining a proper critical distance from the authorities, while those of southern Dalmatia and Herzegovina were allegedly pro-Ustaša for the most part, as were many Jesuits.[68] The report is revealing, in that it provides an 'internal' assessment of the orientation of both the Catholic clergy and its orders toward the regime. It also points to the many divisions – particularly generational and regional – within the ranks of the lower clergy. His assessment of the episcopacy was generally more favourable. Stepinac, the late Mišić, Butorac, Burić and Bonefačić were regarded as passively critical or anti-Ustaše, whereas Šarić and Akšamović were deemed pro-Ustaša.[69] The clergy who were most pro-regime tended to be young and based primarily in Herzegovina, while the hierarchy and orders based in Bosnia and in Croatia proper were far more reserved.

The worst cases of clergy in the Ustaša ranks – the most notorious example is that of the Franciscan friar Tomislav Filipović, who served briefly as commandant of the Jasenovac camp – provoked the Church hierarchy's intervention. In June 1941, the Franciscans of Zagreb province met in Zagreb and decided that not a single Franciscan should serve as a member of the Ustaša Party. The notorious Filipović was eventually defrocked.[70] Don Ivo Guberina, a member of the Ustaša party and an active propagandist for the wartime regime, was forbidden from performing his religious duties in June 1943. This move followed 'a threatening and bloody speech' given in Mostar by Guberina which, in the words of Bishop Čule, was highly 'inappropriate' for even the most extreme nationalist, let alone a member of the Church. He added, in a letter to Stepinac, that '[our] opponents will say, the Church condones all those killings'.[71] Other clergy, including the priest Zvonko Brekalo and the Franciscan friar Emil Orozović, were stripped of their vestments in 1942. The Church hierarchy also had serious difficulties with the Franciscans Dionizije Juričev and Radoslav Glavaš, both of whom took up official posts in government service, the former as head of the Religious Section (VO) responsible for forced conversion policy, and the latter as head of the Religious Department of the Ministry of Justice and Religion.[72] Juričev once allegedly remarked to the papal representative in Croatia that all clergy should be in Ustaša ranks and that, if it were up to him, he would 'persecute not religions but the bishops'.[73]

There is little doubt that many individual members of the Catholic clergy openly sided with and worked for the Croatian authorities. Their collaboration took various forms, occasionally quite brutal and immoral forms. But their participation in the Ustaša ranks was hardly dictated by Church policy. Indeed, in February 1942 Stepinac informed Pavelić that he would uphold a ban on political activities by the Catholic clergy, even if it involved activities on behalf of the Ustaša Party and state. Since this ban was evidently ignored by many clergy as well as the authorities, in September 1943 Stepinac issued a circular to the clergy in which he reminded them of relevant papal encyclicals (1926) and decrees previously issued by the Archbishopric (1935, 1938) forbidding their participation in political parties.[74] The simple fact remains that the Church was hardly the monolithic institution it pretended or wished to be; in Croatia, neither the episcopacy nor the clergy had a uniform view of the war or its many implications. Those who sided openly with the regime did so because of their own nationalist and political convictions.

It should also be said that a good number of clergy eventually sided with the Partisans. According to one estimate, of the approximately 950 Catholic clergy in the Independent State of Croatia in 1941, perhaps a quarter joined or collaborated in some form with the Ustaša movement.[75] On the other hand, a rather substantial number of Catholic clergy (at least 43, and among them at least 18 Croat Catholic clergy) collaborated with the Partisans.[76] Among them was Monsignor Svetozar Rittig, the septuagenarian parish priest of St. Mark's Church in Zagreb, who joined the Partisans in the Italian-occupied Croatia in June 1943. It should also be pointed out, however, that as many as 383 Croat Catholic clergy (including one bishop) were allegedly killed during and immediately after the war, mainly by the Partisans,[77] a fact that undoubtedly reinforced the episcopacy's inability to break openly with the Croatian authorities or to side with the resistance.

The Question of Public Silence

Why did the Catholic Church in Croatia not speak out publicly and systematically against the policies of the Ustaša regime? After all, already in 1941 Stepinac was making private protests and interventions. There is also little doubt that Stepinac was increasingly frustrated and disillusioned with the Ustaša authorities, but could not bring himself to condemn their policies openly and unequivocally. The Croatian authorities were certainly aware that Stepinac and several bishops opposed many of their policies, even though some, notably Archbishop Šarić, supported them. But the private hostility that existed within the bishops' ranks was never expressed forcefully and unequivocally in public, although it was always acknowledged in Ustaša government circles. Stepinac's private protests of 1941 were many and some were even public, expressed in the form of sermons. When, in October 1941, the authorities began demolishing the Zagreb synagogue, Stepinac remarked in a sermon that 'The House of God of whatever faith is a holy thing and whoever tampers with it, will pay with his life. Both in this life and the next, he will be persecuted'.[78]

In the spring of 1942, the number of critical sermons – especially those denouncing racism – increased steadily. In March 1942, as rumours circulated in Zagreb of the imminent deportations of Jews, Stepinac wrote to Interior Minister Artuković, noting that 'irresponsible elements have to be stopped from violating not only the Christian law of love towards one neighbour, but also the most fundamental, natural law of humanity'.[79] In a sermon of October 1942, Stepinac also spoke out against racism: 'All peoples and races stem from God. There really exists only one race, and that is God's race ... that is why the Catholic Church always condemned every injustice and violence perpetrated in the name of theories of class, race and nationality'.[80] Steps were also taken either to remove or defrock the most notorious clergy, and to intervene against the application of Race Laws to Jewish converts to Catholicism and to Jews in Catholic marriages, as well as against the persecution of Catholicised Serbs and deportations of the same. In most cases, these interventions appear to have been reactive, however, and it seems that Stepinac's primary concern was to protest against the government's encroachment onto the Church's realm and interests. One should therefore not be surprised that his harshest private denunciation of Ustaša methods came after he learned of the fate of a group of Slovene Catholic priests in the Jasenovac camp system. These priests had been deported by the German authorities to Croatia, where they were incarcerated as allegedly hostile elements and eventually murdered. On 24 February 1943, Stepinac wrote to Pavelić: 'I must conclude that they were all executed on the assumption that they were antinational. Why were they not brought before the court ... or a court-martial? This is a disgraceful incident and a crime that cries out for vengeance from heaven. Jasenovac camp itself is a shameful stain on the honour of the Independent State of Croatia'.[81]

This complex mix of private protest and disillusionment, on the one hand, and tacit support of Croatian statehood, on the other, was earlier revealed in a set of developments during 1942. In April 1942, Stepinac was visited by a former Yugoslav Army officer, the Slovene Lt. Stanislav Rapotec, who had escaped from Yugoslavia during the April 1941 Axis invasion. Rapotec landed on the Dalmatian coast by British submarine in mid-January 1942, and by April 1942 was in Zagreb, where he spent two and a half months. His mission was to assess the situation in occupied Yugoslavia. In Zagreb he made contact with some of the city's remaining Serb and Jewish leaders.[82] He discovered soon after his arrival in Zagreb, as he later reported, that Stepinac was *persona non grata* with the Ustaša authorities. And much to his surprise, he heard only positive things from remaining Jews and Serbs about Stepinac. Rapotec later reported that he was so impressed with Stepinac's sincerity that he told him openly who he was and why he was there. In total, Rapotec had five meetings with Stepinac. When Rapotec asked him why he had not broken openly with the Ustaše regime, Stepinac stated that had he done so, he would not have been in a position to help anyone. He assured Rapotec that the forced conversions were organised by the Ustaša authorities and priests loyal to them, not by the Church. Stepinac admitted that bishops had gone their own way: Ivan Šarić of Sarajevo had openly sided with the Ustaše, while Alojzije Mišić of Mostar was opposed to them. Stepinac appeared genuinely surprised at Rapotec's claim that many in the West were critical of the Church for not doing enough to stop the killings.

When he arrived in Cairo in late July 1942, Rapotec filed a lengthy report on his journey to Croatia. He described the terror against Serbs and Jews in detail, and noted the 'sad role' of the Catholic Church. Only a few prominent individuals, like Stepinac, Akšamović, and Mišić, were opposed to the regime. Stepinac simply did not, Rapotec concluded, wield enough authority even among his own clergy. Rapotec reported that Stepinac was willing to receive and distribute Yugoslav funds to the Belgrade Red Cross for Croatian Serb refugees in Serbia, as well as Swiss or Turkish passports for persons to be evacuated through the Swiss consulate. The Rapotec report paints a picture of a disillusioned cleric, albeit a cleric who refused to express his disillusionment publicly and forcefully, or to break completely with the regime.[83]

Rapotec's account is buttressed, at least in part, by Nikola Rušinović, who was attached to the Croatian embassy in Rome from June 1941 to July 1942 as liaison to the Vatican. In his recently, posthumously published memoirs, Rušinović claims that in late February 1942, during an official visit to Rome by Marshal Slavko Kvaternik, the head of the Croatian army, the two met privately to discuss the situation in Croatia. According to Rušinović, Kvaternik confirmed that Pavelić and Eugen 'Dido' Kvaternik, the head of the Croatian security police, were displeased with Stepinac due to some of his sermons. During his subsequent visit to Zagreb, Rušinović met with Pavelić, who conceded that he was having 'difficulties' with Stepinac on account of his refusal to actively work with the Ustaša government, in part because of its association with the Third Reich. Shortly afterwards, Rušinović met with Stepinac, who appeared dejected. Stepinac allegedly spoke to him bitterly of both Croatia's 'enemies' and her Axis allies, and spoke poorly of the Croatian government, its laws and administration.[84]

And yet, shortly after meeting with Rušinović and Rapotec, Stepinac made his second journey to Rome in April 1942, where he met with Pope Pius XII and Vatican officials. In the Vatican, Stepinac presented a report to State Secretary Luigi Cardinal Maglione that cited some of the 'positive' aspects of the Ustaša regime, such as its abolition of abortion, campaigns against pornography, 'blasphemy', freemasonry, and its determined struggle against communism. On 5 May 1942, the Croatian Foreign Minister, Mladen Lorković, wrote in the Ministry's logbook, 'Councilor Rušinović reports that Archbishop Stepinac brought with him to the Vatican a written report about the situation in Croatia, which is so positive that even the Poglavnik himself could sign it'.[85] Indeed, in his memoirs Rušinović mentions Stepinac's visit, and their meeting at the Institute of San Girolamo. They discussed Stepinac's meeting with and report to Maglione, and Rušinović confirms that the report was 'favourable'. It cited the sufferings of the Croat people, and dismissed, according to Rušinović, the many 'lies' spread by Croat 'enemies' about the crimes perpetrated by the Croatian authorities. He also alleges that Stepinac expressed optimism for the future of the Croatian state.[86] The Rapotec report and, to a lesser extent, the Rušinović account together reveal a Stepinac disillusioned with the Ustaša government. And yet the reports of Stepinac's trip to the Vatican indicate that, even if disillusioned with the regime, he still supported Croatian independence, in spite of the regime.

Also, in 1942, Stepinac made contact with the German General in Croatia, Edmund Glaise von Horstenau. Like most German military representatives in Croatia and southeastern Europe, Horstenau was a critic of the Ustaša regime and its murderous policies against the Serbs, although not necessarily against the Jews. He recorded a number of negative comments culled from various government sources about Stepinac, his private interventions and, especially in late 1943, his sermons. By spring 1943 Stepinac was visiting Horstenau, normally on Sunday mornings before Mass, with requests and pleas to intervene with the authorities.[87] To be sure, the picture that emerges of Stepinac in this account is incomplete. Stepinac does not come across as a confidant of the Ustaša regime; yet Stepinac's own assertion made to Rapotec, that he did not publicly condemn the regime because he would not be able to intervene in individual instances to help people in need, seems questionable. By 1943, Stepinac was reduced to working through the German General, himself a critic of the Ustaša regime, in order to intervene. Stepinac's links to the Croatian government appear tenuous and weak by this point, but there was still, evidently, no willingness on his part to condemn the regime and its many crimes publicly.

The closest Stepinac ever came to a public break with the Croatian authorities occurred during October 1943. In a 31 October 1943 sermon, he said that the Catholic Church explicitly condemned racism, and that the policy of shooting hundreds of hostages for a crime, particularly when the person guilty of the crime could not be found, was 'a pagan system which only results in evil'. The Church had 'always condemned and condemns today as well every injustice and all violence committed in the name of the theories of class, race or nationality'.[88] The government reacted immediately. The Minister of Education, Julije Makanec, rebuked Stepinac in the 7 November 1943 issue of the government's daily newspaper, *Nova Hrvatska* [*The New Croatia*]. Defending the government's racist policies, Makanec added, in an implicit reference to Stepinac, that 'men who neither know nor have a feeling for secular problems ... who are devoid of every political instinct [...should not] spread political confusion and defection among the soldiers who defend with their lives not only the foundations of the Croatian State but also the Catholic Church'. He went on to add that 'it is best that everyone remain in the field to which he has been called and in which he is competent. This is entirely valid as well for that high ecclesiastical dignitary who has recently, in his sermons, passed beyond the limits of his vocation and began to meddle in affairs in which he is not competent'.[89] This was a blunt public rebuke on the government's part, but like Stepinac, it too seemingly wished to avoid a complete break.

By 1943–44 Stepinac was undoubtedly deeply embittered by the Croatian authorities. Employing papal encyclicals and canon law, Stepinac attempted to distance the Catholic hierarchy from the worst abuses of the Ustaša regime. Private protests were being made regularly – usually with little effect – and a far more critical tenor is evident in his sermons.[90] But do his sermons, which increasingly railed against racial discrimination, violence and killings, collectively represent a public denunciation of the Ustaša regime? To most observers they do not. Why did Stepinac not take the step of withdrawing his support and publicly denouncing the regime in power at Zagreb? After all, when the Allies bombed Zagreb in February 1944, resulting in the deaths of 75 people (including 7 priests) and 160 additional casualties, Stepinac published a circular condemning the bombing.[91] To be sure, this was not a condemnation of the Allies. The circular was used to good effect, however, by Ustaša propagandists; it was reprinted in their press over several days.

Why did Stepinac restrict himself to public criticism of the regime's policies, rather than condemning the Ustaša regime as such? Was it because of Stepinac's support for the regime in power in Croatia? Was it because of cowardice and the potential personal risk involved in challenging what was, after all, a remarkably brutal regime? Neither argument seems particularly convincing. The most compelling reason to explain his silence appears to be his, as well as the other Catholic bishops', support for an independent Croatian state. This applies not only to Archbishop Šarić of Sarajevo, an explicit supporter of the Ustaše to the bitter end,[92] but also to those bishops who were critical of that regime. That the Catholic bishops preferred a Croatian state to Yugoslavia, in whatever form, seems incontrovertible. It is unclear whether Stepinac and the other bishops realised that the Croatian state could not survive the war, given the fact that it was synonymous with the Ustaša regime and, by extension, the Third Reich. Admittedly, it may not have seemed too far-fetched to imagine that a Croatian state might yet exist after the war; in those uncertain times, the post-war political landscape was an open question. In the event, the Croatian bishops were certainly not alone in this regard. Many Croat opponents of the Ustaše, particularly those in the ranks of the HSS, entertained the hope, only later proven to be a facile illusion, that the Croatian state might be preserved after the war, despite the fact that it was an Axis creature and that its regime had perpetrated horrific atrocities. This false impression may have been fuelled by the mistaken belief that the western Allies would prefer, almost at any cost, a post-war non-Communist Croatia (naturally, without the Ustaše) to a Communist Yugoslavia.

Furthermore, Stepinac continued to fear the Communist Scylla much more than the Fascist Charybdis to the very end. His November 1940 diary entry, which noted that a Soviet victory in the war would mean that 'the devil will have authority over both the world and hell', spoke to a mindset that had long remained in place. This fact undoubtedly conditioned Stepinac's understanding of the conflict that was played out in wartime Croatia; there is considerable evidence indicating not only that he found it hard to accept the extent of the Ustaša regime's crimes, but that he understood them as crimes committed within the context of a cruel fratricidal war in which all sides, including the royalist Chetniks and the Communist Partisans, perpetrated horrific atrocities. However shameful and appalling the violence of the Ustaše might be, Chetnik massacres of Croat and Bosnian Muslim civilians as well as Partisan reprisals against their opponents – among whom the Catholic clergy figured prominently – were seen as equally atrocious in his mind. By 1943, it seemed apparent to most observers, and Stepinac was certainly no exception, that the only serious resistance in Croatia and Yugoslavia was the Partisan movement. In Stepinac's mind, to condemn publicly the Croatian government probably would have meant only hastening a catastrophe; such an act would have played into the hands of Josip Broz Tito's Partisans and all opponents of Croatian statehood. Indeed, in a sermon of 18 March 1945, just weeks before the end of the war, he remarked that all peoples were entitled to freedom and statehood; any regime that denied this right to the Croat people would necessarily represent only 'an insignificant minority' that would have to impose itself on the Croat nation.[93] The implicit reference to the Partisans is unmistakable.

One might be tempted to conclude, as his biographer has done, that Stepinac remained to the end of the war politically narrow-minded, unable to grasp either the precarious reality of the NDH's position or the wider implications of the catastrophe which was engulfing Europe.[94] Still, it is doubtful whether a decisive public condemnation of the Ustaša regime would have altered the political situation in Croatia dramatically or brought an end to the abuses of that regime. That such a public condemnation would have saved the moral image, honour and reputation of the Church seems undeniable, however. By not taking such a step, Stepinac and the Catholic hierarchy remained indirectly associated with the Ustaša regime. By 1943 if not earlier, it must have been clear to Stepinac that his hope, expressed in April 1941, that the Church 'would enjoy freedom to carry out its work' in the Croatian state, was illusory. A public condemnation would also have brought the Church in line with a large segment of the Croat population; by most accounts, including those of German military officials stationed in Croatia, the Ustaša regime had, by 1942, lost much and perhaps most of the support it enjoyed in the spring of 1941. By 1943 that regime was in dire straits. This fact gave the politically divided Catholic hierarchy more leverage than it probably realised, had it chosen to exercise it.

Conclusion

Since the appearance of Stella Alexander's biography well over a decade ago, the historiography on the wartime Ustaše's relationship with the Catholic Church has not substantially advanced. Largely, this is due to the fact that few new archival sources have appeared during this period. Some Croatian documents and memoirs have emerged over the last few years which tend, by and large, to reinforce what is already known. If any new light is to be shed on the wartime role of Stepinac and the Catholic Church in Croatia, it will have to come from the Vatican's own archives and those of the Catholic Church in Croatia. We do not know, for example, to what extent Stepinac's own policies were guided, or even dictated, by Pius XII and the Vatican. We have a reasonably good idea of what

Stepinac reported to the Vatican during his three visits there; we do not know, however, what precise instructions or policy directions he was given by the Vatican. It seems most implausible that Stepinac was given no advice at all. In order words, we simply do not know how much direction he received from the Vatican about the policy he should pursue *vis-à-vis* the Ustaša regime. Perhaps we will never know. But Stepinac's policies appear to have closely mirrored those of Pius XII and the Vatican.

Carlo Falconi has shown that the Vatican was well aware of the grave situation in Croatia, but that it chose not to speak out against the Croatian regime. This was recently confirmed by the former Croatian diplomat Nikola Rušinović. He admitted that the Vatican's doors opened to him only with great difficulty, and that he had no success in the Vatican from June 1941, when he took up his duties in Rome, to February 1942. That month, however, he was informed that the Vatican's State Secretary, Luigi Cardinal Maglione, would receive him in private audience. During their first meeting, Maglione allegedly said that both Pope Pius XII and he wanted *de jure* recognition of the Croatian state, but that this was impossible under wartime conditions. Much to his surprise, Rušinović was informed in early July 1942, shortly before his departure from Rome, that Pius XII would grant him a brief private audience. The audience was indeed brief; the Pope simply blessed Rušinović, his family, and Croatia.[95] There is no mention in Rušinović's admittedly one-sided account of a single harsh word uttered by Maglione or Pius XII about the Croatian government or its policies. Stepinac remained to the end critical in his sermons of racist and other immoral policies, yet cautious in his pointed criticisms of the regime; his private interventions were less guarded although almost always diplomatic. The available documentation would appear to show that the official Vatican remained silent publicly and behind closed doors.

The Archbishop Stepinac who emerges from the historical documents is a complex figure. He appears to have been neither an ardent supporter of the Ustaša authorities legitimising their every policy, nor an avowed opponent who publicly denounced its crimes in a systematic manner. He occupied a middle-ground between these extremes. He was certainly delighted at the prospect of Croatian statehood and the gains that the Church might make in the new state, but he was seriously concerned about – and even appalled at – the regime's methods and encroachments with respect to Church prerogatives. Stepinac often intervened for victims and by 1942–43 his sermons were increasingly critical, but he never threatened to withdraw either his personal approval or that of the Church from a government that so often unceremoniously ignored its interests. He may have believed that such an unprecedented act would only further aggravate the existing fissures within the Church. That is why there remains considerable unease in many quarters about the Catholic Church's wartime role in Croatia, and the silence following the war. That silence was undoubtedly conditioned in part by the Church's own difficult predicament after 1945, but it has been interpreted by many as moral failure. Public silence in the face of genocide is not tantamount to supporting genocide. Nor is there a moral equivalency between a divided and publicly timid Church hierarchy with the Pavelićes and others who are ultimately responsible for perpetrating unspeakable crimes in wartime Croatia. But there remains discomfort among many that not enough was done to rescue the innocents or to speak out more forcefully against the rampant abuses of the regime. Pope John Paul II's apology of June 2003 was a belated and implicit attempt to address this failure in wartime Croatia. But as the recent flood of books on this subject attests, it would seem that the controversies surrounding the Catholic Church, both in Croatia and Nazi-occupied Europe generally, will not abate soon.

Notes

1. See John Cornwell, *Hitler's Pope: The Secret History of Pius XII* (New York: Viking, 1999) and Daniel Goldhagen, A *Moral Reckoning: The Role of the Catholic Church in the Holocaust and its Unfulfilled Duty of Repair* (New York: Alfred A. Knopf, 2002). Over the last decade, the debate over Pius XII's conduct during the Holocaust has intensified. In addition to the works of Cornwell and Goldhagen, critical works have appeared by J. Michael Phayer, The *Catholic Church and the Holocaust: 1930–1965* (Bloomington, IN: Indiana University Press, 2000); Garry Wills, *Papal Sin: Structures of Deceit* (New York: Doubleday, 2001); James Carroll, *Constantine's Sword: The Church and the Jews* (New York: Houghton Mifflin Co., 2001); Susan Zuccotti, *Under His Very Windows: The Vatican and the Holocaust in Italy* (New Haven: Yale University Press, 2001); and David I. Kertzer, *The Popes Against the Jews: The Vatican's Role in the Rise of Modern Anti-Semitism* (New York: Alfred A. Knopf, 2001).
2. The western scholarly literature on the Ustaša movement and the NDH is not extensive. See Jozo Tomasevich, *War and Revolution in Yugoslavia, 1941–1945: Occupation and Collaboration* (Stanford: Stanford University Press, 2001), pp.233–579; M. Broszat and L. Hory, *Die kroatische Ustascha-Staat, 1941–1945* (Stuttgart: Deutsche V.A., 1964); Dimitrije Djordjević, 'Fascism in Yugoslavia: 1918–1941', and Ivan Avakumović, 'Yugoslavia's Fascist Movements', in P.F. Sugar (ed.), *Native Fascism in the Successor States, 1918–1945* (Santa Barbara: ABC Clio, 1971); Yeshayahu Jelinek, 'Nationalities and Minorities in the Independent State of Croatia', *Nationalities Papers*, Vol.8, No.2 (1984), pp.195–210; Aleksa Djilas, *The Contested Country: Yugoslav Unity and Communist Revolution, 1919–1953* (Cambridge, MA: Harvard University Press, 1991), pp.103–27; and, Holm Sundhaussen, 'Der Ustascha-Staat: Anatomie eines Herrschaftssystem', *Österreichische Osthefte*, Vol.37, No.2 (1995), pp.497–533. Also useful is Edmund Glaise von Horstenau, *Ein General im Zwielicht: Die Erinnerungen Edmund Glaise von Horstenau*, comp. Peter Broucek, vol. 3 (Vienna: Boehlau, 1998). The literature produced in former Yugoslavia is abundant, although of varying quality. The following works stand out: Bogdan Krizman, *Ante Pavelić i Ustaše* (Zagreb: Globus, 1978), *Pavelić između Hitlera i Mussolinija* (Zagreb: Globus, 1980), and *Ustaše i Treći Reich*, 2 vols. (Zagreb: Globus, 1982); and Fikreta Jelić-Butić, *Ustaše i Nezavisna Država Hrvatska* (Zagreb: Školska knjiga, 1977).
3. Cited in Patrick Moore, 'Former Yugoslavia and Pope John Paul II', Radio Free Europe/Radio Liberty Balkan Report, Vol. 9, No. 11, 9 April 2005.
4. On the beatification of Stepinac, see 'Drugi Papin pohod Hrvatskoj 2–4. listopada 1998', at http://www.papa.hr/papa_u_hrvatskoj_drugi_posjet.html (accessed 12 August 2006).
5. For the standard Yugoslav works on the role of the Catholic Church in wartime Croatia, see Joža Horvat and Zdenko Štambuk (eds.), *Dokumenti o protunarodnom radu i zločinima jednog dijela katoličkog klera* (Zagreb, 1946); Viktor Novak, *Magnum crimen: Pola vijeka klerikalizma u Hrvatskoj* (Zagreb: NZ Matica Hrvatska, 1948); Branko Petranović, 'Aktivnost rimokatoličkog klera protiv sredjivanja prilika u Jugoslaviji (March 1945–September 1946)', *Istorija XX veka: Zbornik radova* 5 (1963): pp.263–313; the two books by Sima Simić, *Tuđinske kombinacije oko NDH* (1958, reprint Belgrade: Kultura, 1990), and *Prekrštavanje Srba za vreme Drugog svetskog rata* (1958, reprint Belgrade, 1990); Dinko Davidov, 'Đakovački biskup Antun Akšamović i Srbi', in *Zbornik o Srbima u Hrvatskoj*, ed. Vasilije Krestić, vol. 2 (Belgrade: SANU, 1991), pp.309–26; Novica Vojinović, 'Odnos Katoličke crkve prema Jugoslaviji', in *Drugi svjetski rat – 50 godina kasnije*, ed. Vlado Strugar (Podgorica, 1997), pp.349–64; Dušan Lj. Kašić, 'Srpska crkva u tzv. Nezavisnoj Državi Hrvatskoj', in *Srpska pravoslavna crkva, 1920–70*, ed. Rajko L. Veselinovic et al. (Belgrade: Sinod SPC, 1971), 183–204; R.V. Petrović, *Genocid sa blagoslovom Vatikana: Izjave Srba-izbeglica* (Belgrade: Nikola Tesla, 1992); Veljko Đ. Đurić, *Prekrštavanje Srba u Nezavisnoj Državi Hrvatskoj: Prilozi za istoriju verskog genocida* (Belgrade: Alfa, 1991); Milan Čubrić, *Između noža i križa* (Belgrade: Knji ževne novine, 1990); Milorad Lazić, *Krstarski rat Nezavisne Države Hrvatske* (Belgrade, 1991); Vladimir Dedijer, *The Yugoslav Auschwitz and the Vatican: The Croatian Massacre of the Serbs During World War II* (Buffalo: Prometheus Books, 1992); and the two books by Milan Bulajić, *Misija Vatikana u Nezavisnoj Državi Hrvatskoj*, 2 vols. (Belgrade: Politika, 1992), and *Ustaški zločini genocida i sudjenje Andriji Artukoviću 1986. godine* (Belgrade: Nova knjiga, 1988). Generally speaking, these views are also expressed by Hervé Laurière (pseud. of Branko Miljuš), *Assassins au nom de Dieu* (Lausanne: Editions l'Age d'Homme, 1951); Edmond Paris, *Genocide in satellite Croatia, 1941–45: A*

record of racial and religious persecutions and massacres (Chicago: American Institute for Balkan Affairs, 1961); and Branko Bokun, *Spy in the Vatican 1941–45* (New York, 1973).

6. The most recent defence of Stepinac and the Church is provided by Jure Krišto: 'Katolička crkva u Nezavisnoj Državi Hrvatskoj', *Časopis za suvremenu povijest*, Vol.27, No. 3 (1995), pp.461–74; and, *Katolička crkva u Nezavisnoj Državi Hrvatskoj*, 2 vols. (Zagreb: Hrvatski institut za povijest, 1998). A recent compilation of Stepinac's sermons and other pronouncements may be found in J. Batelja and C. Tomić, *Alojzije Kardinal Stepinac, Nadbiskup zagrebački: Propovijedi, govori, poruke, 1941–46* (hereafter, *Propovijedi*) (Zagreb: Glas koncila, 1996). For earlier studies, see H. O'Brien, *Archbishop Stepinac: The Man and His Case* (Westminster: Newman Bookshop, 1947); B. Wallace, *The Trial of Dr. Aloysius Stepinac, Archbishop of Zagreb* (London, 1947); Richard Pattee, *The Case of Cardinal Aloysius Stepinac* (Milwaukee: Bruce Publishing Co., 1953); Th. Dragoun, *Le dossier du cardinal Stepinac* (Paris: Nouvelles Editions Latines, 1958); Francis Eterovic, *Aloysius Cardinal Stepinac: A Spiritual Leader* (Chicago, 1970); M. Raymond, *The Man for this Moment: the Life and Death of Aloysius Cardinal Stepinac* (New York: Alba House, 1971); and Aleksa Benigar, *Alojzije Stepinac – Hrvatski kardinal* (Rome: ZIRAL, 1974).
7. Cited in http://www.catarchive.com/detailPages/640315.html (accessed 12 August 2006).
8. See Guenter Lewy, *The Catholic Church and Nazi Germany* (New York: Da Capo Press, 1964); Saul Friedlander, *Pius XII and the Third Reich: A Documentation* (New York: Alfred A. Knopf, 1964); and Carlo Falconi, *The Silence of Pius XII* (Boston: Little Brown, 1970), which originally appeared in Italian in 1964.
9. The first truly critical western account of Stepinac and the Church episcopacy in Croatia and Bosnia-Herzegovina was provided in 1956 by Hubert Butler, in his essay, 'The Sub-Prefect Should Have Held His Tongue.' It is available online at http://www.archipelago.org/vol5-1/butler.htm (accessed 12 August 2006).
10. The most comprehensive and objective work produced outside former Yugoslavia thus far about Stepinac is Stella Alexander, *The Triple Myth: A Life of Alojzije Stepinac* (Boulder: East European Monographs, 1987). She also authored *Church and State in Yugoslavia* (Cambridge: Cambridge University Press, 1979), which is a useful study of both the Catholic Church and Serbian Orthodox Church under Yugoslav Communist rule from 1945 to 1970, and 'Croatia: The Catholic Church and the Clergy, 1919–45', in *Catholics, the State, and the European Radical Right, 1919–45*, ed. R.J. Wolff and J.K. Hoensch (Highland Lakes, N.J.: Atlantic Research and Publications, 1987), pp.31–66. Also useful are Pedro Ramet, 'Religion and Nationalism in Yugoslavia', in *Religion and Nationalism in Soviet and East European Politics*, ed. P. Ramet (Duke: Duke University Press, 1989); Chapter 4 of Sabrina Ramet, *Balkan Babel: The Disintegration of Yugoslavia from the Death of Tito to the War for Kosovo* 3rd ed. (Boulder: Westview Press, 1999). Two balanced and judicious treatments of Stepinac and the Catholic Church may also be found in Ivo Goldstein (with Slavko Goldstein), *Holokaust u Zagrebu* (Zagreb: Globus, 2001), pp.559–78; and, Jozo Tomasevich, (note 2), Chapter 12, pp.511–79.
11. I have tried to outline the relationship between religion, religious identity and Croat nationalism in my article, 'Religion and Nation in Wartime Croatia: The Ustaša Policy of Forced Religious Conversion, 1941–42', *Slavonic and East European Review*, Vol.83, No.1 (January 2005), pp.71–116.
12. On Starčević, the 'state right' ideology and the movement he spawned, see Mirjana Gross, *Povijest pravaške ideologije* (Zagreb: Institut za hrvatsku povijest, 1973), recently updated as *Izvorno pravaštvo* (Zagreb: Golden Marketing, 2001).
13. The party's nomenclature changed many times. It was known as the HPSS from 1904 to 1920, then as the Croat Republican Peasant Party (HRSS, 1920–25), and finally as the Croat Peasant Party (HSS, after 1925).
14. The original Party of (Croatian State) Right split in 1895 into two fractions: the Pure Party of Right (or so-called Frankists, named after their leader, Josip Frank) and the larger group, known as the *domovinaši* (after their newspaper, *Hrvatska domovina*). In 1908 the Frankists fractured, with a splinter group forming the Starčević's Party of Right (named after its leader, Mile Starčević). In 1910 a Frankist youth group, known as the Young Croats, briefly came to the fore.
15. Stadler's conversion programme was not supported in all Catholic quarters, and even the Herzegovinan Franciscans did not share his views. See Ivo Banac, *The National Question in Yugoslavia* (Ithaca: Cornell University Press, 1984), p.364.
16. Cited in P. Ramet, 'From Strossmayer to Stepinac: Croatian National Ideology and Catholicism', *Canadian Review of Studies in Nationalism*, Vol.12, No.1 (1985), p.131.
17. Cited in ibid., p.130.
18. Banac, (note 15), pp.349–54. While the Croat People's Party pursued an autonomist political platform to 1929, the Croat Party of Right belonged from the outset to the 'hard' opposition and believed that it was engaged, in the words of one of its exiled followers, in a struggle against a

Great Serbian policy 'which with unbending consistency is working to destroy Croatdom.' See Stjepan Sarkotić, *Radićevo izdajstvo* (Vienna, 1925), p.27. By the late 1920s, there was a consensus within the ranks of the Croat Party of Right that 'a new movement [far more radical than the HSS] had to be created which would be the bearer of an uncompromising and revolutionary struggle [against Belgrade]'. See Eugen Dido Kvaternik, *Sjećanja i zapažanja, 1929–1945: Prilozi za hrvatsku povijest*, comp. by Jere Jareb (Zagreb: Hrvatski institut za pavijest, 1995), p.271.

19. On the origins and pre-1941 development of the Ustaša movement, see Fikreta Jelić-Butić, (note 2), pp.13–57; and Bogdan Krizman, *Ante Pavelić i Ustaše* (Zagreb: Globus, 1980).
20. On the Catholic youth organisations, e.g., the *Orlovi* [*The Eagles*], *Domagoj* (the name of a medieval Croatian ruler), and so on, see the essay by Sandra Prlenda, 'Young, Religious and Radical: The Croat Catholic Youth Organizations 1922–1945,' in *Ideologies and National Identities: The Case of Twentieth-Century Southeastern Europe*, ed. John Lampe and Mark Mazower (New York/Budapest: Central European University Press, 2004).
21. Jelić-Butić, (note 2), p.5.
22. See Alexander, 'Croatia: The Catholic Church and the Clergy, (note 10), pp.31–66.
23. Jelić-Butić, (note 2), p.43.
24. See, for example, the following articles: 'Još jedan ustaški proglas hrv. narodu!', *Nezavisna Hrvatska Država*, 22 April 1939, p.8; Mile Starčević, 'Slava Anti Starčeviću!' *Hrvatski narod*, 24 February 1939, p.1; Mile Budak, '11. i 13. lipnja', *Hrvatski narod*, 9 June 1939, p.1; Ur., 'Naša prva riječ!' *Hrvatski narod*, 9 February 1939, p.1; and Ivan Oršanić, 'Dr. Ante Starčević', *Hrvatski narod*, 1 March 1940, p.1.
25. See, for example, 'Ne damo Bosnu!,' *Nezavisna Hrvatska Država*, 3 June 1939, p.2; 'Opomena vodstvu HSS,' *Hrvatski narod*, 28 July 1939, p.1. Luka Grbić, 'Još o Srbo-Cincaro-Vlasima,' *Nezavisna Hrvatska Država*, 4 November 1939, p.4; and, 'Hrvatska politika u Bosni,' *Hrvatski narod*, 28 July 1939, p.6. See also, M.O., 'Vlasi a ne Srbi', *Nezavisna Hrvatska Država*, 1 June 1940, p.2. Muhamed Hadžijahić, 'Nacionalna obilježja bosansko-hercegovačkih Muslimana', *Hrvatski narod*, 24 March 1939, p.7. See also, I.Z.H., 'Još nešto o muslimanima istočne Bosne', *Hrvatski narod*, 26 May 1939, p.1; and, d., 'Tragedija Hrvatske krajine', *Hrvatski narod*, 26 May 1939, p.5; Petar Preradović, 'Na prošlosti budućnost se snuje', *Hrvatski narod*, 9 June 1939, p.5; and M.G., 'O Hrvatstvu', *Hrvatski narod*, 7 July 1939, p.7.
26. M.S., 'Srpski apetit', *Nezavisna Hrvatska Država*, 24 December 1938, p.4.
27. See, for example: Mladen Lorković, *Narod i zemlja Hrvata* (Zagreb: Matica Hrvatska, 1940); Krunoslav Draganović's *Katolička crkva u Bosni i Hercegovini* (Zagreb, 1934); and X., 'Katolička crkva u Bosni i Hercegovini', *Hrvatski narod*, 5 May 1939, p.5.
28. Ivo Pilar, *Južnoslavensko pitanje: Prikaz cjelokupnog pitanja*, trans. by Fedor Pucek (1943; reprint Zagreb: Matica Hrvatska, 1990), 112, 215. Originally published as L. von Südland, *Die Südslawische Frage und der Weltkrieg* (Vienna: Manz, 1918).
29. See the discussion in Robert O. Paxton, *Europe in the Twentieth Century*, 3rd ed. (New York: Harcourt, 1997), pp.361–2.
30. Ivan Oršanić, 'Posljedice Versaillesa', *Hrvatski narod*, 5 May 1939, p.1.
31. Ivo Guberina, 'Naš katolicizam i poljska tragedija', *Hrvatski narod*, 10 November 1939, p.3.
32. In 1939 the Split-based Catholic newspaper *Katoličke riječi* [*Catholic Words*] accused *Hrvatski narod*, which was edited by Mile Budak, and the 'Croat nationalists' generally of possessing racist and National Socialist views, which prompted Budak to dismiss such claims as untrue. See 'Onima, koji ne znaju ideologiju hrv. nacionalista,' *Hrvatski narod*, Christmas 1939, p.1.
33. Krsto Spalatin, 'Prvi glasovi iz Francuske,' *Hrvatska revija*, Vol.14, No.7 (1941), pp.382–4.
34. Ibid.
35. Cited in Slavko Goldstein, 'Beatifikacija kardinala Alojzija Stepinca,' *Ha-kol* (November 1998), p.14. Strictly speaking, this was not a 'diary'; entries were made by Stepinac and his aides.
36. Alexander, (note 10), p.53.
37. Cited in Ramet (note 10), pp.137–8.
38. Alexander (note 10), p.52.
39. Cited in ibid., pp.23–4.
40. Alexander (note 10), 36–8. On the Concordat and its demise, see ibid., pp.28–38.
41. Cited in Goldstein (note 10), pp.562–3.
42. Cited in ibid., p.41.
43. Dragutin Kamber, *Slom NDH: Kako sam ga ja proživio*, ed. Božica Ercegovac Jambrović (Zagreb: Hrvatski informativni centar, 1993), p.5. During the war Kamber belonged to the Ustaša movement, and in April–May 1941 participated in the Ustaša commission which ran Doboj district in Bosnia. In 1945 he emigrated, and eventually made his way first to the United States and then Canada, where he died in 1969.

44. Cited in Alexander, (note 10), pp.61–2.
45. Archbishops Stepinac of Zagreb and Šarić of Sarajevo; and Bishops Antun Akšamović of Đakovo, Josip Marija Carević of Dubrovnik, Kvirin Klement Bonefačić of Split, Alojzije Mišić of Mostar (after 1942, Petar Čule), Jeronim Mileta of Šibenik, Josip Garić of Banja Luka, Josip Srebrnić of Krk, Miho Pušić of Hvar, Viktor Burić of Senj-Modruš, Pavao Butorac of Kotor, and Janko Šimrak, the Apostolic Administrator of the Greek Catholic Bishopric of Križevci. The bishoprics of Đakovo, Senj-Modruš, and Križevci all fell under the Zagreb Archbishopric, while those of Mostar and Banja Luka fell under the Sarajevo Archbishopric. The five Dalmatian bishoprics of Šibenik, Split, Hvar, Kotor, and Dubrovnik fell under the Zadar (Zara) Archbishopric, which was part of Italy at the time.
46. On 13 June 1941 Mgr Ramiro Marcone, the Benedictine Abbot of Monte Cassino, who was not a member of the regular Vatican diplomatic corps, was appointed apostolic visitor to the Croatian Bishops' Conference (*not* to the Croatian state, as is sometimes incorrectly claimed) in summer 1941. He arrived in Zagreb on 3 August 1941 in the company of his secretary, Don Giuseppe Masucci. He remained in Croatia until late 1945, and spent the entire time in Stepinac's palace in Zagreb; ibid., pp.66–7.
47. This letter is reproduced in Pattee, (note 6), Doc. XXVI, pp.300–302. One month earlier, on 23 April 1941, Stepinac had written to Artuković reminding him that many Jews had turned to the Church, were 'good Catholics of the Jewish race,' and several had also 'excelled as good Croatian patriots.' See ibid., Doc. XXV, pp.299–300.
48. Cited in Goldstein, 'Beatifikacija kardinala Alojzije Stepinca,' pp.15–16.
49. Alexander (note 10), pp.71–2.
50. See *Actes et documents du Saint Siège relatifs à la seconde guerre mondiale*, vol. 4 : *Le Saint Siège et la guerre en Europe, Juin 1940–Juin 1941* (Rome: Libreria editrice vaticana, 1967), Doc. 347, dated 15 May 1941, p.491.
51. *Documents on German Foreign Policy*, Volume XII (Washington: US Government Printing Office, 1962), Doc. 603, pp.977–81.
52. Count Galeazzo Ciano, *Diplomatic Papers*, ed. by Malcolm Muggeridge (London: Odhams Press, 1948), p.472.
53. Kamber (note 43), pp.18–19.
54. Cited in Batelja & Tomić (note 6), pp.283–4.
55. Alexander (note 10), p.74.
56. Ibid., p.75.
57. Alexander, *Church and State in Yugoslavia* (note 10), pp.27–8.
58. On 4 November 1941, Bishop Josip Garić of Banja Luka wrote to Archbishop Stepinac about the persecution of Serbs in his region. However, Garić placed most of the blame on the local Muslims in the Ustaša ranks who committed, he claimed, numerous crimes against local Serbs. He added that many local Serbs who had converted to Catholicism had been killed by Muslims, and some were apparently even forced to convert to Islam. On 15 November 1941, the Archbishop of Sarajevo, Ivan Šarić, wrote to Stepinac on the problems relating to the conversion of Serbs. He complained mainly of the Muslims employed in the civil administration who were, upon receiving written requests for conversion by Serbs, not following up on these requests. He even complained about the propaganda of the Evangelical Church; Protestant pastors were telling Serbs that they need not convert to Catholicism, and could convert to Protestantism. See Alexander, *Church and State in Yugoslavia* (note 10), p.33; Carlo Falconi (note 8), p.286; and, Đoko Slijepčević, *Istorija Srpske pravoslavne crkve*, vol. 2: *Od početka XIX veka do kraja Drugog svetskog rata* (Munich, 1966), pp.675–8.
59. Alexander, *Church and State in Yugoslavia* (note 10), p.32.
60. Cited in Alexander (note 10), pp.80–2.
61. Cited in Goldstein, *Holokaust u Zagrebu*, p.570.
62. Cited in Alexander, *Church and State in Yugoslavia* (note 10), p.34. The letter to Pavelić is reprinted in Pattee, *Stepinac*, Doc. LII, pp.384–395. Stepinac's 3 December 1941 letter to Pope Pius XII, summarising the proceedings of the Catholic Bishops' Conference, is reproduced in *Actes et documents* (note 50), vol. 5, Doc. 216, pp.368–9.
63. Cited in Ciano (note 52), p.472.
64. See note 11.
65. Tomasevich (note 2), pp.576–9.
66. *Hrvatski Državni Arhiv* (HDA), *Državno ravnateljestvo za ponovu, Vjerski odsjek*, Box 1: Broj 282/41 ('Teški udarac hrvatskoj nacionalnoj politici u slučaju prelaza grčkoistočnjaka na grkokatoličku vjeru'), 11 December 1941.
67. Aleksa Djilas (note 2), p.209, n.24.

68. Cited in Jure Krišto, *Sukob simbola: Politika, vjerail ideologije u Nezavisnoj Državi Hrvatskoj* (Zagreb: Globus, 2001), p.96.
69. Jure Krišto (note 6), vol.1, p.77.
70. Goldstein (note 10), p.565.
71. Cited in ibid., p.573.
72. Krišto (note 68), pp.98–104.
73. Cited in G. Masucci, *Misija u Hrvatskoj* (Madrid: Drinina knjižica, 1967), p.44.
74. The letter and circular are reprinted in Pattee (note 6), Documents I and IV, pp.245–6, pp.254–5.
75. Sabrina Ramet (note 10), pp.136–7.
76. Goldstein (note 10), p.565.
77. Tomasevich (note 2), p.572. In a written statement given to Yugoslav investigators on 20 September 1946, Stepinac alleged that at least 260–270 priests and about one dozen nuns had been killed by Partisans from the beginning of the war. See Batelja and Tomić (note 6), p.279.
78. Cited in Goldstein (note 10), p.570.
79. Cited in ibid., p.572. See Pattee, *Stepinac*, Doc. XXVIII, p.306.
80. Reprinted in Pattee Ibid. Doc. XXXV, pp.319–22.
81. Cited in Alexander (note 10), p.91.
82. See Stevan Pavlowitch, *Unconventional Perceptions of Yugoslavia, 1940–1945* (New York: Columbia University Press, 1984).
83. Alexander notes that on 19 June 1946, Ilija Jukić, the former Under-Secretary of State in the Ministry of Foreign Affairs of the Yugoslav government in exile (1941–43), wrote to the *New York Times* confirming that London had sent Rapotec to occupied Yugoslavia, and that Rapotec had met with Stepinac. He also confirmed that Stepinac had agreed to distribute funds to victims of the Ustaša regime. Alexander also cites a 14 July 1942 report by the Yugoslav ambassador to Turkey, who informed the Yugoslav government in exile, after his meeting with Rapotec: 'According to reports from Serbs in Zagreb Stepinac is behaving well. He has interceded for Serbs on many occasions, helped them and defended them but he has not always been successful. He might well have resigned because of the Ustaša crimes but found that it would not be tactically a good thing.' Cited in Alexander (note 10), pp.95–101.
84. Nikola Rušinović, *Moja sjećanja na Hrvatsku* (Zagreb: Meditor, 1996), pp.120–26.
85. Mladen Lorković, *Ministar urotnik: Mladen Lorković*, comp. by Nada Kisić-Kolanović (Zagreb: Golden Marketing, 1998), p.153. Rušinović was replaced in 1942 by Prince Erwin Lobkowitz.
86. Rušinović, (note 84), pp.127–8.
87. Peter Broucek (note 2), p.293f. There is nothing in Horstenau's memoirs to suggest that Stepinac actively collaborated with the Ustaša government.
88. Alexander (note 10), pp.98–9. This sermon followed closely on the heels of the execution of Stepinac's brother, who happened to be a Partisan sympathiser, as well as the SS execution of a priest and a dozen peasants in a village north of Zagreb, all in October 1943. See, Broucek (note 2), pp.299–300, pp.314–15. The sermon is reprinted in Pattee (note 6), Document XVI, pp.281–7.
89. Alexander (note 10), pp.99–100.
90. In late June 1942, he remarked in a sermon that the Church opposed forcible conversion to Catholicism and would defend as best it could all converts, and blamed 'irresponsible elements' in the Croatian government for the killing of innocent people. In March 1943, when the Ustaša authorities issued a decree ordering all remaining Jews of Zagreb to register with the police, Stepinac protested, and in a sermon of 14 March 1943 denounced racist policies. But even at this stage there is still no indication of an attempt to assist those Jews who had not converted to Catholicism; ibid., pp.96–7.
91. Ibid., pp.108–9.
92. Archbishop Šarić and Bishop Garić of Banja Luka were the only two Croat members of the Catholic hierarchy to flee the country in 1945. The Slovene Bishop Gregorij Rožman of Ljubljana also fled in 1945. Šarić eventually found asylum in Franco's Spain. In the mid-1990s he was reburied in Sarajevo, the Bosnian capital. Garić died in Austria, evidently in 1946.
93. Batelja and Tomić (note 6) p.260.
94. Alexander (note 10), p.107.
95. Rušinović (note 84), pp.116–17, p.130.

The NDH's Relations with Italy and Germany

MARIO JAREB
Croatian Institute of History

The Ustaša leader in Croatia, Colonel Slavko Kvaternik, proclaimed the Independent State of Croatia on 10 April 1941. The activities of the Croatian Banovina's [*Banovina Hrvatska*] authorities during the period from spring 1940 to March 1941 almost destroyed the Ustaša groups in Croatia. Only the war and the collapse of Yugoslavia allowed the Ustaše to revive their activities in late March and April 1941.[1] After the *coup* in Belgrade, the Third Reich decided to invade and destroy the Kingdom of Yugoslavia. The Germans realised that their efforts to occupy and stabilise the former Yugoslav territory might be easier if cooperation with local elements could be established. They therefore attempted to exploit Croatian dissatisfaction with Yugoslavia. They were hoping that the Croatian Peasant Party (*Hrvatska seljačka stranka* – HSS) and its president, Dr. Vladko Maček, would accept the establishment of an independent Croatian state, and initially ignored Ustaša elements in Zagreb.[2] For the Germans, the HSS was the real representative of the Croatian nation.[3] As such, it was considered a guarantee of political stability and order in a future Croatian state. As a result, the Germans treated the Ustaše as a group with minor political influence and strength.[4] Pavelić himself was treated as an Italian *protégé*.[5]

It soon become clear that Maček was rejecting cooperation with the Germans.[6] Only then did the German special envoy in Zagreb, Edmund von Veesenmayer, decide to give support to Ustaše, then led domestically by Kvaternik. However, Ustaša activities in Croatia did not have any influence on the course of events from the beginning of April 1941 to the breakout of the war on 6 April of that year. The first days of war did not change the situation in Zagreb; and Ustaša elements were forced to hide in order to avoid arrest or internment.[7]

Still, the Yugoslav military collapse was evident and it became obvious that the Germans would occupy Zagreb and the rest of Croatia within the next several days. Under such circumstances, a mutiny of Croatian soldiers took place in the town of Bjelovar on 8 April.[8] Finally, Kvaternik decided to act on 10 April. He re-established contacts with his followers as well as the German envoy in Zagreb; simultaneously, a German advance forced the leadership of the Banovina of Croatia to leave Zagreb the same day. The HSS president, Maček decided to stay.[9] Circumstances were favourable for Kvaternik, and he obtained support from local police and Croatian Peasant and Civic Protection forces. With power in his hands, Kvaternik was able to proclaim the independence of Croatia over Radio Station Zagreb.

On the same day, Maček released a short proclamation to his followers and invited them to cooperate with the new authorities. During the war, Communist propaganda used this proclamation to accuse him of betrayal, or used it as 'evidence' of his alleged adherence to the Ustaše.[10] Any analysis of the proclamation, as well as of the circumstances and events that contributed to its creation, would show that these accusations were not based on facts. For Maček had rejected all German offers before that, thus he could not be charged with any cooperation with the Nazis or their allies. Moreover, on 8 April he had issued a proclamation in which he appealed to Croats to be loyal to the Yugoslav Army and to fight the enemy.[11]

On 10 April 1941, the situation changed radically. The Yugoslav army was already defeated, the Banovina of Croatia and its administration had collapsed, and German troops started their advance to the centre of Zagreb.[12] On the same day the Ustaše, led by Kvaternik, established a government and proclaimed the independence of Croatia.[13] Thus overnight Maček became a person without power and influence. However, as president of the HSS and the legitimate Croatian leader, he was still an important political figure who could not be simply ignored. This is why von Veesenmeyer and Kvaternik decided to visit Maček and gain some sort of approval.[14] Maček actually issued the proclamation and appealed to his followers to cooperate with the new authorities.[15] However, there is no single word that could be understood as constituting approval of Kvaternik's acts. There is also no word that can be understood as implying the transmittal of his leadership to Kvaternik or the new authorities. He simply accepted the fact that Kvaternik had already proclaimed independence. Therefore, his words can be understood as those of a person aware of an impending reality. On 10 April 1941, he could only hope that the end of conflict would prevent the meaningless loss of life in the future.[16] He also thought that the war was primarily a matter between Great Powers; small nations could await its outcome. He was deeply convinced that the western powers would win that war, and that any alliance with Germany and Italy would be harmful for Croatia. He decided to wait, and to prepare the HSS to reclaim its leadership of the Croats at the end of the war.[17]

Many Croats initially welcomed the founding of the NDH. For many it looked as if the old Croatian dream of a free Croatian state had finally come true. The fact that, simultaneously, an unjust and odious Yugoslavia had collapsed was also well accepted. It is important to note that many Croats believed that the establishment of the NDH would spare Croatia from the ravages of war and foreign military occupation. Very soon, however, it became obvious that these hopes were nothing but illusions.[18]

The policy of the Ustaša regime led by *Poglavnik* [chief of state and of the Ustaša Movement] Dr. Ante Pavelić was, from the very beginning, limited by the strong German and Italian influence in the NDH. German and Italian zones of influence and military presence in the NDH were first established at the meeting of Galeazzo Ciano and Joachim von Ribbentrop in Vienna on 21–22 April 1941.[19] The

German presence throughout 1941 was not overtly visible to the public, although there is no doubt that German representatives, institutions and troops deployed in northern parts of the country had a major impact on the internal situation and policy.

During that period, the Croatian public was primarily concerned about relations with Fascist Italy, and was focused on negotiations about the new Croatian–Italian border. On territory occupied by the Italian armed forces their behaviour also worried the Croatian public. Italian military authorities attempted to completely subordinate local authorities on the Adriatic coast to their power. Italian occupation was also followed by strong propaganda intended to present Dalmatia as Italian land, and to support Italian territorial claims. Italian control in the hinterland was not as strict, but local Croatian authorities were subjected to Italian military command, and the NDH government was not in position to effectively administer the occupied areas.

The fears on the part of the Croatian public were justified, due to the fact that, according to the Rome treaties [*Rimski ugovori*], of 18 May 1941, the NDH had to accept the cession of a major part of the Croatian coast to Italy.[20] Thus, Italy annexed the area of Sušak-Čabar; the islands of Krk and Rab; the entire hinterland of Zadar; the districts of Biograd and Šibenik; the town of Trogir; the Kaštela area between Trogir and Split; the city of Split; the islands of Čiovo, Šolta, Korčula and Mljet, as well as part of Konavle and Boka Kotorska [the Bay of Kotor].[21] The city of Split and its surroundings (both suburbs and the Kaštela area), alongside the island of Korčula, would be governed by a common Italian-Croatian administration.[22] However, Italian authorities ignored these provisions, and both the Split area and Korčula were exposed to Italianisation and subjected to Fascist terror. Furthermore, a wide strip of NDH territory was demilitarised.[23]

Agreements also guaranteed complete Italian control of the NDH Adriatic littoral. The NDH agreed not to organise its own navy, and allowed the Italians to control its territorial waters. Yet Italian occupation troops were stationed on territories recognised as part of the NDH. They simply changed their status and remained in their posts as allied troops.[24] Only then were the NDH authorities allowed to establish their administration on these territories, and to deploy their own police, and army.

Numerous Italian officials favoured the idea of an Italo-Croat customs, monetary and personal union. Croatia would thus become a state only nominally, and power would remain in Italian hands.[25] Pavelić and his associates declined Italian advances, and the NDH formally retained all authority to organise and execute its own economic policy.[26] A proposal that Croatia would become a kingdom with an Italian duke as a king was formally accepted, although this was never implemented.[27] However, the strong Italian presence and the impotence of the NDH authorities to establish effective control on large territories in zones of Italian influence allowed the Italians to become the real masters in these areas.[28] The Italian army and other Italian representatives therefore established almost complete control over Zone II, and exerted strong influence on developments in Zone III. Attempts by the NDH authorities to protect Croatian economic interests were limited to fruitless negotiations with the Italians and endless letters, memoranda and protests.[29] None of these documents changed anything, despite containing much data that can be useful in future research on Italo-Croat wartime relations. The Italian presence on these territories had devastating effects on their economy – indeed, upon the economy of the entire NDH.[30] Italian troops committed numerous war crimes in zones under their control, and contributed much to the disorder within them. The Italian presence in the NDH prevented Zagreb from establishing effective control over the majority of its territory belonging in Zones II and III. On the other hand, however, while the Italian moves increased the level of disorder they could not prevent the NDH authorities from committing numerous war crimes in these territories, especially during 1941.[31]

The German presence in the NDH was initially less evident than the Italian. Unlike Italy, the Third Reich had no territorial intentions to impinge upon Croatian national interests. This fact enhanced the image of Germans among Croats in 1941. In regard to their views of Jews and Serbs, however, the Ustaše decided to copy German National Socialist internal policy in order to gain support from the Third Reich and to become an integral part of the 'New Order' in Europe. This resulted in racial decrees against Jews being issued as early as the end of April 1941.[32] The NDH established concentration camps for those whose racial origin, religious denomination or political beliefs were considered a threat to the regime.[33]

At the same time, the Ustaša leadership attempted to construct an ideology based on the Italian Fascist and German National Socialist regimes.[34] The persecution of Serbs was not based on racial or similar views, but instead rested upon the idea that they should be punished for crimes against Croats committed by Serb-dominated interwar Yugoslav regimes. The Ustaše believed that Serbs' loyalty to the NDH was questionable; they were consequently considered to be a potential threat. Mass crimes against the Serb population, mostly in the rural areas of Lika, Kordun, Bosnia, and Eastern Hercegovina, forced them to defend themselves. By the end of summer 1941, large parts of the NDH (primarily in Zones II and III) had become battlefields. However, the NDH authorities soon realised that the mass persecution of Serbs would only harm their own interests; so, by the end of 1941, they decided to change their policy. In 1942, they even assisted in the establishment of the Croatian Orthodox Church.[35] Serbs were not recognised under their national name, but as so-called 'Orthodox Croats' and their position (primarily in cities and towns) gradually improved.[36]

At the beginning, most Serbian rebels were united in their efforts to defend their lives, but very soon they split into two main groups. The first group, led by Communists (Tito's partisans), decided to fight not only against the NDH, but also against the Italians and Germans. From the very beginning numerous Croats (primarily in Zone I) fought along with them.

The second group was dominated by interwar Serbian nationalistic elements (primarily Chetnik leaders), ready to cooperate with the Italian occupation.[37] In reality most of the Chetnik detachments in Zones II and III established very close cooperation with the Italians, and assisted the Italian troops in their efforts to annihilate Tito's partisans in these territories.[38] However, the Chetniks were notorious for their numerous crimes against civilian population.[39] Croats and Muslims were the main targets, but they did not hesitate to kill Serbs who did not support them. The best known among Chetnik leaders and units were Momčilo Đujić and his Dinara Chetnik Division (founded in spring 1942).[40] Đujić's Chetniks were based in the Knin area, but participated in anti-Partisan operations in the wider area of southern Lika, Western Bosnia, and Northern Dalmatia. During the autumn of 1941 it became obvious that the Partisans constituted the main obstacle to the realisation of Chetnik goals. So, even in northern parts of the NDH, the Chetniks were trying to find a way to fight the Partisans. The modified policy of the NDH towards the Serbs from the beginning of 1942 and the German desire to unite all anti-Communist forces to fight against the Partisans fostered the establishment of Chetnik cooperation with the Germans and even with the NDH authorities.[41]

After the capitulation of Italy, Chetnik units in former Italian occupation zones immediately joined the Germans as their new protectors. Among these were Momčilo Đujić and his Dinara Chetnik Division. Đujić's Chetniks remained loyal to the Germans to the very end of the war.[42] Following the liberation of Knin in December 1944, the Dinara Chetnik Division left that area and with German assistance arrived in Slovenia.[43] In May 1945, they surrendered to the Allies in Northern Italy.

The totalitarian character of the NDH regime was evident in its relation to other Croatian political parties and groups. All were banned, and the ruling Ustaša movement was the only political organisation allowed to exist.[44] Moreover, following German and Italian patterns, the Ustaša regime attempted to embrace all aspects of public and professional life in the Independent State of Croatia. All professional, class, and sports organisations were obliged to become members of the *Savez staliških postrojbi* [The Alliance of State Organisations], just as such organisations in Italy and Germany were organised within fascist corporations and various national-socialist organisations.[45]

Unsurprisingly, the NDH and the Third Reich had established diplomatic relations by the end of April 1941. The German legation in Zagreb was formally established as a major German institution in the country; and the German ambassador to Zagreb, Siegfried Kasche, played an important role in the relations between the Third Reich and the NDH.[46] Still, he was only one among many German representatives and institutions. The position of the German Plenipotentiary General in Croatia was also important. From 1941 to 1944, General Edmund Glaise von Horstenau held this position. His approach was moderate. Later in the war, he lost faith in a German victory, but there is no question about his loyalty to the Third Reich and that he protected German interests in the Independent State of Croatia.[47] Other German institutions, such as the Nazi Party [NSDAP], the *Gestapo*, and the SS were also present in the NDH.[48] The German minority [*Volksdeutsche*] were granted special provisions.[49] In return, the German Ethnic Group in Croatia [*Deutsche Volksgruppe in Kroatien*] formally recognised the sovereignty of the Independent State of Croatia. In reality, various parts of the *Volksgruppe* showed little respect for the NDH authorities. It maintained special relations with German institutions in Croatia, and also established direct connections with institutions in the Third Reich.[50]

German economic factors were also heavily present in the NDH during the entire period from 1941 to 1945, and they enjoyed strong support from representatives of the Third Reich.[51] However, a strong German economic position in the NDH was also a result of old economic ties between Croatia and lands of the Third Reich (especially Austria and Bohemia-Moravia). Indeed, the German economic position was dominant from the very beginning. However, in 1941 the NDH authorities tried to gain political advantage through their alliance with the Third Reich, and to preserve the public image of an independent Croatian economy.[52] Due to the ravages of war and a stronger German military involvement by 1942, that image had faded, and it became obvious that the NDH economy depended upon wartime Germany's. The German war industry demanded the export of raw materials and other goods to Germany, which in turn had a devastating effect on the Croatian economy in the final stages of the war.

Economic links were only one aspect of the relationship between the NDH and the Third Reich during the war. While German influence was generally pervasive between 1941 and 1945, German domination grew much stronger in late 1942 and at the beginning of 1943. During 1942, the majority of NDH territory became a battlefield. It became obvious that the NDH authorities and armed forces were not able to stop the resistance and growth of Tito's Partisan movement. Already in mid-1942, the NDH armed forces were engaged in large-scale military operations in alliance with German armed forces and under German command.[53] Operations in the Kozara mountain region in spring and summer 1942 proved that. Ustaša and *Domobran* [the Home Guard] units, as well as some Chetnik detachments, were commanded by German general Stahl and fought in close cooperation with the Germans. The weakness of the NDH armed forces, especially of the *Domobranstvo* [the Home Guard Army], forced the Germans to deploy more troops.[54] The Germans also insisted on the complete reconstruction of the NDH armed forces, in order to transform them into an efficient and powerful army.[55] In addition, the Germans decided to send back to Croatia all those Croatian volunteers and mobilised soldiers who were supposed to join the Croatian legion on the Eastern front. However, they decided not to include these soldiers in the existing Domobran or Ustaša units, but to keep them under their direct command. In August 1942, therefore, the Germans formed the 369th Infantry Division of the *Wehrmacht*, the 'Devil's Division', as a Legionary Division. By the end of the war, the Germans formed two more Croatian Legionary divisions of the *Wehrmacht*.[56] Finally, at the beginning of 1943, all combat units of the NDH armed forces were placed under German command.[57]

The German role became even more significant after the capitulation of Italy in September 1943. The Croatian public and the NDH authorities accepted that fact with joy and enthusiasm, due to the destructive Italian policy towards the Croatian population on the Eastern Adriatic. In a special statement at that time, Pavelić annulled the Rome agreements and declared the NDH's right to reclaim territories lost in May 1941.[58] However, the NDH authorities desired even more – they wanted to claim even those Croatian territories that had been within Italian borders before April 1941 (Istria, Rijeka-Fiume, Zadar-Zara and Lastovo-Lagosta).[59] It seemed to the Croatian public that the Germans were not against such claims, and Hitler's recognition of the NDH's right to include territories on the Adriatic into its borders was well received in Berlin. In his speech of 10 September 1943, General Glaise von Horstenau invited 'sons of the Croatian homeland' to raise 'the flags of Croatia not only in Senj and Dubrovnik, but in Rijeka and Sušak, in Zadar, Šibenik and Split as well.' By so doing, he contributed greatly to the impression that Germans would allow the NDH to extend its sovereignty to territories belonging to Italy before April 1941.[60]

It soon became clear however that the Germans only had in mind those territories that had been ceded to Italy in May 1941. In addition to that, the NDH authorities were prevented from establishing their institutions and deploying their armed forces even on some territories which were nominally recognised by the Third Reich as the part of the NDH. For example, in Boka Kotorska, the Germans established full control of the area, and strictly prevented the NDH officials and military personnel from entering the area. In Zadar (Zara in Italian), the local German command preferred the existing Italian authorities and attempted to prevent all activities that might place the town under the control of the NDH authorities.[61] In the area of Sušak-Čabar-Krk the Germans allowed the deployment of Croatian personnel, but included the entire area in the *Operationszone Adriatisches Küstenland* [The Zone of Operations Adriatic Coastland].[62] The zone was composed of various Croatian, Slovenian, and Italian regions, and was put under the direct control of German administration led by the *Gauleiter* [Nazi party Provincial leader] of Carinthia, Dr. Friedrich Alois Rainer.[63] All local authorities in the zone, including the NDH authorities, were primarily responsible to the German administration.

Still, the situation was not so different there from the situation in the entire NDH. German military and political domination was more than evident, and in reality the NDH was just one among many European states under German military occupation,[64] despite the fact that it was a nominally independent state with its own government and armed forces.[65]

German domination, as well as the advance of the Allies on all fronts and evident prospects of their victory, encouraged some members of the Ustaša leadership to think about other solutions. Already in autumn 1943, some Ustaša leaders initiated negotiations with some members of the HSS about the possible inclusion of that party in the NDH government.[66] In that case not only Allied victories, but also the German desire to stabilise conditions in the NDH, allowed these negotiations. They ended soon after their beginning due to the fact that the two sides (Ustaša and the HSS) could not agree about basic principles.

A more serious attempt to change the course of events was the well-known Lorković-Vokić *coup d'etat*.[67] In reality, the Minister of Foreign Affairs, Dr. Mladen Lorković, and Minister of Armed Forces, Ustaša General [*krilnik*] Ante Vokić, were trying to find a way for Croatia to leave the alliance with Germany and join the Allies.[68] They soon realised that their efforts could be successful only without Pavelić and the Ustaša Movement in power. It appears that such a prospect, as well as fears that Germans might find out what was going on, pushed Pavelić to arrest Lorković, Vokić, some prominent members of the HSS and numerous Home Guard Army officers.[69]

The only certainty is that Pavelić decided to follow Germany to the very end. The end was near, and, in early May 1945, the NDH disappeared from the map. Clearly, the establishment of the NDH was closely related to the actions of Italy and Germany in 1941. Nazi Germany's initial desire to establish a stable regime in Croatia led by the HSS failed due to Maček's refusal to cooperate with them. Only then did the Germans agree to support the Ustaše and to accept the Italian protégé, Pavelić, as the leader of an independent Croatia. Although the German role in the establishment of the new regime was of major importance, the fact is that, in 1941, Italian authority in the country had a greater influence upon the course of events. Both the Rome treaties and the fact that Italian armed forces controlled almost half of its territory had a particularly negative impact on the situation in the NDH: Italian control had a devastating impact on the economy; Italian domination prevented NDH authorities from protecting Croatian interests; so their efforts were limited to impotent protests and memoranda. The German presence in the NDH was less evident in 1941, but was nevertheless of the same importance for the internal political and economic development of the country. German influence and pressure encouraged the Ustaša regime to copy a number of National Socialist policies – especially regarding race. From the beginning, the character of the NDH was defined by its subjugation to the power of Germany and Italy.

Notes

1. For details about Ustaša activities in Croatia before April 1941, and on the Ustaša-Domobran Movement during the 1930s and at the beginning of 1940s see my book *Ustaško-domobranski pokret od nastanka do travnja 1941. godine* [*The Ustaša-Domobran Movement from its Emergence to April 1941*] (Zagreb: Školska knjiga and Hrvatski institut za povijest, 2006). For details of the emergence of the Ustaša organisation and its activities during the 1930s, see James Sadkovich, *Italian Support for Croatian Separatism 1927–1937* (New York and London: Garland, 1987).
2. This is why Germany sent two special envoys to Croatia. Walter Malletke was a high official of the Foreign Policy Office of the NSDAP [*Aussenpolitisches Amt der NSDAP*]. His task was to convince Maček to cooperate with the Germans and to proclaim Croatia's independence (See Bogdan Krizman, 'Njemački emisar W. Malletke kod V. Mačeka uoči napada na Jugoslaviju 1941 [German Envoy Walter Malletke by Vladko Maček before the German attack on Yugoslavia]', in *Časopis za suvremenu povijest*, Vol.7, No.1 (1975), pp.152–63. Edmund von Veesenmeyer met Maček, too. For details about Veesenmeyer's activities in Zagreb see Igor Phillip Matic, *Edmund Veesenmeyer. Agent und Diplomat der nationalsozialistischen Expansionspolitik* [*Edmund Veesenmeyer: The Agent and Diplomat of the National Socialist Expansion Policy*] (Munich: R. Oldenbourg Verlag, 2002), pp.125–56.
3. More on German arguments to support Maček as the leader of Croatian State can be found in Jozo Tomasevich, *War and Revolution in Yugoslavia, 1941–1945: Occupation and Collaboration* (Stanford, Calif.: Stanford University Press, 2001), pp.49–50. Alfred Rosenberg, who was in charge of the Foreign Policy Office of the NSDAP, was in favour of Maček and the HSS. For details see Matić (note 2), p.131. High officials of the *Auswärtige Amt* [Foreign Office] had similar views on the situation in Croatia.
4. This was characteristic for Ustaša–German relations during the period from 1933 to 1941. The Third Reich was then primarily interested in the maintenance of good relations with the Kingdom of Yugoslavia. Thus, Ustaša attempts to gain German support failed. The case of Pavelić's memorandum entitled *Die kroatische Frage* [*The Croatian Question*] from October 1936 shows how German authorities treated Ustaša attempts to approach them. In this case, Pavelić handed over the manuscript of *Die kroatische Frage* to Professor Carl von Loesch, who promised to present it to the German Foreign Office. The manuscript was ignored by German diplomats and was destined to spend several years hidden from the public. Yet the new political circumstances in early April 1941 inspired German authorities to publish Pavelić's study. So it was published by the 'Institut für Grenz und Auslandstudien' in Berlin-Steglitz as a pamphlet intended for 'the official use only'. For Ustaša–German relations from 1933 to 1939 see Dušan Biber, 'Ustaše i Treći Reich: Prilog problematici jugoslovensko-nemačkih odnosa [The Ustaše and the Third Reich: Contribution to the issue of the Yugoslav–German relations]', in *Jugoslovenski istorijski časopis* (1964), no. 2, pp.37–55. The author stresses the fact that various German institutions had different views on the Croatian question and on the Ustaše. The author provides data demonstrating that the Third Reich did not favour the Ustaše. Some of his conclusions do not entirely correspond with the data presented, but one should have in mind that Biber published his article in Communist Yugoslavia. Historiography there had to follow some official interpretations of historical events. One of these was the image of the Ustaše only as Fascist and Nazi servants, whose cooperation with 'enemies of our peoples' was evident and indubitable from the very beginning.
5. As late as 8 April 1941, German representatives still resisted the idea of Pavelić as a future leader of Croatia. See Bogdan Krizman, 'Pavelićev dolazak u Zagreb 1941. g. [Pavelić's Arrival to Zagreb in 1941]', in *Zbornik Historijskog instituta Slavonije*, vol. 1 (1963), p.166.
6. Malletke and Veesenmeyer realised how Maček would never agree to cooperate with the Germans. Only then did they recommend negotiations with the Ustaše.
7. Some of them later published their memoirs of these events. Ernest Bauer's are entitled *Život je kratak san. Uspomene 1910–1985* [*Life is a Short Dream. Memoirs 1910–1985*] (Barcelona-Munich: Knjižnica Hrvatske revije, 1986), pp.78–85.
8. Some Croatian NCOs initiated the mutiny; the rebels were primarily mobilised soldiers. Members of the local authorities in Bjelovar joined rebels and attempted to organise a new Croatian administration.
9. Maček announced on 8 April 1941, in his proclamation to the Croatian nation, that he had decided to remain in Croatia. American consul in Zagreb, John James Meily, reported later that Maček said: 'I shall remain with you and share with you, as before, everything, good or evil', NARA, M1203, roll 16, Meily to the Secretary of the State on 'The Ustaše [sic] Coup d'etat in Croatia', 13 June 1941, p.4.

10. For communist propaganda against Maček and the HSS at the end of the war, see Zdenko Radelić, *Hrvatska seljačka stranka 1941–1950*. [*The Croatian Peasant Party from 1941 to 1950*] (Zagreb: Hrvatski institut za povijest, 1996), pp.37–42.
11. On 8 April Maček also demanded from Croats 'complete order and discipline in every place, be it at home or in the army.'
12. Meily described the situation in Zagreb during 9 April and early hours of 10 April 1941 with the following words: 'On Wednesday, 9 April, it was rumoured that the entire HSS town guard went over to the Frankists [Ustaše – sic]; Serbian officials in Zagreb, among whom was the Vice-Ban, prepared to leave the city. The following day, 10 April, the citizen (Gradjanska) and at least part of the peasant (Seljacka) guard openly declared themselves for the Frankists; about 10:00 a.m. the Vice-Ban received a representative of this office with the words "Debacle! complete debacle!" At noon the Cabinet Chief of the Ban informed this office that it was finished with Yugoslavia; that in few hours German troops would enter the town; that Croatia will be declared independent; and that the HSS would be obliged to seek a compromise with the Frankists', NARA, M1203, roll 16, Meily to the Secretary of the State on 'The Ustaše Coup d'etat in Croatia', 13 June 1941, pp.4–5. On 11 April, von Veesenmeyer sent to the German Foreign office a detailed report about events that took place on the previous day. The entire report was published in *Akten zur Deutschen Auswärtigen Politik 1918–1945 (ADAP)*, Series D (1937–1941), vol. XII.2, 6 April to 22 June 1941 (Göttingen: Vandenhoeck & Ruprecht, 1969), pp.429–30.
13. Slavko Kvaternik later described his activities during 10 April 1941. For his notes and memoirs, see Nada Kisić Kolanović, ed., *Vojskovođa i politika: Sjećanja Slavka Kvaternika* [*The Field Marshall and the Politics. Memoirs of Slavko Kvaternik*] (Zagreb: Golden marketing, 1997). 10 April is described on pp.147–54. Kvaternik stated that he proclaimed Croatian independence for the first time around noon on the same day in *Banski dvori* [Ban's palace in Zagreb's Upper town].
14. Kvaternik and Veesenmeyer visited Maček during the early afternoon, and only then could Kvaternik have left for the radio station to proclaim the independence of Croatia to the Croatian public. If Kvaternik's claims that the proclamation happened before he visited Maček is accepted as credible, the proclamation over the radio should be viewed only as a public announcement intended to inform the Croatian public. American consul Meily failed to mention the content of Kvaternik's proclamation. However, it was published in the contemporary Croatian press, including Zagreb's daily *Hrvatski narod* [the Croat Nation]. For the English translation of Kvaternik's and Maček's proclamations see Tomasevich (note 3), p.53.
15. An English translation of Maček's proclamation can be found in Meily's report, NARA, M1203, roll 16, Meily to the Secretary of the State on 'The Ustaše [sic] Coup d'etat in Croatia', 13 June 1941, p.5. In his proclamation, Maček also called 'upon the whole Croatian nation to obey the new authorities. I enjoin all members of the Croatian Peasant Party who are at various posts, all members of township administrators, etc., etc., to remain at their posts and sincerely to cooperate with the new government'. In Autumn 1945, Ivan Bernardić, Maček's follower and editor-in-chief of the only issue of the oppositional newspaper *Narodni glas*, published the article entitled 'Predsjednik Hrvatske seljačke stranke dr. Vladko Maček [The President of the Croatian Peasant Party dr. Vladko Maček]', *Narodni glas*, 20 October 1945, pp.3–4. He stated that Kvaternik and Veesenmeyer demanded that Maček hand over the leadership of the Croatian nation to Kvaternik or bloodshed would occur. Maček refused to hand over the leadership, but agreed to issue a proclamation. Bernardić added that Maček's original declaration was different from the one broadcast. According to Bernardić, the original declaration still existed in Zagreb at that time (autumn 1945). For details about *Narodni glas* see Radelić (note 10), pp.73–82.
16. Tomasevich (note 3), p.740, concluded that in 'actuality ... the Germans forced Maček to issue this statement of support, a fact that has never been acknowledged in Serbian or Yugoslav writings. Uppermost in his mind seems to have been the desire to preserve peace and conclusion that Maček never voluntarily made a deal with either the Ustaše or the Germans and Italians. He was held in the Jasenovac concentration camp by the Ustaše for about five months and spent the remainder of the war under strict house arrest.'
17. For Maček's ideas and policy in 1941, and especially during the period from March to April 1941 see Radelić (note 10), pp.21–3; and Ljubo Boban, *Maček i politika HSS-a* [*Maček and the Policy of the HSS*], vol. 2 (Zagreb: Liber, 1974), pp.386–436.
18. For more details on the establishment of the NDH, see Mario Jareb (note 1), pp.568–95.
19. For details, see Bogdan Krizman, *Ante Pavelić i Ustaše* [*Ante Pavelić and the Ustaše*] (Zagreb: Globus, 1978), pp.445–55; H. James Burgwyn, *Empire on the Adriatic: Mussolini's Conquest of Yugoslavia 1941–1943* (New York: Enigma Books, 2005), pp.34–5; Nada Kisić Kolanović, *NDH i Italija*:

Političke veze i diplomatski odnosi (*The NDH and Italy: Political Connections and Diplomatic Relations*) (Zagreb: Naklada Ljevak and Hrvatski institut za povijest, 2001), pp.86–7.

20. Details about negotiations between the NDH authorities (and Pavelić personally) and the Italians are well known. One of the most detailed overviews is the one written by Bogdan Krizman (note 19), pp.455–74. Nada Kisić Kolanović (note 19), pp.86–97, describes how the Rome treaties were concluded and presents the main elements. Burgwyn (note 19), pp.31–40, provides a detailed account of the negotiations and briefly presents the main elements of the Rome treaties. However, he attempted to write about Croatian history without taking into account documents in Croatian archives, documents published in Croatia and in former Yugoslavia in Croatian and other South-Slavic languages, as well as numerous articles and monographs published by Croatian historians. Consequently, some pages of his book contain inaccurate data. This could have been easily avoided if all available sources had been taken into account. Italian documents related to these issues were published in Italian, see *I documenti diplomatici italiani*, series IX, VII (24 April–11 December 1941) (Rome: Istituto poligrafico e Zecca dello stato: Libreria dello stato, 1987). For Ciano's views see his diaries; in this article, the following edition was used: *Ciano's Diary 1939–1943*, edited by Malcolm Muggeridge (London/Toronto: William Heinemann, 1947), pp.333–46.

The Rome treaties were published in Croatian and Italian in 1941, in the collection of international treaties entitled *Međunarodni ugovori* [*International Treaties*] (Zagreb: Nezavisna Država Hrvatska. Ministarstvo vanjskih poslova, 1941), pp.49–70. The agreement was entitled 'Ugovor o određivanju granica između Kraljevine Italije i Kraljevine Hrvatske [Treaty About Borders Between the Kingdom of Italy and the Kingdom of Croatia]', pp.49–51; the agreement about the establishment of demilitarised zone in the Adriatic areas of Croatia was entitled 'Sporazum o pitanjima vojnog značaja, koja se odnose na jadransko obalno područje [Agreement on Military Issues related to the Adriatic Coastal Areas]', pp.53–4. The Rome treaties were also published in Italy.

21. More details about the new border can be found in the above-mentioned 'Treaty About Borders Between the Kingdom of Italy and the Kingdom of Croatia', ibid. A map signed by Pavelić and Mussolini showing the new borders was an integral part of that agreement. The map was published in *Međunarodni ugovori* as an insert between p.52–3. A copy of the map with the original signatures of Pavelić and Mussolini can be found in the Croatian State Archives [*Hrvatski državni arhiv*] in Zagreb; records of the Ministry of the Foreign Affairs of the NDH [*Ministarstvo vanjskih poslova NDH*]. A facsimile of the map was published by Kisić Kolanović (note 19), pp.442–3.

22. In a letter dated Rome, 18 May 1941, Mussolini informed Pavelić about Italian intentions to compose a draft of an agreement which would become an integral part of the Rome treaties. The letter was published in Italian and in Croatian translation in *Međunarodni ugovori*, p.61. Pavelić's reply to Mussolini was published on p.63.

23. Tomasevich (note3), p.247, briefly describes the composition of Croatian territories occupied by Italy: 'The three areas of Croatian territory between the Adriatic Sea and the German–Italian demarcation line specified in the Rome treaties were henceforth referred to as three zones: Zone I, the area annexed by Italy; Zone II, the demilitarised zone; and Zone III, the remainder of the territory to the demarcation line'. A useful map showing all three zones was published by Vjekoslav Vrančić, *Urota protiv Hrvatske* [*Conspiracy against Croatia*] (Zagreb: Nakladna knjižara Velebit, 1943), p.11. The territory of the Zone II was already indicated on 18 May 1941, on the map signed by Pavelić and Mussolini attached to the 'Agreement on Military Issues related to the Adriatic Coastal Areas'. Its facsimile was later published in the collection of documents entitled *Narodnooslobodilačka borba u Dalmaciji 1941–1945.* [*The People's Liberation Struggle in Dalmatia 1941–1945*], vol. 1 (the year of 1941) (Split: Institut za historiju radničkog pokreta Dalmacije, 1981), inlay between pages 440–41.

24. See the order issued by the command of the Italian Second Army on 20 May 1941 to all subordinated commands and troops. A Croatian translation of the order was published in *Narodnooslobodilačka borba u Dalmaciji 1941–1945*, pp.443–4. That order followed Mussolini's directive, see Burgwyn (note 19), p.56.

25. According to that, Croatia would not have any control over its economy and defence. The Italian king (or some other member of the House of Savoy) would become the Croatian king as well. These ideas were similar to Italian solutions in Albania after its occupation in 1939. The Italian side presented them to Pavelić when he met Count Ciano on 23 January 1940. Documents related to that meeting were published in *I documenti diplomatici italiani*, series IX, vol. III (Rome: Libreria dello stato, 1959), pp.162–6. Pavelić insisted on preserving the image of the future Croatian state as an independent state, and Ciano finally agreed that Croatian government should be composed of all ministries.

26. For details, see Kisić Kolanović (note 19), pp.235–7. In the fourth paragraph of the 'Treaty about the Guarantees and Cooperation between the Kingdom of Croatia and the Kingdom of Italy' the Croatian and Italian governments pledged to establish more comprehensive and stronger customs and monetary relations. That treaty was one of the Rome treaties, and was published in *Međunarodni ugovori* (note 20), pp.55–7.
27. According to the Rome treaties, the NDH would become a kingdom with a king from the House of Savoia. Following Pavelić's invitation, Italian king Vittorio Emmanuele designated Aimone di Savoia-Aosta, Duke of Spoleto, for that position. So, the NDH skipped the proposed personal union with Italy. Pavelić's invitation, entitled 'Riječi Poglavnika glavi savojske kraljevske kuće [The Words of *Poglavnik* to the head of the Royal House of Savoia]', was published on the front page of Zagreb's daily *Hrvatski narod*, no. 96, 19 May 1941. The presence of an Italian duke as King of Croatia would have jeopardised Pavelić's position as sole dictator of Croatia, and would have spoiled the image of the NDH as a formally independent state. This is why, from the very beginning, Pavelić and his regime ignored Aimone di Savoia–Aosta, who remained in Italy. For details about the issue of a Croatian king see Bogdan Krizman, *NDH između Hitlera i Mussolinija* [*Pavelić between Hitler and Mussolini*] (Zagreb: Globus, 1983), pp.101–17.
28. Tomasevich (note 3), p.249, noted that, according to a statement of Mladen Lorković to 'von Ribbentrop in late November 1941, the Italians had about 200,000 troops in Zones II and III'. On the same page, he wrote that the strength of the Italian Second Army 'was estimated at close to 300,000 men at the end of July 1942'. For details about the strength of the Italian 2nd army from spring 1941 to September 1943, see Kisić Kolanović (note 19), pp.175–80.
29. Probably the most important NDH institution for the research of Italian–Croatian economic relations was the State Economic Commision [*Državno gospodarstveno povjerenstvo – DGP*]. It was very active during the presidency of Field Marshall Slavko Kvaternik, from August 1941 to September 1942. Documents related to the activities of the *DGP* were published as a collection of documents entitled *Državno gospodarstveno povjerenstvo Nezavisne Države Hrvatske od kolovoza 1941. do travnja 1945.* [*The State Economic Commision of the Independent State of Croatia from August 1941 to April 1945*], Jere Jareb (ed.) (Zagreb: Hrvatski institut za povijest, Hrvatski državni arhiv, Dom i svijet, 2001).
30. For more details about the NDH–Italian economic relations from April 1941 to September 1943 see Kisić Kolanović (note 19), pp.235–55.
31. For details, see Kisić Kolanović (note 19), Burgwyn (note 19), and Krizman (note 27). See also Zdravko Dizdar, 'Italian Policies Toward Croatians in Occupied Territories during the Second World War', *Review of Croatian History* 1 (2005), pp.179–210.
32. These were 'Zakonska odredba o rasnoj pripadnosti [The Law Decree on Racial Belonging]', and 'Zakonska odredba o zaštiti arijske krvi i časti hrvatskoga naroda [The Law Decree on the Protection of Aryan Blood and Honour of the Croatian People]' from 30 April 1941. They were both published in *Narodne novine*, no. 16, 30 April 1941. Some decrees issued before that contained some anti-Jewish provisions too. In spring and summer 1941 there were more decrees issued.
33. The largest and most important was the notorious Jasenovac concentration camp, which operated from summer 1941 to late April 1945. For details about Jasenovac, see Nataša Mataušić, *Jasenovac 1941–1945: Logor smrti i radni logor* [*Jasenovac from 1941 to 1945: The Death Camp and Labour Camp*] (Jasenovac and Zagreb: Javna ustanova Spomen-područje Jasenovac, 2003). Today, the number of approximately 80,000 victims of Jasenovac and Stara Gradiška camps is widely accepted. For example, Serbian researcher Dragan Cvetković from Belgrade's Museum of Genocide Victims recently announced the number of 79,872 victims in book (with co-author Igor Graovac) entitled *Ljudski gubici Hrvatske 1941–1945 godine: pitanja, primjeri, rezultati…* (*Human Losses of Croatia from 1941 to 1945: Questions, Examples, Results…*) (Zagreb: Zajednica istraživača *Dijalog* and Zaklada Friedrich Naumann, 2005), p.72. For details on the numbers of war victims in former Yugoslavia and manipulations of these numbers, see Tomasevich (note 19), pp.718–50. See also Vladimir Žerjavić, *Population Losses in Yugoslavia 1941–1945* (Zagreb: Dom i svijet, Hrvatski institut za povijest, 1997).
34. The prewar Ustaša-Domobran Movement failed to formulate a consistent ideology and political programme. It is only possible to talk about some basic Ustaša-Domobran ideas, including a determination to destroy Yugoslavia as the precondition for the establishment of independent Croatia. For details of the Ustaša-Domobran ideas and programme before April 1941 see Mario Jareb (note 1), pp.112–63. Most researchers, such as Fikreta Jelić Butić and Jozo Tomasevich, agree that the prewar Movement could not be characterised as purely Fascist. Tomasevich (note 19), p.32, wrote that the Ustaša organisation was modelled 'on the Internal Macedonian Revolutionary Organization'. He added that Pavelić accepted Italian Fascist principles by the late 1930s, and that his

72 *The Independent State of Croatia 1941–45*

fascist inclinations are 'best seen in his book *Strahote zabluda* … Written from the Fascist point of view, this lightweight anti-Communist tract shows Mussolini in a very favorable light and mentions Hitler only in passing.'

35. For details of the persecution of the Serbian Orthodox Church, the foundation of the Croatian Orthodox Church, and other churches and religions in the Independent State of Croatia see Jure Krišto, *Sukob simbola. Politika, vjere i ideologije u Nezavisnoj Državi Hrvatskoj* [*The Conflict of Symbols. Politics, Religions and Ideologies in the Independent State of Croatia*] (Zagreb: Nakladni zavod Globus, 2001).

36. Later Serbs ('Orthodox Croats') could even serve in the NDH Armed Forces. They served in special labour battalions, and at the end of the war they could serve in combat units as well. For details see Nikica Barić, *Ustroj kopnene vojske domobranstva Nezavisne Države Hrvatske 1941-1945.* [*The Organisation of the Ground Forces of the Home Guard of the Independent State of Croatia from 1941 to 1945*] (Zagreb: Hrvatski institut za povijest, 2003). The same author published an article entitled 'Položaj Srba u domobranstvu Nezavisne Države Hrvatske [The Position of Serbs in the Home Guard Army of the Independent State of Croatia]', *Polemos, Časopis za interdisciplinarna istraživanja rata i mira,* Vol. 5, No.1–2 (2002): pp.159–75.

37. For details about the Chetniks see: Jozo Tomasevich, *War and Revolution in Yugoslavia, 1941–1945: The Chetniks* (Stanford, Calif.: Stanford University Press, 1975); Fikreta Jelić-Butić, *Četnici u Hrvatskoj 1941–1945* [*Chetniks in Croatia from 1941 to 1945*] (Zagreb: Globus, 1986); Mihael Sobolevski and Zdravko Dizdar, ed., *Prešućivani četnički zločini u Hrvatskoj i Bosni i Hercegovini 1941–1945.* [*Hidden Chetnik Crimes in Croatia and Bosnia and Herzegovina from 1941 to 1945*] (Zagreb: Hrvatski institut za povijest i Dom i svijet, 1999), Summary in English pp.717–28; and Zdravko Dizdar (ed.), *Četnički zločini u Bosni i Hercegovini 1941–1945* [*Chetnik Crimes in Bosnia and Herzegovina from 1941 to 1945*] (Zagreb: Hrvatski institut za povijest i Dom i svijet, 2002).

38. For details about the beginnings of the Chetnik–Italian cooperation in summer 1941 see Jelić Butić (note 37), pp.37–64.

39. Numerous documents about Chetnik crimes can be found in *Genocid nad Muslimanima 1941–1945. Zbornik dokumenata i svjedočenja* [*Genocide against Muslims. The Collection of Documents and Testimonies*], Vladimir Dedijer and Antun Miletić, ed., (Sarajevo: Svjetlost, 1990). Many documents can be found in collections edited by Mihael Sobolevski and Zdravko Dizdar (note 37), and Zdravko Dizdar (note 37).

40. For details see Jelić Butić (note 37), and Jovo Popović, Marko Lolić and Branko Latas, *Pop izdaje* [*The Priest Betrayed*] (Zagreb: Stvarnost, 1988).

41. Numerous documents about Chetnik cooperation with the Germans and Italians, as well as with the NDH authorities, can be found in book entitled Branko Latas (comp.), *Saradnja četnika Draže Mihailovića sa okupatorima i ustašama (1941–1945): Dokumenti* [*The Cooperation of Draža Mihailović's Chetniks with Occupants and the Ustashas (1941–1945): Documents*] (Belgrade: Društvo za istinu o antifašistiškoj narodnooslobodilačkoj borbi 1941–1945, 1999). Most of these documents were previously published in various publications, mainly in some volumes of *Zbornik dokumenata i podataka o Narodnooslobodilačkom ratu jugoslovenskih naroda* [*The Collection of Documents and Data about the People's Liberation War of Yugoslav Peoples*].

42. For details about Đujić's cooperation with Germans see Popović, Lolić, Latas (note 41), pp.266–380.

43. On 21 December 1944, *Poglavnik* Pavelić even issued an order, based on the agreement concluded between 'Croatian and German government', that 'Chetnik group of priest Đujić, all together 6000 men strong' would be transported from the area of Bihać to Germany (today the territory of Slovenia), Latas (note 41), pp.312–13.

44. The HSS was banned on 11 June 1941. Later, in summer 1941, the Ustaša regime attempted to attract former members of that party to join the Ustaša ranks. Some members, including several high party officials did precisely that. However, the majority of party members and officials refused to do so. Some of them later joined Josip Broz Tito's Partisans.

45. This Alliance was established in January 1942.

46. Siegfried Kasche arrived in Zagreb on 20 April 1941 and remained there until the end of the war. British troops in Austria arrested him after the war and extradited him to Yugoslav authorities. In 1947, he was sentenced to death and executed. As the German Envoy and Plenipotentiary Minister in Zagreb, he was a strong supporter of the Ustaše regime.

47. For details about Glaise von Horstenau and his stay in Zagreb, see *Ein General in Zwielicht. Die Erinnerungen Edmund Glaises von Horstenau* [*One General in Twilight. The Memoires of Edmund Glaise von Horstenau*], volume 3, Peter Broucek (ed.) (Vienna – Cologne – Graz: Hermann Böhlaus Nach., 1988). He opposed the extremist policy of the Ustaša regime.

48. In 1943 SS founded the *Waffen-SS* Handschar Division, composed of personnel from the NDH and German commanding cadre. Members of the Handschar division were mainly Bosnian

Muslims. For details, see George Lepre, *Himmler's Bosnian Division. The Waffen-SS Handschar Division 1943–1945* (Atglen, PA: Schiffer Military History, 1997). On 10 March 1943, SS established the common German-Croatian Police [*Deutsch-Kroatische Polizei*]. For details, see N. Thomas and K. Mikulan, *Axis Forces in Yugoslavia* (Oxford: Osprey Publishing, 1995), p.20.

49. It was based on the 'Law Decree on Temporary Legal Position of the German Ethnic Group in the Independent State of Croatia', from 21 June 1941. It was published in *Narodne novine*, no. 56, 21 June 1941, p.1. More Law Decrees were issued later, in 1941 and 1942. Law Decrees allowed *Volksgruppe* to organise the life of its members in all areas – political, educational, economic, and even military. The history of the *Volksgruppe* has not been a matter of serious research yet. Some data can be found in two documents published by Vladimir Geiger: 'Saslušanje Branimira Altgayera vođe Njemačke narodne skupine u Nezavisnoj Državi Hrvatskoj u Upravi državne bezbjednosti za Narodnu Republiku Hrvatsku 1949 godine [The Interogation of Branimir Altgayer, the Leader of the German Ethnic Group in the Independent State of Croatia, by the Administration of the State Security for the People's Republic of Croatia]', in *Časopis za suvremenu povijest*, Vol.31, No.3 (1999), pp.575–638; and 'Smrtna presuda Branimiru Altgayeru vođi Njemačke narodne skupine u Nezavisnoj Državi Hrvatskoj Okružnog suda u Zagrebu 1950, godine [The Death Verdict of the District Court in Zagreb from 1950 to Branimir Altgayer, the leader of the German Ethnic Group in the Independent State of Croatia]', in *Folksdojčeri pod teretom kolektivne krivnje* [*Volksdeutschers under the Faith of Collective Guilt*] (Osijek: Njemačka narodnosna zajednica, 2002), pp.77–89.

50. They maintained special relations with the *Volksdeutsche Mittelstelle* [*Vomi* – Ethnic German Central Office]. For details about the *Vomi*, see, *The Encyclopedia of the Third Reich*, Christian Zentner and Friedemann Bedürftig, eds. (New York: Da Capo Press, 1997), p.242.

51. For details about the NDH–German economic relations, see Holm Sundhaussen, *Wirtschaftsgeschichte Kroatiens im nationasozialistischen Großraum 1941–1945* [*The Economic History of Croatia in National-Socialist Greater Area*] (Stuttgart: Deutsche Verlags-Anstalt, 1983). Much data can be found in the collection of documents of the *Državno gospodarstveno povjerenstvo* (note 29).

52. The Germans and the NDH authorities tried to present economic relations with the Third Reich to Croatian public only as fruitful cooperation. For example, in autumn 1942, German Legation to the NDH, German Ministry for Food-Supply and Agriculture and the NDH Ministry for Peasant Economy, organised in Zagreb *Hrvatsko-njemačka poljopriradna smotra/Kroatisch-deutsche Landwirtschaftsschau* [*The Croatian-German Agrucultural Exhibition*]. The catalogue of the exhibition was published under the same title in Croatian and German.

53. A brief overview of the structure, battle order and activities of the NDH armed forces can be found by N. Thomas and K. Mikulan (note 48), pp.12–21 and 38–46. The book published in Croatian by Krunoslav Mikulan and Siniša Pogačić, *Hrvatske oružane snage 1941–1945.* [*Croatian Armed Forces from 1941 to 1945*] (Zagreb: P.c. grafičke usluge, 1999) contains data about the structure of the NDH Armed Forces during the Second World War.

54. According to Barić (note 36), p.287, during 1942 several German divisions were transferred to the NDH from Serbia, due to the growth of Partisan activities during that year. The activities of those divisions were considered only temporary at the time.

55. On 2 February 1943 Pavelić agreed to accept German plan for the reconstruction of the NDH Armed Forces under German control. Subsequently, in September 1943 German general Hans Juppe became Inspector of the Ground Forces by the German plenipotentiary general in Croatia [*Heeresinspektor bei Deutschen Bevollmaecthiger General in Kroatien*]. Juppe remained on that position by the end of war. For details see Barić (note 36), p.294.

56. Basic data about 369th 'Devil's' Division and 373th 'Tiger Division' can be found by Thomas and Mikulan (note 48), p.7. More on all divisions (two previously mentioned divisions and 392th 'Blue Division' can be found by David Littlejohn, *Foreign Legions of the Third Reich*, Vol. 3: Albania, Czechoslovakia, Greece, Hungary and Yugoslavia (San Jose, CA: R. James Bender Publishing, 1994), pp.187–9. See also Barić (note 36), pp.295–7.

57. For details see Barić (note 36), pp.288–90.

58. His Statement from 10 September 1943 entitled '*Državopravna izjava o razrješenju Rimskih ugovora* [Statement about the Destitution of the Rome Agreements]' was published in contemporary NDH press. On 9 September 1943 Pavelić gave a speech, broadcasted by the State Radio Station Zagreb, in which he declared that Italian moves 'released Croatian people and Croatian state from all obligations' provided by 'imposed treaties [Rome treaties]'. His speech was published in a special edition of Zagreb's daily *Nova Hrvatska*, 9 September 1943, p.1. Pavelić also said that Hitler recognised the belonging of 'separated Croatian lands on the Adriatic' to the NDH.

59. On 11 September 1943 Pavelić appointed Dr. Oskar Turina to the position of 'the Head of the Civil Administration of Gorski Kotar, Hrvatsko Primorje and Istria'. Pavelić's decision was published

in Zagreb's daily *Nova Hrvatska*, no. 214, 12 September 1943, p.1. On 13 September 1943, Pavelić sent a letter to Hitler, in which demanded the inclusion of Eastern Istria in the NDH. For details see Antun Giron and Petar Strčić, *Poglavnikovom vojnom uredu. Treći Reich, NDH, Sušak – Rijeka i izvješće dr. Oskara Turine 1943*. [*To the Poglavnik's Military Office. The Third Reich, the NDH, Sušak-Rijeka and the Report of dr. Oskar Turina from 1943*] (Rijeka: Povijesno društvo Rijeka, 1993), p.8. Finally, on 20 September 1943 the NDH Government concluded that in the Statement of 10 September 1943 Pavelić declared that the NDH should claim not only territories that were lost in May 1941, but also those that belonged to Italy during the interwar period. So, the government decided to issue a law about the administration in liberated areas, and to found new Greater Counties for the area of Ravni Kotari with the town of Zadar, and for the area of Rijeka and 'Croatian part of Istria'. The NDH government's conclusions and decisions were published in *Hrvatski narod*, no.845, 28 September 1943, p.1, under the title 'Zakon o upravi u oslobođenim krajevima na Jadranu. Zaključak hrvatske državne vlade donešen na sjednici od 20. rujna 1943. [The Law about the Administration in Liberated Areas of the Adriatic. The Conclusion of the Croatian State Government brought on the Session of 20 September 1943]'.

For details about the NDH attempts to include Istria into its borders see Mario Jareb, 'Istra u medijima, promidžbi i publicistici Ustaško-domobranskog pokreta i Nezavisne Države Hrvatske od kraja dvadesetih godina do 1945. godine [Istria in Media, Propaganda and Publications of the Ustaše-Domobran Movement and the Independent State of Croatia from the end of 1920s to 1945]', in M. Manin. Lj. Dobrovšak, G. Črpić and R. Blagoni (ed.), *Identitet Istre – Ishodišta i perspektive* (Zagreb: Institut društvenih znanosti Ivo Pilar, 2006), pp.217–28.

60. His speech was broadcasted by the State Radio Station Zagreb. The complete text of his speech was published under the title 'Napried na hrvatsko more! [Go ahead to the Croatian Sea!]', in *Hrvatski narod*, no. 831 (11 September 1943), p.1.
61. Prior to April 1941 Zadar was part of the Kingdom of Italy, and lived as an Italian enclave surrounded by Yugoslav territory. It became Italian after the First World War. For details about political and demographic changes in Zadar between 1918 and 1943, see Josip Vidaković, 'Egzodus Hrvata iz Zadra pod talijanskom upravom od 1918. do 1943. godine [Exodus of the Croats from Zadar under Italian Administration between 1918 and 1943]', in *Talijanska uprava na hrvatskom prostoru i Egzodus Hrvata (1918–1943)* (Zagreb: Hrvatski institut za povijest i Društvo 'Egzodus istarskih Hrvata', 2001), pp.347–71.
62. For details about the Zone see Roland Kaltenegger, *Operationszone 'Adriatisches Küstenland'. Der Kampf um Triest, Istrien und Fiume 1944–5* [*The Zone of Operations 'Adriatic Coastland'. The Struggle for Trieste, Istria and Fiume in 1944/1945*] (Graz-Stuttgart: Leopold Stocker Verlag, 1993). He focused primarily on military operations during 1944 and 1945. More on the foundation of the Zone in September 1943 and on the activities of Rainer and his administration (primarily in relation to the Sušak-Rijeka area) can be found in Antun Giron and Petar Strčić (note 59), pp.10–1 and p.18–21.
63. The Zone was founded already on 10 September 1943.
64. Probably the most comprehensive source of data about NDH–German relations from summer 1943 to 1945 are the two volumes of Bogdan Krizman's book *Ustaše i Treći Reich* [*The Ustaše and the Third Reich*](Zagreb: Globus, 1986). Krizman published many documents, excerpts from hundreds of other documents, and added his comments and remarks.
65. It is possible to compare the status of the NDH during 1944 and 1945 with the status of Hungary and Slovakia. The Third Reich occupied Hungary in spring 1944, and Slovakia in fall of the same year. Both states retained their nominal independence, governments and armed forces, but in reality they were subjected to German military occupation.
66. For details about these negotiations, see Nada Kisić Kolanović, *Mladen Lorković. Ministar urotnik* [*Mladen Lorković. Minister Conspirator*] (Zagreb: Golden Marketing and Hrvatski državni arhiv, 1998), pp.63–71, Jozo Ivičević, 'Politički program ratnoga HSS-a i 'puč Lorković-Vokić' [Political Program of the Wartime Croatian Peasant Party and 'Vokić-Lorković coup']', *Časopis za suvremenu povijest* 27/3 (1995), pp.493–4, and Radelić (note 10), pp.27–8. They all mentioned that the HSS did not want to compromise itself by accepting the cooperation with the Ustaše. The HSS demanded the formation of neutral, non-party government, but Ustaše representatives did not want to accept that.
67. For details see Kisić Kolanović (note 65), pp.74–98.
68. Lorković and Vokić renewed negotiations with the HSS representatives in June 1944 with the knowledge of Pavelić.
69. Lorković, Vokić and prominent HSS members Ivanko Farolfi and Ljudevit Tomašić were killed in Lepoglava prison at the very end of the war, probably on 30 April 1945. It is not certain what really happened or why were they killed.

The NDH's Relations with Southeast European Countries, Turkey and Japan, 1941–45

NADA KISIĆ KOLANOVIĆ
Croatian Institute for History (Zagreb)

This article is based on the documentation of the NDH embassy in Sofia, which is an irreplaceable source for the analysis of communication among Southeast and Central European countries in the period from 1941 to 1945. Vladimir Židovec, an exceptionally analytical and perceptive Croatian ambassador, left behind him around 2000 pages of diplomatic reports.[1] Židovec was not a professional diplomat, although he possessed a solid education, analytical talent and spoke four languages. He was descended from a respectable family of lawyers from Karlovac, and earned a doctor's degree in law from Zagreb University in 1930.

For those less informed on Yugoslav history, it might be useful to repeat several key historical moments related to the history of the Independent State of Croatia (NDH), which was proclaimed in Zagreb on 11 April 1941. Its international sponsors were Mussolini's Italy and Hitler's Germany, which accordingly led the NDH to join the Tripartite Pact on 15 June and the Anti-Comintern Pact on 15 November 1941.

The NDH was internationally recognised by Germany, Italy and Slovakia (15 April 1941), as well as Bulgaria (19 April 1941), Romania (7 May 1941), Spain (27 June 1941), Finland (2 July 1941), Denmark (10 July 1941) and Manchukuo (2 August 1941). In recent Croatian historiography, a great number of texts have been printed on the NDH, reviving a number of ideological controversies as to its character.[2] The problems related to the NDH's relationship with Germany and Italy have been relatively well considered, whereas when it comes to its connections with Eastern and Central European countries, analytical comparisons sections are still missing. The fact is, by concluding the Roman Treaties with Mussolini's Italy on 15 May 1941, NDH entered the orbit of Fascist Italy. This treaty was responsible for the NDH losing the most valuable part of the Adriatic coast, while the Second Italian Army occupied a considerable part of the hinterland. There was a tendency by some Ustaša ministers to proclaim the pro-Italian policy of the head of state, Ante Pavelić, to be a mistake, because much more could have been achieved within the orbit of Germany. Nonetheless, the available documentation shows that for the high Berlin circles the NDH was on a political sidetrack and that, even during the war, German diplomacy was unwilling to use its influence with the Italians for a more favourable Croatian-Italian border. As a matter of fact, Germany did not always approve of the Italian methods for the 'albanisation' of NDH, but the former adhered to the principled division on the spheres of interest in the Balkans, and did not want to meddle in the Croatian–Italian relationship.

Hopes and Doubts in the New European Order

When the subject in question is Southeast Europe during the 1920s and 1930s, historians tend to perceive that space as agriculturally oriented toward the German market, with Great Britain as not economically favourably disposed to the countries situated there. Questions on the neutrality of the Balkans remained topical until November 1939, but even then the great powers had different standpoints. The Balkan neutral bloc was supposed to encompass the countries of the Balkan Agreement (Turkey, Greece, Romania and Yugoslavia), as well as Bulgaria and Hungary. The Italian variant of the neutral Balkan bloc excluded Turkey because it was leaning toward the western powers. The possibility of the Balkan neutral bloc coming under the influence of Turkey or even Italy, regardless of the alliance between the two countries, did not suit Germany. British diplomacy was interested in the neutral Balkan bloc under the patronage of Italy, but only as long as it believed that it was possible to keep Italy away from Germany. A Balkan neutral bloc under western influence, however, did not suit the Soviet Union.[3]

Immediately before the outbreak of the war, Southeast Europe was rather an empty space of power – that is, available to Germany as a new political power on the rise. As is known, in 1940 the Tripartite Pact was joined by Hungary (20 November), Romania (23 November) and Slovakia (24 November) while Bulgaria joined in 1941 (1 March). In doing so, the governments of these countries largely appealed to their own national interest. However, the development of events soon compelled them to pose the question as to whether German diplomacy had a complete political conception of South-East Europe at all.

The first crack in the bloc of German 'satellites' appeared in the relationships between the NDH and Bulgaria, on one hand, and Italy on the other. Zagreb and Sofia could not accept Italy as a sincere ally for the simple reason that it looked at the Balkans as its own national *Lebensraum*. In turn, a tense relationship between Croatia and Hungary appeared after the Hungarian annexation of the Medjimurje region. Hungarian revisionism continued to be oriented towards these countries, which were previously part of the Austro-Hungarian Monarchy. Hungary annexed Croatian Medjimurje, and the Hungarian political elite kept expressing scepticism as to the survival of the independent Croatian state.[4] Bulgaria supported the territorial expansion of Hungary at the expense of Yugoslavia but was reserved in the Croatian-Hungarian dispute over Hungary's annexation of Medjimurje. Even though Bulgarian politicians believed that Croatia had majority rights over Dalmatia and Medjimurje, Sofia was not actively engaged on Croatia's part, justifying itself with the claim that Bulgaria did not have great power status.

At the same time, Bulgaria hoped for good relations with Hungary in order to strengthen its position *vis-à-vis* Serbia. Bulgarian national liberals, such as Simeon Radev, believed that the most favourable international political option for Bulgaria was to create a defensive bloc with Croatia and Hungary against Serbia.[5]

For their part, the Slovaks thought that Bulgaria should not risk its friendship with Croatia and Slovakia on account of the pact with Hungary, since Sofia had already had enough enemies, including the Turks, Greeks and Serbs. The friendship between Hungary and Romania, which had to give up northern Transylvania in favour of Hungary, was considered far more unstable. Romanians were embittered because they had to leave about 1.3 million of their fellow-countrymen in Transylvania in order to enable Hungary to gain sovereignty over 800,000 Romanian Hungarians.[6]

Yet, the NDH did not want to bind itself to Romania because both countries had a territorial dispute with Hungary. The Croatian government believed that a pact with Bucharest would damage Croatian–Hungarian relations even further. Indeed, Bulgaria approved of Croatian reservations toward Romania. The friendship between Bulgaria and Romania, which displayed constant distrust toward Sofia due to the loss of southern Dobrudža, was fragile. The problems over relocation of the population, as well as financial recompense that Bulgaria had to pay to Romania by way of investment, were sources of permanent tension.[7]

On the other hand, Romanian diplomacy had a tendency to equate Bolshevism and all Slavic states. Stojan Comakov Petrov, the Bulgarian envoy in Bucharest, warned his Croatian colleague Branko Benzon not to fall for Romanian propaganda, which 'identifies all the Slavs with the Bolsheviks'. Yet Benzon, as a prominent Germanophile, said that he 'does not understand' the 'great Slav emotions of Bulgarians'.[8] Still, Romania's trust in Bulgaria's friendship was not sincere.

In November 1941, the Romanian ambassador in Sofia, Caranfil said to Židovec:

> I understand the suspicions toward Romania and I have talked to you about that before, but today Bulgaria is especially afraid of Romania because it fears that Romania will expand toward the East and thus become by far the largest state on the Balkans and in the East of Europe and will gain a dominant position. For that reason Bulgaria would certainly like to see the entire Erdelj belong to Hungary.[9]

In the Bulgarian-Romanian dispute, the NDH took the side of Bulgaria because it thought the latter would strengthen its position towards Hungary in return. Zagreb maintained only basic contacts with Bucharest. Židovec confirmed that the closeness between Croatia and Romania 'might be a momentary need and political game with a certain goal, whereas our relationship toward Bulgaria has to be a corner-stone upon which we shall build our politics and our future.'[10]

There is no doubt that Romania wished for collaboration with the NDH as a natural ally against Hungary. Mihail Antonescu, who in the meantime had assumed the post of Foreign Minister, believed that Hungarian revisionism jeopardised the national interests of both countries to the same extent. In January 1942, Antonescu tried to convince Branko Benzon, the Croatian Ambassador to

Bucharest, that he was well acquainted with Croatia's circumstances and that, in the Croatian-Hungarian dispute over the Medjimurje region, Romania was completely on Croatia's side. Antonescu was also extremely distrustful toward Italy, claiming that it had a pact with Hungary and Bulgaria against Croatia: 'Italy is assisting Hungary, and is trying to bring them and Bulgarians as close as possible. The tendency of Italian policy is to squeeze Croats between these two blocs and to force them to seek refuge with Italy as much as possible. Perhaps Italy will soon try to give even more to the Hungarians at the expense of Croatia.' Benzon concluded that Antonescu clearly wanted to find 'an ally anywhere against Hungary, and he would also like to be insured against the Bulgarians', and that he 'did not entirely give up Dobrudža'. The Romanian press took the lead in the campaign against Hungary, and for the same reason it gave much coverage to positive articles about Croatia and Slovakia.[11]

Even though these satellite regimes did not want to put their mutual disputes above the Axis war efforts, Croatia and Bulgaria secretly hoped that Germany would restrain Italian appetites. However, very soon it was to become apparent that Germany would stick to the binding logic of interest spheres, and therefore it did not want to question the territorial advantages of Italy in the NDH.[12] In fact, in 1941 all German satellites in Central and Southeast Europe were confronted with similar temptations, and in their own way they realised that a new European order would not provide decisive national answers. Subordinating everything to war logic, Germany neglected the small allies and their national interests, for Germany believed that they had no other goals except to serve the Axis' global interests. Satellite governments were thus supposed to refrain from mutual quarrels, which reflected common wartime goals in a negative way. Such a view was openly presented by all German ambassadors in the satellite countries who were orthodox National Socialists and *Obergruppenführers* of Nazi assault orders – including Adolf Beckerle in Sofia, Siegfried Kasche in Zagreb, Hanns Ludin in Bratislava, Manfred Killinger in Bucharest and Dietrich Jegow in Budapest.

Collectively, their rhetoric was a reflection of that cold-blood military doctrine reducing everything to brute force, losing sight of political values in consequence. Židovec recorded Beckerle's statement that Germans saw the background of the conflicts in the Balkans and elsewhere but, since they were in military control, it was not important what local governments thought. Although he could not precisely define the flaws of German politics at that moment, Židovec thought that Germans tended to 'underestimate events' and to interpret power relations in a 'very simplified manner'. Moreover, the Japanese intelligence service in charge of the sector of the Balkans and Southeast Europe claimed that German politics often relied on 'naïve plans' and it 'underestimated adversaries'.[13]

Manfred Killinger, the German ambassador in Bucharest, reacted promptly to the vigorous growth of anti-Hungarian propaganda in Romanian circles. When a possibility of the outbreak of Hungarian-Romanian conflict over Transylvania was openly discussed in summer 1942, Killinger said that there would be no test of strength among the Tripartite Pact signatories, because 'Germany cannot allow private wars in Europe either in autumn or even later, but all controversial issues will be solved slowly and soberly'.[14]

However, it was natural that the governments of the satellite countries constantly demonstrated the will to impose their vital interests. At home, all these governments kept publicly emphasising that it was due to national interests that they waged war on the side of Germany. Such a conception was incompatible with German policy, which in their allies' countries started to provoke contrary effects to those desired ones. In the satellites' diplomatic circles it could be quickly heard that Germany manifested the chauvinism of a great power and that it monopolised intergovernmental negotiations. Indeed, the then Romanian Ambassador in Sofia had always been more critical towards the Germans than his colleagues. In December 1942, Caranfil expressed an overt suspicion that Germany could 'rule Europe for many years at the dissatisfaction and against the will of all other nations'. In his opinion, 'the Germans are remarkable organisers and in their own country they managed to bring about real miracles. However, their understanding of other nations' souls and needs is poor so everywhere they keep disappointing those nations with their politics, so there are more and more pro-ally sympathisers every day.'[15]

Yet, while Germany persisted in holding to a logic based on force and self-serving interests, the prospects of resolving territorial disputes among satellite countries were grim. This is quite clear if we recall the warning the German ambassador in Sofia, Adolf Beckerle, gave to Židovec in December 1941 on Croatia not being allowed to have secret negotiations over Medjimurje with Hungary. Intimidating the satellite countries in order to keep them from getting involved in squaring accounts with one another was justified with the argument that all such disputes would be resolved after the war through German arbitration. Therefore, the Croatian Foreign Minister, Mladen Lorković, kept refusing unacceptable suggestions by the Hungarians on the pretext that the Germans would 'look very much askance' at it.[16]

In Bucharest, Croatian Ambassador Benzon could already feel opposition to the Axis trends. In pursuit of allies against Hungary – which expanded in Transylvania at the expense of Romania – Romanian Foreign Minister Antonescu proposed a bilateral pact to Croatia in February 1942.[17] However, the German Ambassador in Bucharest, Manfred Killinger, nipped the idea of regional coalitions in the bud, warning Benzon to 'reduce to a proper measure' 'Antonescu's strong pressure' toward bilateral cooperation. The two countries were thus allowed only 'to deal with cultural relations and alliances'; therefore in political terms he 'recommends an extreme restraint'. Individual countries were not supposed to solve their problems independently of the Axis' global interests. Therefore Killinger claimed that 'the Germans would be reluctant to see the relations among the Slovaks, Croats and Romanians becoming strongly pronounced, and that these relations can be only cultural'.[18]

For its part, the Slovakian government was also aware of constraints imposed by Germany. The Deputy President of the Slovakian government, Stefan Polyak told Židovec that 'Croats, Slovaks and Romanians could conclude a pact against Hungary in five minutes, but in this moment it would not be justified, nor would Germany want or tolerate that.'[19]

Germany's political *diktat* to satellite regimes could be conditionally conceived as erasing the national background from their politics. Those satellites whose borders were dictated by Italy – and Židovec himself called this situation 'the absurdity of the Balkan situation' – most painfully felt this. Although he did not provide a precise definition of the problem, Židovec claimed that relationships within the Axis had been encumbered with previously unsolved issues, and that Germany's small allies had not yet reached the status of satisfied nations. In short, 'the new European order' incurred not only public enemies but also secret ones throughout the Balkans. Židovec realised that German war policy could hardly be translated into other countries' national languages. In his summary report for 1942, he revealed that the new European order in the Balkans was bogged down in contradictions because 'malcontents' against Germany 'were rising everywhere'. Insurgent movements outgrew local character, and 'even the entire nations or parts of the nation' rebelled along the length and breadth of the Balkans. Yet even Židovec could hardly avert his eyes from the fact that the Germans tolerated Italian expansion at the expense of Croatia, as a result of which antifascist mobilisation increased rapidly. The NDH government was thus losing control over the rebellion at home day after day. The call of partisan arms was most strongly felt in annexed Dalmatia, where the anti-Italian – but also the anti-Ustaša – spirit assumed the character of a general uprising. From the very beginning, Ustaša politics was lacking any appeal or perspective for Croats living in the zones occupied by the Italian army. As a result, the Partisan liberation movement found its meaning in the ideology of national liberation. Therefore it is no wonder that Židovec, analysing the new European order, raised a question of the relationship between the means and the goal. He said:

> The Germans keep telling us it is more important to achieve a complete victory, but one can talk like that to politicians, and one can talk like that to people who have some general view and can understand the necessities and the needs imposed by time. One cannot talk like that and cannot win over, let us say, a Croat peasant somewhere in Dalmatia to whom, suppose, the Italians have burnt down the house and killed his father and brother, and to whom, let us say, the Chetniks of so-called the anti-communist gang had killed his wife and children.

Since this was how matters stood, Partisan movements based their propaganda on a promise that occupied peoples would get back everything that had been taken away from them, as well as what belonged to them. Such a development of events, in Židovec's opinion, made it possible for 'Bolshevism' to impose itself permanently on the Balkans through national liberation movements.[20] Indeed, time proved his assumptions to be correct.

Major German allies, such as Japan, were also critical regarding the capacity of the new European order to absorb restored national movements. Rioci Umeda, an intelligence officer filling the post of Press Envoy in the Japanese Embassy in Sofia, was convinced that German politics 'brings about equally bad consequences everywhere'. Mentioning small nations, Umeda used the Ukraine as an example of the essential shortcomings of German foreign policy. For example, the Germans fed Ukrainian nationalists the story about 'waiting' and 'patience' until a full war victory was achieved. Židovec personally witnessed the frustration of Ukrainian nationalists who considered the Germans responsible for spreading war in the country. In December 1942, Ukrainian nationalist Nikola Kovalevski told Židovec that banner carriers of the fight against Germany 'are not at all Bolsheviks, but these are rather Ukrainian malcontents.'[21]

Since the alliance with Germany did not geopolitically strengthen its small allies, faith in the new European order consequently started to melt. The Croatian ambassador in Bucharest, Benzon, would thus note down the words of his Slovak colleague who told him in early 1942 that he 'does not believe in the fairness of the new order, which has already affected Slovaks, Romanians and Croats', and that he had completely lost hope 'that the wrongs will be rectified after the war, but instead this promise is only for smearing the eyes of small nations'.[22]

The defeat of the Axis in Northern Africa (as the loss of Tunis turned out to be) created a new situation and paved the path toward a raising of awareness by the satellite regimes. The surrender of 225,000 German and Italian soldiers at Cape Bona on 12 May 1943 shook the German satellites' faith in the positive outcome of the war. Židovec's report, addressed to Pavelić on 11 May 1943, implied an effective crisis, which was induced in the governments of the Balkan satellites by the fall of Tunis. From that moment on, it was only a matter of time before an Allied invasion of the continent. In satellite circles, the German retreat in Africa was viewed as a tremendous military and moral defeat for the Axis. Yet the frame of mind with regard to Italy was even worse. The state of mind in the Balkan countries is best expressed by the succinct statement of the Romanian military envoy, Plesioianua: 'Italy is the heaviest ballast for Germany'. Analogously to the role of Austro-Hungary in the defeat of Germany in the previous war, he believed that, in this war, Italy would play 'a fatal role for Germany' and would bring Germany to a 'similar ending' to 1918.

Turkey: The barrier to the expansion of Soviet hegemony in Central Europe

Turkey was not only the hegemonic power in the Middle East; it also had a significant place in the balance of powers in the South-East of Europe. In May 1939, Turkey signed a bilateral agreement with Britain and France and made a commitment to comply with international regulations on its straits. In 1941 Turkey formally opted for a neutral position; in Ankara on 18 June 1941, it signed with Germany the Pact of Non-Aggression and Friendship, which was only to be cancelled on 2 August 1944. During 1941 and 1942, Germany did not expect Turkey to be involved any further in war events. After the war broke out, Turkey adhered to international provisions on strait navigation control in addition to the ban on passage of warships over 100 tonnes. Germany reckoned that it could get Turkey on its side because, throughout its history, Turkey had taken an interest in the destiny of Europe by assigning itself the role of strait keeper. Moreover, in Turkey there was an active pro-German conservative group, which nurtured economic and cultural relations with Germany.

Even though on 25 March 1941 Turkey signed a declaration on friendship with Moscow, it unreservedly accepted Hitler's aggression on the USSR, dubbed 'Operation Barbarossa'. German ambassador Beckerle believed that Turkey observed German actions against the Soviets with sympathy, and that it disapproved of the British policy in Iran. Beckerle was also aware of the fact that Turkey's attitude towards Germany depended on the outcome of the war with the USSR and that, in the case of Germany's defeat, Turkey would 'immediately start to negotiate with the Americans and the English'.[23] In the same time, due to the strategic importance of the Asia Minor strip for the defence of British interests in the Near East, Turkey found itself at the focus of the British politics. Germany's satellites were secretly hoping that London would not allow the Soviet Union to jeopardise British interests in Turkey, Greece and further afield in Egypt and on the Suez, the main communication artery to their dominions in Asia.

Whereas in 1941 the Turkish government tried to be neutral toward Germany, the Turkish press kept encouraging the pro-Allied trends in the Balkan satellite countries, especially in Bulgaria and Romania. To be sure, overt sympathy toward the western Allies predominated in the Turkish press and public life, or example in the Constantinople daily *La Republique*, the European edition of *Džumhurijjet* which was printed in French. Yet, Turkish policy toward the Balkan countries could be more clearly discerned in Sofia, because it was from this capital that the Turkish diplomats pulled the strings in order to bring together the Balkan states against Bolshevik Russia. Above all, Sofia's friendly attitude toward Turkey reflected a realistic need for Bulgaria to defend itself from Soviet involvement. The first step in that direction was the signing of a pact between Bulgaria and Turkey in Ankara on 17 February 1941.

That said, the NDH could not rely upon a more serious diplomatic initiative from Turkey as long as the latter continued to recognise Yugoslavia. The activities of continuing Yugoslav diplomacy through the consulate general in Constantinople were particularly unfavourable to Croatia. The Yugoslav government-in-exile monitored the developments of the NDH through Vladimir Perić, an intelligence officer in Turkey, who operated within the framework of the Intelligence Department of the Yugoslav troops' Command in the Middle East, with headquarters located in Cairo. His mainly negative reports on the NDH also found their way to the intelligence services of the western Allies and the Soviet Union. Still, there is no doubt that the NDH officials kept receiving certain encouragements from Turkey. What remains to be seen is to what extent these influences coincided with the interests of the Croatian government.

In late 1941, certain episodes came to light which might lead to the conclusion that Turkey was willing to recognise Croatia at the diplomatic level – if the end of the war would result in a new form of independence for the individual peoples of Yugoslavia. The Turkish ambassador in Sofia, Ali Sevki Berker, who held that office since 1934, commented on that when the first meeting between him and Židovec took place on 11 October 1941. Berker had asked the Croatian Embassy to issue Croatian visas to some Turkish citizens. The Turkish ambassador took the greatest interest in the Muslim community in Croatia as well as in the construction of the mosque in Zagreb.[24] Even though the conversation had no special political meaning, Berker's statement on Turkey's willingness 'to recognise Croatia, so that sooner or later normal relations between our states will be established' is indicative. Indeed, in 1941 the Croatian government had already taken the initiative in that direction. In November 1941, the Croatian government sent Munir Šahinović Ekremov, a Sarajevo-born journalist and writer, to Turkey. His trip was primarily related to the NDH's effort to achieve some form of Turkish recognition, if only through a trade agreement. During the conversation with Židovec, Ekremov said that he travelled to Turkey 'unofficially, but if achieving success, it will be official'. Šahinović personally briefed Berker on the character of his mission. On that occasion, the Turkish ambassador said that he 'deems it necessary to regulate the consular relationships between the NDH and Turkey, because all roads from Turkey to Europe lead through Croatia'.[25] Yet Šahinović's mission in Turkey failed to achieve satisfactory results. He did not seem to be the most suitable person, since his book *Turska, danas i sjutra* [*Turkey, Today and Tomorrow*], provoked certain reservations and hesitations in Turkey. Although he acknowledged Turkey's primacy as 'the leading country in the Islamic world', Šahinović did not hesitate to conclude that Turkey had not yet become 'a modern European state', which doubtless displeased his Turkish contemporaries.[26]

In summer 1942, the NDH decided to move forward with the Croatian Turkish commercial treaty. As instructed by the government, Židovec officially proposed to get the Croatian–Turkish commercial negotiations started in the Turkish Embassy. In June 1942, the Turkish charge d'affaires informed Židovec that:

> for the time being the Turkish government would not like to abandon the manner of trading with Croatia they have had so far; that is, entirely private business deals by individual merchants based on compensation, because it is considered to be the most appropriate under current circumstances. For that reason the Turkish government believes the time for direct Turkish-Croatian commercial negotiations has not come yet.[27]

Late in May, the 1942 Croatian Ministry for Foreign Affairs sponsored a new trip for Croatian observers to Turkey. Muhamed Mujagić, supreme sheriat judge in retirement, and Hivzija Košarić, a clerk in the NDH consulate in Maribor, stayed in Turkey as private citizens from 30 May to 10 July 1942. Mujagić and Košarić got in touch with religious dignitaries relatively easily, but they failed to establish any contact with official Turkish representatives – with the exception of meeting Nevzet-beg Naderizović, mayor and *valia* [great prefect] in Ankara, with family roots in Travnik. Indeed, Turkish religious circles expressed positive attitudes toward the Croatian government much more openly.[28]

In the meantime, Turkish observers were visiting Croatia as well. There is no doubt that a trip round the NDH, undertaken in autumn 1942 by Hakir Čečene, a newspaper reporter accredited with the Turkish embassy in Sofia, was related to intelligence tasks. Čečene, among other things, was supposed to examine the efficacy of the Partisan resistance movement for the British secret service. In Zagreb, Čečene talked to August Košutić, secretary of the Croatian Peasant Party (HSS). Židovec confirmed that the Turkish government had sent Čečene to Croatia and Bosnia in order to look into the mood of the local Muslims as well as the possibility of their joining the war effort against the Axis should Turkey go to war with Germany and Bulgaria. Židovec found out that the Ustaša regime had made a very unfavourable impression on Čečene.

Nonetheless, the Ustaša top leadership continued attempting to establish relations with Turkey. It was precisely in the anti-communist logic of Turkish politics that Croatian policy-makers saw the opportunity to gain diplomatic recognition. In November 1942, the press attaché in the Croatian embassy in Sofia, Stjepan Mosner, travelled to Turkey to brief official Turkish circles on the Croatian conditions. Mosner's report leaves no room for doubt that Turkey was ready to establish cultural relations with Croatia, albeit not diplomatic ones. Editors of various newspapers accepted the offer to print material on Croatia. The editor-in-chief of *Džumhurijjet* spoke positively about Croatian policy toward the Muslims and gave credit to the Croatian army, which was engaged on the Eastern Front against Bolshevik Russia.[29] In the same month, the press directorate in Constantinople agreed to a Croatian proposal to have a Croatian Muslim newspaper distributed in Turkey, one which would be subject to Turkish censorship. By April 1943, this Turkish Croatian newspaper, *East-West* [*Dogu ve Bati*] was printed in Zagreb.

Yet, even though Croatian representatives did not manage to establish official contacts with government representatives, Turkey nevertheless had no intention of cutting off the NDH completely from the regional or international community. The interest of Turkish foreign policy in events transpiring in the South-East of Europe was proportionate to its fear of Soviet expansion. In consequence, the

Turkish initiative for creating a bloc of Southeast European states, which would be strong enough to resist the pressure of the Soviet Union and international communism, was growing increasingly strong at this time.

In early December 1942, Berker was assigned a new ambassadorial post in Vichy, and the Turkish embassy in Sofia was entrusted to Vasfi Mentes. Mentes came from the embassy in Bern and, unlike his predecessor, his attitude toward the NDH embassy was not passive. Mentes' generally more lively diplomatic activity was related to a new direction in Balkan policy after the Italian surrender to the Allies. As soon as Italy left the Axis, Turkey, as a Balkan power, would confer to Bulgaria, Romania and Hungary in order to create a formally neutral – but in fact anti-Soviet – bloc. The Soviets allegedly knew of these plans. Mentes undoubtedly made it known to Židovec that Turkey expected the Croats to join the security system against the Bolshevik Soviet Union.[30]

Although it was still early to talk about formal recognition, Mentes nevertheless created a new climate in relationships with Židovec. On 19 December 1942, Mentes informed him semi-officially that Turkish politics aimed at a stable European South-East, which included Turkey's obligation to protect that space from the Communist invasion. During this conversation Mentes explicitly stated that Turkey 'has the greatest interest in the Balkans', which included developments in Croatia, Hungary and Romania. Therefore Turkey would be glad to see these countries gathered in an anti-Bolshevik defensive alliance. Turkey 'looks on Croatia with sympathies, and believes that Croatia will be able to build its state with excellence in peace, because the Croats are an old, cultural people'. Mentes further discussed Turkey as a world power, which advanced the principle that 'all nations have right to freedom and independent life'. It was especially relevant that Mentes hinted Turkey would establish diplomatic relations with Croatia after the war. Židovec emphasised that the Turkish ambassador spoke in 'friendly terms' and that his analyses were congruent with the goals of the British.[31] Mentes unequivocally confirmed this, saying that Turkey was 'always ready to engage in war … on the side of the Balkan states'. He called this readiness 'natural', and concluded that the first line of Turkish defence extended along the river Dnjestra. Later Židovec was to confirm that in spring 1942 he had information that Turkey was conducting a similar diplomatic action in Hungary, Romania and Bulgaria, trying to draw the line of defence from the expansion of communism in those countries as well.[32]

With this in mind, Suphi Tanriörf, the Turkish ambassador in Bucharest, specifically approached Croatian ambassador Benzon on this matter. When in November 1942 it became clear that the Axis powers were losing the war in both North Africa and the Eastern Front, Suphi declared that the defeat of Germany on the Eastern Front would, in the long-term, establish the geopolitical predominance of USSR in Southeast Europe. Suphi claimed that 'all nations under German occupation, even including the Croatian nation, which was allegedly liberated from the Serbian slavery', expected the arrival of Anglo-American troops in Europe. It was from 'this phenomenon' that Suphi drew the conclusion that 'Europe is not with Germany, quite the contrary, it is against it, but Germany usurps the right to speak on behalf of the whole Europe'.[33]

At the beginning of 1943, Germany started to react more and more nervously to Turkey's protective role toward the Balkan countries, which formally remained under German occupation. Therefore, the Turkish Ministry of Foreign Affairs had to make additional efforts to convince Germany that Turkey was not going to deviate from its policy of neutrality. Sückrü Saracoglu, during his conversation with the German ambassador Franz von Papen on 19 March 1943, stated that 'Russia remains the great common adversary' for both Turkey and Germany. [34]

But, having left Sofia in December 1943, Židovec expressed his suspicion of Turkey's willingness to make some concessions to the Croatian government. This was at least partly due to the prevalence of Allied sympathisers in Turkey as well as the preponderance of strong Serbian espionage and propaganda, which operated within the Yugoslav consulate general in Constantinople. Indeed, according to Židovec, 'our Moslems from Turkey were completely pro-Yugoslav', while 'our people who live in Turkey are Yugoslavs as well.'[35] Yet as late as April 1944, Turkish representatives in Sofia established contact with the Croatian embassy again. The Turkish commercial attaché, Basher, asked for a meeting with the new Croatian Ambassador, Nikola Rušinović. There was no doubt that Basher, otherwise a declared Anglophile, followed instructions from above. He approached Rušinović with the following proposition:

> Mister Minister, your government is closely linked with Germany. We hope everybody in Croatia is clear that Germany will lose the war. With Germany goes Croatia too. There is a possibility for Croatia to save itself. It is in Turkey's interest that Croatia remains an independent state, which is certainly your wish too. We Turks have been and will be working on it, but you have to take part in it as well. For that reason you need to send a group of Croats to Turkey immediately, who will be transferred to London. Your people must be irreproachable in every respect.

Moreover, Turkey was willing to bear material expenses of transferring some 20 or 30 Croatian representatives to London, and Rušinović was asked to forward the offer to Pavelić. Forty-eight hours later, Rušinović found himself in Zagreb and was immediately received by the *Poglavnik*, who heard him out with a certain interest. Pavelić then said he would think everything through, although he never responded to the Turkish initiative, which in the meantime died out completely.[36]

In the first half of 1944, the USSR advanced alongside the entire southern half of the Soviet–German front, with the final goal of invading the Danube region and even further west in Europe. Conservative circles in Turkey thought that the western Allies were going to leave Southeast Europe to the Soviets. Numan Menemencioglu, the Turkish Minister of Foreign Affairs, was compelled to resign from his office in July 1944 because it was discovered that, during May and June, Germany managed to pull 13 warships out through the straits disguised as commercial transports. During July 1944, the German Ambassador, Franz von Papen, was preparing the evacuation of the Embassy.

Then in August 1944 Turkey announced a break in diplomatic relations with Germany. On the same day, the Turkish Ambassador in Sofia officially informed the Croatian Ambassador, Rušinović that, despite the diplomatic rupture, 'Turkey's relations toward German allies will not change'. During another conversation with the Turkish Commercial Envoy, Basher, Rušinović concluded that Turkey had no intention of pitting itself against Germany: Basher confirmed that there was no 'national interest' which his government could use to justify entering the war with the Turkish general public. For its part, Turkey feared that a secret agreement between the Anglo-Americans and the Soviets on the division of the zones of influence had been reached in respect of the Balkans. At the same time, the government believed that Turkey was not technically ready for war, supporting this by the claim that the British had not fulfilled their promise, given in Adana, about delivering modern arms.[37] Still, at the Allies' conference in Yalta (4–11 February 1945) it was decided that countries which did not go to war on the side of the anti-fascist powers before 1 March 1945 would not take part in creating a new European order. Unsurprisingly, therefore, on 23 February 1945 Turkey declared war on Nazi Germany.

Japanese Diplomacy and the NDH

The topic of Croatian–Japanese relations may seem rather out of place when discussing the notion according to which Europe was not within the Japanese sphere of interest. Japan was oriented toward the East Asian space, that is, as evidenced by war against China (1937) and the US (1941), even though Southeast Europe had a secondary meaning for Japan, and events that took place in that area were not unknown to Japanese intelligence officers. The activity of the Japanese intelligence service in the Balkans was, in the first place, directed at obstructing the formation of any British directed anti-Axis monolith in that space. As a result, Croatia occupied a certain place within this concept.

When the European war first broke out in 1939, Japan was formally neutral. Hitler's initial successes in Europe, especially the entry of the German army in Paris in June 1940, led the Japanese government to conclude a pact of mutual assistance with Germany and Italy on 27 September 1940, and thus to become an ally of the Axis powers. In 1941, Japan considered the USSR a natural ally, whereas Great Britain and the US were its natural enemies. Wishing to strengthen its position in relation to America, in April 1941 Japan concluded a five-year pact of neutrality with the Soviet Union. From Japan's point of view, the pact with the USSR was conceived as a means of deterring American intervention in the Far East. At the same time, in joining the Tripartite Pact, Japan made no commitment to take part in any German–Soviet war, because Japan had only committed itself to go to war against any country that joined the British side.

On 7 June 1941, Japan officially recognised the NDH. In the second half of 1941, a group of Japanese journalists accredited in Rome visited the NDH, after which the Japanese press released several positive articles on the Croatian state. Yet by relying on the reports of its ambassadors in Rome and Berlin, the Japanese government had no immediate intention of opening a permanent diplomatic office in Zagreb. It was from the Japanese embassy in Sofia that positive initiatives in that direction first arose (further discussed below). But here it is worth emphasising that the Japanese embassies in Berlin and Rome often judged events through a German prism, whereas the Japanese Embassy in Sofia tried to establish contact with all the warring sides. It was thus from the Japanese Embassy in Sofia that preparations were initiated for opening a regular Japanese diplomatic office in Zagreb. On 18 June 1942 Židovec found out that Rioci Umeda, the Japanese press representative to the Embassy in Sofia, printed in some German newspapers in May – with no official instructions from his government – the news that a Japanese Ambassador in Sofia would also be accredited as an ambassador in Zagreb. Umeda stated that his reason for this was that he wanted to gauge the reaction in Italian circles.[38] Židovec believed that Umeda had not taken independent action, and that the Japanese government had entrusted him with a special political mission in the Balkans. Yet this assumption was immediately denied by Akira Jamaji, the Japanese Ambassador to Sofia, who insisted that his government had no intention of opening a permanent diplomatic mission in Croatia, because if it did the government would find itself in a 'delicate' position in relation to Italy. Indeed, late in April 1942, Jamaji was allegedly instructed by his government that 'it is not the time to travel to Croatia'.[39]

The Japanese embassy in Sofia was in charge of maintaining permanent contact with Židovec and exchanging information with him. Although Umeda stayed in Zagreb several times, these visits were of an unofficial nature. Nevertheless, the Germans frowned upon his activity. The German Ambassador in Sofia, Beckerle, called the Japanese 'meddling in internal European affairs' 'absurd'. Beckerle thought little of Umeda and his 'impossible Pan-Slavic ideas' which were picked up during the latter's 17 years of living in Warsaw. In Beckerle's opinion, Umeda's enquiries on whether the Bulgarian emperor 'would be willing to take over, if the situation presented itself, the Ukrainian crown' were the pinnacle of amateurism.[40] Umeda's trips around Macedonia and Dobrudža in June 1942 were also frowned on in Italian circles.

Umeda met the NDH Minister for Foreign Affairs, Mladen Lorković, in Zagreb on 22 August 1942, suggesting that he take formal steps to arrange for the Sofia embassy to represent Japanese interests in Croatia. Lorković stated that he would 'greet' such a decision, but remarked that the Croatian ministry was not formally authorised to take an initiative of this kind. Umeda confirmed that Japan had a 'vivid interest' in the 'independency and strengthening of the states of the South-East of Europe, especially Croatia and Bulgaria'.[41]

In mid-January 1943, after the German troops started to withdraw from the Caucasus, Umeda requested official authorisation from the Croatian government to take steps to open a permanent mission in Zagreb. But the situation was not yet conducive to establishing regular Japanese–Croatian diplomatic relations: the territory of the NDH remained within the competence of the Japanese Embassy in Berlin. It was only in February 1944 that the Tokyo government sent a *chargé d'affaires* to Zagreb, Kazuichi Miura, who had previously filled the post of Japanese consul in Moscow and cultural envoy in Bern. Miura first opened his office in the Hotel Esplanade in Zagreb, before receiving official premises. He addressed the Croatian public for the first time in a radio broadcast on 29 April 1944. He stated that 'Japan is not an insular empire distantly separated from Croatia. Both nations are closely and cordially connected with treaties, as well as with sympathies and friendship. Japan is now fighting side by side with Croatia.'[42] Simultaneously, a Croatian-Japanese society was founded in Zagreb, whose president was both a writer and the deputy head of state, Mile Budak.

The documentation of the Croatian Embassy in Sofia reveals, among other things, that Japanese diplomacy entertained an idea of founding a Japanese-Soviet defence bloc, which was to be joined by the Southeast European Slavic states. The intelligence service in the Japanese Embassy was the main collector of information for the entire Southeast European sector as well as for Turkey. The embassy in Sofia kept in constant touch with the Japanese intelligence department in Switzerland and Hungary. Akira Jamaji, the Japanese Ambassador in Sofia, formerly the Consul General in Vienna, was relatively well informed about the situation in the Balkans. Jamaji made a good impression on Croatian representatives in Sofia, and the new Croatian Ambassador there, Nikola Rušinović, later said that he was 'serious and very well briefed about the world events'.[43]

Yet on the subject of the Japanese intelligence service in Sofia, Rioci Umeda is certainly the most interesting person. He formally filled the post of Press Envoy in the Japanese Embassy. Umeda was rather knowledgeable about the European situation; he spoke Russian, Polish and Bulgarian, and he frequently travelled to Italy, Romania, Greece, Turkey and elsewhere. In the meantime, he took over the role of intermediary between the Japanese government and the Balkan countries. He had relatively good knowledge of Croatian and Yugoslav history, and he called himself 'the first' European diplomatic representative in Europe to send 'warm reports' on Croatia to Tokyo.[44] In Bulgarian circles, the assessments of Umeda's role ranged from the conviction that he was 'one of the most influential and most significant Japanese in Europe' to the assertion that he was a person of no significance at all. The Croatian Ambassador in Bucharest, Benzon, learned from his Japanese colleague that Umeda 'has no political significance or political position'. Židovec, for his new part, assessed that the Japanese 'intentionally hide Umeda's significance and work'. In any case, Židovec believed that 'the connection with the Japanese is very interesting and useful, and that Croatian politics can make use of his data in many ways, of course after they are stripped off of the colour and the tendency he sometimes likes to add to things'. Umeda confirmed to Židovec that:

> he, that is the secret service he was the head of, is entrusted with the task to observe the USSR from the Balkan Peninsula in the first place. His second task is to observe, from the Balkans, the English influence and English policy on the Near East, while his third task is to build links between the Balkan states that is between Bulgaria and Croatia on one side and Japan on the other side.[45]

As already stated, Japan never managed to identify itself with the German war against the USSR, although the Germans were trying to win over the Japanese by suggesting they occupy Vladivostok. The Imperial Council, however, wanted to protect itself from a war on four fronts (in China, Southeast Asia, the Pacific, and in Siberia). Moreover, Germany attacked the USSR with no previous consultations with Tokyo. After the German-Soviet conflict, Japan continued its neutral policy toward Moscow.

It was from exactly this neutral perspective that the Japanese diplomatic representatives judged events, let alone the new world order to be created after the war. Thus as early as 1943, Umeda was to lay out an entirely accurate prognosis that a new antagonism between the USSR and Anglo-American bloc was looming. That conflict was to be expected after the end of the European war, when Japan would be on the side of the USSR. In this scenario, the Japanese intelligence service assigned a particular role to the Balkan countries.

The Japanese thought that Hitler, in his war against the Soviet Union, started from a wrong estimate of the real power relations. Germany was more technically and materially superior, but the USSR had much greater and more enduring manpower. The analyses of Japanese intelligence officers monitoring the Eastern front pointed to the strategic advantage of the Soviet Union which, according to Japanese estimates, had preserved 70 per cent of its military-industrial resources. Therefore, in September 1942, Umeda declared that the most convenient situation for Japan was to conclude a separate peace with Moscow and Berlin, in that way Germany would avoid war on multiple fronts and would be able to contribute more efficiently to the fight against the US since late 1941.[46]

The Japanese also deemed that the war on the Eastern Front pulled German ground troops away from occupied Europe, where resistance movements had started to get organised. Umeda explained to Židovec that the settlement between Germany and the Soviet Union was of extreme strategic importance to Japan. In April 1943, he predicted that 'the only salvation for Germany is to conclude peace with the Soviet Union as soon as possible, with the help of Japan, with or without Turkey'. The cooperation among Japan, Germany and the USSR would be, in Umeda's words, 'good and natural'. Based on those suggestions, Židovec wrote that it would be Japan that would play a considerable role in creating a compromise peace because it was in Japan's interest that Germany not lose the war, though the Japanese did not want to see Germany become too strong at the expense of the other great powers. Umeda assured Židovec that German military potential at the Soviet front was 'very limited', meaning that the Germans could endure not longer than the end of 1942. The Japanese thought that German aggression against the Soviet Union had been 'an endless folly' because it provided Great Britain and the US with some breathing space and enabled them to raise their military readiness, whereas Germany was bleeding on the East. Umeda further believed that the main goal of British policy was to have 'Germany and Russia weakened as much as possible'. Japan was thus against a large-scale German–Soviet conflict, believing that Germany had neither the resources nor the strength for any strong military escalation on the Eastern front.[47]

In August 1942, Židovec arrived in Zagreb to describe to Pavelić all the difficulties of the German position on the Eastern Front, although he failed to convince the *Pogknvik* of this version of events. Pavelić continued to be convinced that 'the Russians will never march to Berlin for sure'.[48] For their part, Japanese intelligence officers undoubtedly attempted to soften the anti-Soviet attitude of the Croatian government. As early as late-1942, Umeda assured Židovec that Japan was going to build some support of its own in Europe, for which 'Ukraine, Bulgaria and Croatia' could be of use; Japan therefore supported a firmer alignment of these countries. In early August 1942, Umeda visited Zagreb and had a secret meeting with Pavelić. Židovec confirmed that, during this conversation, Umeda showed a particular interest in Ukrainian–Croatian relations.[49]

At the same time, Umeda advocated a firmer line by Bulgaria and Croatia towards Italy. He declared that Japan was interested in seeing 'Italy going to Africa as much as possible', because its geopolitical dictate on the Balkans proved to be harmful to the collective security of the Axis powers. The Japanese Ambassador in Bucharest confirmed that in their long-term vision of Europe, his country counted on Germany playing the main role while Italy should not be allowed to meddle in high European diplomacy; indeed, even Italy's maritime primacy was questionable, meaning that the Mediterranean Sea should not be the space of exclusive Italian hegemony.[50]

Several times during spring 1942 Umeda also showed his interest in the problem of the Italian annexation of Dalmatia. He even entertained the idea of persuading Hiroshi Oshima, Japanese Ambassador in Berlin, to intervene with Hitler over Croatia. Early in 1943, the Japanese intelligence service quite unexpectedly became interested in the crimes the Italian army had committed in Dalmatia. In January 1943, the Japanese government kept enquiring specifically into the violence of the Second Italian army in occupied Croatia. For its part, the Japanese Embassy in Sofia received a coded request from the government to deliver more precise information regarding the issue, causing the Croats to speculate on what Japan actually wanted to achieve. Židovec suggested that the enquiry from Tokyo about 'why the Italians did this' was in fact a hint to Croatia that 'the Italians are carrying out that policy as German allies'. Umeda reported stories to Židovec declaring that the Germans had taken 'the war in Russia beyond the scope of the fight against communism and have turned it into a racial war, that their goal is to destroy the Slavs, which after all may be seen from their conduct in Croatia'. From all that, Židovec concluded that the sudden Japanese interest in Croatia was a signal to the government that Italy would go over to the anti-fascist coalitions soon, and that the Balkan satellites were not supposed to follow Italy.[51]

Umeda's interest in Croatia was particularly active in April 1943, after he had concluded that 'new times are coming' for the NDH, in which it 'must lead an independent policy' and 'put the home front in order and strengthen the army'. He also believed that the time was coming when Italian hegemony in the Balkans would deteriorate, and that the Croatian government needed to establish friendly relations with all of its neighbouring countries, including Serbia.[52]

There is no doubt that the Japanese intelligence service came to believe that, by further protraction of the war with the Soviet Union, Germany was courting a military collapse. If this happened, there would be no way out for Germany but to conclude peace with Britain and the US. This was the most dangerous scenario for Japan, since Anglo-American forces, freed from the war in Europe, would be able to concentrate on Japan. In this context, Umeda used the term 'the third world war' and predicted the emergence of a coalition of western democracies to defend themselves against the Soviet Union. In the case of such a conflict between the USSR, on the one side, and the US and Britain on the other, there was only one option left for Japan: to take the side of the Soviets. Umeda laid out the following scenario to Židovec: if Germany were to strike a deal with the Anglo-Americans, Japan would hold out for a Japanese-Soviet defensive bloc to be joined by the Southeast European Slavic states. Umeda tried to express to Židovec the benefits Croatia and Bulgaria would gain from the joining that bloc, rather than the British and US bloc. At the same time, Japan was very anxious about the possible change of regime in Italy, because then, with Turkey's support, Italy would pull the Balkan states to its side and strike against the Germans. With this in mind, in February 1943 Židovec went to Zagreb to submit a verbal report to Pavelić (and Lorković). But his bosses did not believe in such a development, particularly in the possibility of some defensive pact between the Soviet Union and the Balkan states. Židovec noted afterwards that the conversation 'might have been interesting, but nothing more, because they were still lulled into the safe assumption of German victory'.[53]

It was Japan's belief that Moscow was not going to give up the 1941 Japanese-Soviet Non-Aggression Pact. This hope kept Japan going in the final stages of the war and influenced the Japanese prognosis that peace in Europe would inevitably bring about the conflict between the USSR and the US; thus it was reasonable to assume that the Soviet Union would embrace Japan as a natural ally. Of course, the predictions of the Japanese intelligence service on the conflict between the USSR and western democracies proved to be wrong. In April 1945 the USSR announced that it was not going to renew the Soviet-Japanese Non-Aggression Pact, and on 8 August declared war on Japan.

Conclusions

The most important element in interpreting the policies of the Central European countries which during the Second World War joined the Axis bloc is their readiness to accept the revisionism advocated by a Germany dissatisfied with peace treaties from the previous war. Croatian nationalists attempted, with the help of Berlin and Rome, to get a viable independent state, but the domestic situation in the NDH dramatically changed when Italy occupied and annexed Croatian coastal regions in Dalmatia. The NDH and Southeast European countries joined the Axis camp in an attempt to either realise their national interests or obtain territorial gains. However, during the war the Axis regimes increasingly found that Germany considered only its own military-political interest, dictating policy to its satellites – policy which can be usefully conceived as obliterating the national underpinnings of countries like the NDH. This situation deeply influenced the Croatian masses, causing them to increasingly reject the Ustaša regime and its nationalistic elite, to the point of finally putting up armed resistance against German and Italian occupation.

Indeed, the NDH example demonstrates that geo-strategic factors played a significant role in relationships between the Balkan countries and then-neutral Turkey. The Turkish policy toward Southeast Europe could be more clearly discerned from Sofia, where Turkish diplomacy clearly pulled the strings in order to bring the Balkan states together against the expected regional invasion by the USSR. Although Croatian representatives did not manage to establish official contacts with government representatives in Ankara, Turkey still had no intention of completely cutting off the NDH from the international community, because Turkish foreign policy interests in the NDH centred on the latter's Soviet expansion.

Not even major Eastern powers, such as Japan, could keep their complete distance from the NDH and the Southeast European countries. Japan was more critical where the capability of Germany to win the USSR was concerned, as well as the capability of Hitler's 'new European order' to meet the needs of the satellite regimes. At the same time, the Japanese intelligence agents attempted to soften the anti-Soviet attitude of the NDH and Bulgaria. As early as late-1942, the Japanese intelligence service attempted to build its own support in Zagreb and Sofia, as well as in the Ukraine. On the other hand, Japanese diplomacy advocated a stronger alliance between those countries, predicting that conflict between western democracies and the USSR might break out, in which case Japan would have preferred to have the Balkan countries on the side of the USSR.

Notes

1. Židovec was on duty in Sofia from 29 July 1941 to June 1943. After the collapse of the NDH, he withdrew first to Austria and then to Italy where, in 1946, he managed to get Nansen's passport and Argentinean visa. However he failed to cross the ocean because he was arrested by the British agents in Genovese harbour on 4 March 1947 and was shipped to the Allied prison in Rome. He was extradited to Yugoslav authorities on 27 April 1947 as a 'war criminal'. In early 1948 Židovec was sentenced to death in a political process held in Zagreb. However, there is evidence that the sentence was not carried out on 3 March 1948 as declared in police documents, and that in prison he wrote analytical reports for the use of the Communist intelligence service.
2. Due to limited space I have singled out the following works of my own choice: Hrvoje Matković, *Povijest Nezavisne Države Hrvatske* [*The History of the Independent State of Croatia*] (Zagreb, Naklada Pavličić, 1994); *Tko je tko u NDH, Hrvatska 1941–1945* [*Who is Who in the NDH, Croatia 1941–1945*] (Zagreb, Minerva, 1997); Tomislav Jonjić, *Hrvatska vanjska politika 1939–1942* [*Croatian Foreign*

Policy 1939–1942] (Zagreb, Libar, 2000); Nada Kisić Kolanović, *Mladen Lorković, Ministar urotnik* [*Mladen Lorković, The Minister Conspirator*] (Zagreb, Hrvatski državni arhiv – Dom i Svijet, 1998); and, *Vojskovođa i politika, sjećanja Slavka Kvaternika* [*Army Leader and Politics, The Memoirs of Slavko Kvaternik*] (Zagreb, Golden marketing, 1997); and, *NDH i Italija, političke veze i diplomatski odnosi* [*NDH and Italy, Political Connections and Diplomatic Relations*] (Zagreb, Naklada Ljevak, 2001); and *Zagreb-Sofija, Prijateljstvo po mjeri ratnog vremena 1941.–1944* [*Zagreb-Sofia, Friendship Tailored by War Time 1941–1944*] (Zagreb, Dom i svijet - Hrvatski državni arhiv, 2003); Jure Krišto, *Katolička crkva i Nezavisna Država Hrvatska 1941–1945* [*The Catholic Church and the Independent State of Croatia 1941–1945*] (Zagreb, Hrvatski institut za povijest, 1998); Jere Jareb, *Zlato i novac NDH iznesen u inozemstvo 1944. i 1945* [*The NDH Gold and Money Taken Abroad in 1944 and 1945*] (Zagreb, Hrvatski institut za povijest – Dom i svijet, 1997); V. Žerjavić, *Opsesije i megalomanije oko Jasenovca i Bleiburga: Gubici stanovništva Jugoslavije u drugom svjetskom ratu* [*Opsessions and Megalomanias over Jasenovac: The Population Losses of Yugoslavia in WW II*] (Zagreb, Globus, 1992).

3. For more details on the position of these countries towards the neutral Balkan bloc between 1939 and March 1941, see Lj. Boban, *Maček i politika Hrvatske seljačke stranke 1928/1941* [*Maček and the Politics of Croatian Peasant's Party 1928/1941*] (Zagreb, 1974), vol.2, pp.303–415.
4. In elite Hungarian circles at one time, one could hear that the NDH was 'an unhealthy attempt, an unhealthy state formation, which allegedly will not be able to hold its own, where there are incessant riots, and which faces an immediate Communist revolution'. Nada Kisić Kolanović, ed., *Poslanstvo NDH u Sofiji, diplomatski izvještaji 1941–1945* [*The NDH Embassy in Sofia, Diplomatic Reports 1941–1945*] (Zagreb, 2003), vol.1, p.63.
5. Ibid., vol.2, p.265.
6. Ibid., vol.1, pp.26–27 and p.32. In a conversation with Židovec, Bulgarian foreign minister Ivan Popov confirmed that Hitler had reluctantly accepted arbitration in the Romanian–Hungarian dispute over Transylvania, stating to Popov: 'I will never get involved in such arbitrations again. Now neither are Hungarians satisfied, who think that he has ruined for them St. Stephen's Kingdom, nor are Romanians who have lost so many of their people'.
7. Ibid., vol.1, p.31. After gaining the Southern Dobrudža, Bulgaria agreed to pay 1 billion Romanian leis to Romania on account of realised investments. Bulgarian foreign minister Popov claimed that Romania 'has done nothing at all' in Dobružda; on the contrary, he claimed that considerable damage was done intentionally on public buildings when they were leaving the area. Popov also asked for an extension of the voluntary emigration period, since Romania had stalled the issue on purpose.
8. Hrvatski državni arhiv [Croatian State Archive; here after HAD] Zagreb, Poslanstvo NDH u Bukureštu [NDH Embassy in Bucharest], microfilm [mf.] 2, image [im.] 175: Branko Benzon, *Tjedno izvješće*, [Weekly Report] no. 9/42, 2–8 March 1942.
9. Kisić Kolanović (note 4), vol.1, pp.92–3.
10. Ibid., p.258.
11. HDA, MVP NDH, Poslanstvo NDH u Bukureštu, mf. 2, im. 162; mf. 2, im. 179.
12. Kisić Kolanović (note 4), vol.1, pp.74–5. Nonetheless, the German ambassador Beckerle could not completely devalue the territorial problem of Dalmatia, so in October 1941 he commented that 'he is familiar with the problem of Dalmatia, that he knows it is Croatian land, which belongs and must belong to Croatia'. When Secretary of German Embassy Ewald von Massow said to Židovec that 'Germany has an intention to settle all European problems, including this one, not before this winter is over, after the victory over Russia', he had in mind Dalmatia.
13. HDA, 013.0.56; V. Židovec, *Moje sudjelovanje u političkom životu* [*My Participation in Political Life*], p.249.
14. HDA, Poslanstvo NDH u Bukureštu, mf. 2, im.253.
15. Kisić Kolanović (note 4), vol.1, p.98. Caranfil also judged that Germany's chances to end the war through compromise were growing slim. Since he thought that Berlin could not 'sit at a green table as an equal partner', Caranfil predicted that 'in 1943 Germany would try everything in order to achieve a decisive success in Russia, thus gaining a free hand for waging war in the Near East and Africa so it could finally reach an equal position with England and force her to conclude a compromise peace'.
16. Ibid., pp.222–3.
17. HDA, Poslanstvo NDH u Bukureštu, mf. 2, im. 171 and 172.
18. HDA, MVP NDH, Poslanstvo u Bukureštu, mf. 2, im. 177–9; Branko Benson (note 8), no. 11/42, 9–15 March 1942.
19. Kisić Kolanović (note 4), vol.1, pp.114–15.
20. Ibid., pp.781–2. Židovec was not at all surprised by the fact that the Communist idea of a 'free Soviet Republic of Macedonia' had become increasingly popular in Macedonia.

21. Ibid., pp.2, 137–8. Kovalevski also asserted that Ukraine 'has a great interest in Southeast Europe and especially in gaining the passage to the Adriatic Sea, which will render the friendship between the Ukrainian state and Croatia to the utmost importance in the future'. It is no surprise that Židovec's interpretation of the conversation gave preference to his anti-Bolshevik attitude, so in his report to Pavelić he pointed out that such statements were an expression of 'that natural and traditional Russian policy for gaining an access to the Mediterranean Sea, only this time it should be in the friendship with the Croatian state and no longer with the Serbs'.
22. HDA, Poslanstvo NDH, Poslanstvo NDH u Bukureštu, mf. 2, im. 171.
23. Kisić Kolanović (note 4), vol.1, p.291.
24. The Ustaša leadership decided to construct the Zagreb mosque in August 1941. The Museum of Visual Arts served this purpose (with a number of interior alterations), and three minarets were erected around it. The mosque was ceremoniously opened in August 1944.
25. Kisić Kolanović (note 4), vol.1, pp.133–5.
26. Šahinović's criticism of Turkey is undoubtedly related to his views on the Croatian 'ethnic character' of Bosnian-Herzegovian Muslims. He also believed that Turkey had a pan-Islamic mission, which he understood as 'pan-Islamic in a modern sense'. Therefore he rejected all considerations and pointed out clearly the need of even greater liberalisation in Turkey. M. Šahinović-Ekremov, *Turska, danas i sjutra, presjek kroz život jedne države* [*Turkey, Today and Tomorrow, Cross-section through a State's Life*], (Sarajevo, 1939), pp.192, 135 and 145.
27. Kisić Kolanović (note 4), vol.1, p.510.
28. HDA, Zbirka mikrofilmova 301449 – Mladen Lorković, Izvješće Hivzije Košarića M. Lorkoviću, ministru vanjskih poslova, o putovanju u Tursku od 20. srpnja 1942. godine [Collection of microfilms 301449 – Mladen Lorković, Report of Hivzija Košarić to M. Lorković, foreign minister, on the trip to Turkey of 20 July 1942].
29. Kisić Kolanović (note 4), vol.2, pp.119–34.
30. HDA, RSUP SRH SDS, 012.0.60, Dosje V. Židovec [The V. Židovec File].
31. Kisić Kolanović (note 4), vol.1, p.762.
32. HDA, RSUP SRH SDS, 013.0.56; V. Židovec (note 13), pp.255–6.
33. HDA, MVP NDH, Poslanstvo u Rumunjskoj [Embassy in Romania], mf. 2, im. 299, Poslanstvo u Bukureštu, Izvješće B. Benzona [Embassy in Bucharest, Report of B. Benzon], V.T. no. 72/42, TI, 23–29 November 1942.
34. Dušan Lukač, *Treći Rajh i zemlje jugoistočne Evrope 1941–1945* [*The Third Reich and the Southeast European Countries 1941–1945*], (Beograd, 1987), vol.3, pp.502 and 527.
35. Kisić Kolanović (note 4), vol.1, pp.751–2.
36. Nikola Rušinović, *Moja sjećanja na Hrvatsku* [*My Memories of Croatia*] (Zagreb, 1996), p.184.
37. Kisić Kolanović (note 4), vol.2, pp.638–46. Rušinović confirmed that the rupture of diplomatic relations with Germany caused 'panic' in Turkey. As a result the government kept officially emphasising that this was in no way tantamount to a 'declaration of war'. Diplomatic staff were evacuated from Ankara, and a large number of civilians retreated from big cities to villages.
38. Ibid., p.44–5.
39. Ibid., vol.1, p.446.
40. Umeda asked the director of the Bulgarian press, Aleksandar Nikolaev, to make enquires at court as to whether the 'Bulgarian emperor would like to become in the same time Ukrainian ruler'. The answer was that the emperor 'does not see any possibility at all of something like this becoming reality'. Umeda also kept convincing Židovec that 'a close alliance between Ukraine and Bulgaria would be in the interest of Germany'; ibid., vol.2, pp.45–7.
41. N. Kisić Kolanović, Mladen Lorković, Ministar urotnik, Zagreb, 1998, p.228.
42. Kazuichi Miura, *Japanac o Japanu* [*A Japanese on Japan*], Nakladna knjižara Velebit, Zagreb 1944, p.12.
43. Rušinović, *Moja sjećanja* [*My Memories*], p.182.
44. Kisić Kolanović (note 4), vol.1, pp.357–8. For Umeda it was not unexpected that 'war will take place, that Yugoslavia will be ruined and that free Croatia will be created under the leadership of *Poglavnik*'. He had sent such a report before the breakdown of Yugoslavia, and when the NDH was proclaimed, he did not hide his interest in taking over the duty of Japanese 'observer' in Zagreb.
45. Ibid., vol.2, pp.428–30.
46. Ibid., pp.68–73.
47. Ibid., pp.169–72.
48. HDA, RSUP SRH, SDS, V. Židovec, Moje sudjelovanje u političkom životu, p.252.

49. Kisić Kolanović (note 4), vol.2, p.150. Also see: HDA RSUP SRH, 012.0.60, V. Židovec, Dodatak sistemtskom i stvarnom kazalu, Bilješka od 12. ožujka 1948. godine [Appendix to Systemic and Actual Index, Annotation of 12 March 1948].
50. Ibid., pp.428–9. It is interesting that as early as September 1942 the Japanese ambassador in Bucharest presented the view that 'Italy, as a matter of fact, must be rewarded for its victims, but the Mediterranean Sea cannot become Italian sea because the Germans also have interest in it for its trade'. He also stated that Japan expected that in the new order 'Europe will be under the leadership of Germany', while Japan would dominate in Asia, which would need a lot of industrial products, which would be supplied 'from settled Europe'. Also compare: HDA, Poslanstvo NDH u Bukureštu, mf. 2, im. 265, Poslanstvo u Bukureštu, Izvješće B. Benzon, V. T. no.60/42, 27 September to 4 October 1942.
51. HDA, RSUP SRH, V. Židovec, Zapisnik saslušanja kod Udbe za Hrvatsku od 1. listopada 1947. godine [Minutes of interrogation at Udba for Croatia of 1 October 1947].
52. Kisić Kolanović (note 4), vol.2, pp.497 and 501.
53. HDA, RSUP SRH, V. Židovec, Zapisnik saslušanja kod Udbe za Hrvatske od 1. listopada 1947. godine [Minutes of interrogation at Udba for Croatia of 1 October 1947].

Personalities in the History of the NDH

Compiled by SABRINA P. RAMET
Checked and corrected by MARIO JAREB and JAMES J. SADKOVICH

Artuković, Andrija (1899–1988) served as Minister of the Interior in the NDH. As a young man, Artuković studied at the Franciscan monastery at Široki Brijeg, Herzegovina. In 1932 he led the Ustaša uprising in Lika. As the minister responsible for overseeing the network of concentration camps in the country, Artuković was implicated in the mass murder of Serbs, Jews, Roma, and others. After the war, he escaped from the country and made his way to California. After repeated requests from the Yugoslav government for his extradition, he was finally extradited in 1986 and stood trial, receiving the death sentence for his war crimes. Given his advanced age, the authorities decided against execution and Artuković died in a prison hospital at the age of 88.

Budak, Mile (1889–1945) served as Minister of Education and Religious Affairs in the NDH, later becoming Foreign Minister. The author of novels and plays glorifying the peasantry, Budak earned a law degree from the University of Zagreb in 1920 and became an active member of the Croatian Party of Right (HSP). After surviving an attempt on his life in 1932, he moved to Italy and joined the Ustaša movement. He became *doglavnik* (deputy commander) of the Ustaše in 1934 – a title which he continued to hold during the war. In summer 1938 he returned to Zagreb, and in 1939 he launched the weekly newspaper, *Hrvatski narod,* which was banned in 1940. His first post in the NDH was serving as the NDH's envoy in Berlin and minister-plenipotentiary to the Third Reich. In his capacity as Minister of Education and Religious Affairs, he co-signed (with Ante Pavelić) a decree on the Croatian language in August 1941, in which people were forbidden to pronounce or spell words in ekavian (Serbian) or to use non-Croatian words to identify shops, companies, or associations. Captured by Tito's Partisans in May 1945, he was put on trial, convicted, and executed. Budak is remembered today, among other things, for a speech in spring-summer 1941, in which he expressed his desire to expel 'disloyal' Serbs from Croatia.

Draganović, Krunoslav (d. 1982) was a Catholic priest and one of the principal coordinators of the 'ratlines' through which Ustaše war criminals escaped to Argentina, Paraguay, and other countries. He is thought to have been instrumental in arranging for Pavelić's escape to Argentina. Born in Travnik and educated at the Papal Oriental Institute and the Gregorian Institute in Rome, Draganović served as secretary to Archbishop Ivan Sarić in Sarajevo. In August 1943 he returned to Rome, where he became secretary of the Croatian Papal Institute of Saint Jerome. In 1967, Draganović was kidnapped by Yugoslav authorities and brought back to Sarajevo, where he gave a press conference in which he praised communist leader Josip Broz Tito's political system. He died in Sarajevo in June 1982.

Filipović-Majstorović, Miroslav (1915–46) was the commandant of the Jasenovac concentration camp during the Second World War. Born Miroslav Filipović, he joined the Franciscan Order in 1938 and completed his theological examinations in Sarajevo in January 1942. At that point, he became a military chaplain for the Ustaše. After his unit raided three Serb Orthodox villages, killing some 2,730 Serbs, he was suspended from the Franciscan order, and following an investigation into the incident, he was expelled from the order. Meanwhile, Filipović was rising in the ranks of the Ustaše under the name Miroslav Majstorović. He served for four months as commandant of the Jasenovac concentration camp beginning in autumn 1942. Although he had been expelled from the Franciscans, he continued to wear clerical robes while running the Jasenovac camp. He was sentenced to death and hanged.

Francetić, Jure (1912–42) was commander of all active service brigades of the Ustaša Militia, with the rank of colonel. Born in Otočac, he studied law in Zagreb, joining the Ustaša organisation in 1931. Arrested in Zagreb in 1933 on charges of hostile propaganda, he was exiled for five years. During this time, he went to Hungary, becoming adjutant to Vjekoslav Servatzy, commander of the Janka Puszta camp. After the assassination of King Aleksandar, he was interned but later amnestied. He returned to Croatia in November 1939, and, after the formation of the NDH, Francetić was named captain of the Poglavnik Bodyguard Battalion in June 1941. In September 1941, he formed the Battle Group Francetić, better known as the Black Legion, fighting primarily against the Partisans, but also against the Chetniks, in eastern Bosnia and earning a reputation for brutality. Francetić rose rapidly through the ranks, and by June 1942 had been promoted to colonel. In August of that year, he was named commander of all active service brigades of the Ustaša Militia. In December 1942, in combat with Partisan units he suffered head wounds, and a few days later he died in captivity in Slunj. In March 1943 he was posthumously promoted to the rank of Ustaša general.

Kasche, Siegfried (1903–1947) was the German envoy in Zagreb from April 1941 to May 1945 and SA-Obergruppenführer (SA-Higher Group Leader). In 1925, Kasche joined the SA (*Sturmabteilung*, usually translated as Storm Troopers), and in January 1926 he joined the Nazi Party. By September 1930, he was a deputy in the Reichstag (the German parliament). In November 1937, he was named leader of the SA Group in Hansa, attaining the rank of Obergruppenführer. On 17 April 1941, he was appointed Ambassador First Class to the NDH. During the war years, he tried to justify the terror against Serb civilians living in the NDH. As the military situation in Croatia deteriorated, Kasche's influence in Berlin diminished. After the war, he was turned over to Yugoslav authorities by the Allies. He was put on trial and sentenced, on 7 June 1947, to be hanged. The sentence was carried out in Zagreb on 19 June 1947.

Kulenović, Džafer (1891–1956) was vice president of the NDH for most of the war. Born in Rajnovići, Sandžak, he became president of the Yugoslav Muslim organisation in 1939, upon the death of Mehmed Spaho. The post of vice president of the NDH was initially held by Džafer's elder brother, Osman, but Džafer assumed the post in November 1941, retaining the position until the collapse of the NDH. Kulenović championed the idea of the unity of Catholic and Muslim Croats. After the war, he moved to Damascus, Syria, where he remained until his death in 1956.

Kulenović, Osman (1889–1947) served as vice president of the NDH government from April to November 1941, when his brother Džafer succeeded him. Born in Rajnovići, Sandžak, he worked in the NDH Ministry of Foreign Affairs from November 1941 until his retirement in May 1943. He surrendered to the British in May 1945, but was turned over to the new Yugoslav communist authorities, who put him on trial and executed him on 7 June 1947.

Kvaternik, Eugen Dido was one of the original members of the Ustaša movement when it was organised in exile. He was the leading figure in the plot to assassinate Yugoslav King Aleksandar in 1934. He headed the Directorate of Public Order and Security in the Ministry of the Interior during the NDH's first 18 months. Later, he and his father Slavko had a falling-out with Pavelić, and in autumn 1942 his father resigned his posts; in 1943, father and son took refuge in Slovakia. In 1957 Eugen Dido Kvaternik died in a car accident in Argentina, together with his two daughters.

Kvaternik, Slavko (1878–1947) was a founding member of the Ustaša movement in 1931 and served as deputy leader of the Ustaša regime during the Second World War. He had been a lieutenant-colonel in the Austro-Hungarian Army during the First World War, defecting to the new army of the National Council of Slovenes, Croats, and Serbs, which was established at the end of 1918, assuming the post of army chief of staff. In that capacity, he commanded Croatian troops in Medjimurje in a successful campaign against the Hungarian army. A close confidant of Ante Pavelić, Kvaternik was the one who proclaimed the establishment of the NDH on 10 April 1941. From April 1941 to October 1942, Kvaternik served as commander-in-chief of the NDH armed forces. After the war he lived for a while in Austria, before local authorities turned him over to the Yugoslav government, which put him on trial and had him executed.

Lorković, Mladen (1909–1945) was named foreign minister in the second NDH government, Pavelić having held the post briefly during the first months of the NDH. In that capacity, it was Lorković who agreed that the NDH would accept a portion of the population being expelled by German occupation authorities from Slovenia, in 'exchange' for an equal number of Serbs to be expelled from the NDH to Serbia. In the 1930s, he had written a highly influential book, *Narod i zemlja Hrvata* (*The People and the Land of the Croats*), published in 1939. He served as Minister of the Interior from 13 October 1943 to 31 August 1944. In summer 1944, Lorković and Ante Vokić, a fellow Ustaša, both of whom had become disenchanted with NDH policies and wanted to secure a separate peace with the Allies, hatched a plot to remove Pavelić from power and install a government headed by the Croatian Peasant Party. Their plot was discovered and Lorković was executed, together with Vokić.

Luburić, Vjekoslav 'Maks' (1913–69) held several important posts in the NDH, including that of commander of the Army of the Drina in the initial months of the war. Born Vjekoslav Luburić in a mountainous area of Herzegovina, he lost his father shortly after the end of the First World War and grew up in poverty. As a student, he took part in demonstrations and came into conflict with the police, spending time in jail. In the early 1930s, he made his way to Hungary, where he made contact with Croatian émigrés and joined the Ustaša organisation. Arriving at the Ustaša training camp Janka Puszta, he met Jure Francetić, who became a lifelong friend and who gave him the name 'Maks'. When he first arrived, Gustav Perčec was commander of Janka Puszta, but in late 1933, Vjekoslav Servatzy became camp commander. Later, after the establishment of the NDH, he organised the concentration camp at Jasenovac and served as its first commandant. After the end of the war, he briefly commanded a small paramilitary group of former Ustaša militiamen. In May 1945, Luburić led remnants of the NDH army to British lines in order to surrender to Great Britain. But the British turned them over to the Yugoslav communists, who slaughtered most of them. Luburić managed to escape and later took part in the activities of Croatian émigré organisations in Germany, Spain, Sweden, Canada, and elsewhere. On 20 April 1969, Luburić was killed by an agent of UDBa, the Yugoslav secret service.

Maček, Vladko (1879–1964) was head of the Croatian Peasant Party (CPP) after the assassination of the erstwhile head of the party, Stjepan Radić, in 1928. Born in Jastrebarsko (southwest of Zagreb), Maček earned a law degree at the University of Zagreb and in 1908 opened a private law practice. He was a member of the CPP from its inception. As head of the party, Maček was confronted with the same challenge with which Radić had been faced: how to end the widespread discrimination against Croats and the persistent assault on Croatian values, culture and institutions. Soon after Maček became party leader, King Aleksandar proclaimed a royal dictatorship, banned the CPP, and placed half a dozen Croatian politicians, including Maček, under constant surveillance. During the years 1929–34, Maček remained in contact with Ante Pavelić and August Košutić, Radic's son-in-law and vice president of the CPP. In November 1932, Maček joined other leading opposition politicians in signing the 'Zagreb Points', charging the authorities with Serb hegemonism and the destruction of Croatian values and institutions. Because of this, Maček was arrested on 31 January 1933, convicted of having violated the law on the security of the state, and sentenced to three years in prison (though he was amnestied in December 1934 after having served just 20 months of his sentence). Given the proliferation of pro-regime and Serb nationalist paramilitaries, the CPP decided to create self-defence units to protect Croat villagers. The first such units emerged in 1934–35, but in 1936, a more formal structure was created, giving birth to the Croatian Peasant Defence forces, comprised of able-bodied Croats of ages 25–40. In spite of this, Maček continued to try to work within the system and, in the 11 December 1938 elections, his list garnered 1,364,524 votes against 1,643,738 claimed for the government list. Since the elections were, in fact, fixed, this strong return induced Belgrade to rethink its policies and, in August 1939, the new prime minister, Dragiša Cvetković, signed an agreement with Maček (the 'Sporazum'), creating the Banovina (governorate) of Croatia, which was sanctioned by royal decree and which was to enjoy wide autonomy. When Axis forces attacked Yugoslavia in April 1941, the Germans asked Maček to agree to serve as prime minister. Maček declined. Distrusted by the Ustaše, he was arrested and incarcerated in Jasenovac concentration camp in October 1941, being transferred a few months later to house arrest in the village of

Kupinec near Jastrebarsko. After the war, he maintained contact with other anti-communist politicians. He died in 1964 in Washington D.C. In 1996 his remains were transferred to Croatia and buried in the Mirigoj cemetery next to the remains of Stjepan Radić.

Pavelić, Ante (1889–1959) was the Poglavnik (leader) of the Independent State of Croatia (NDH) during the Second World War. Born in the village of Bradina, north of Konjic in Herzegovina, Pavelić moved to Zagreb as a young adult, to study for a law degree. He joined the Croatian Party of Right [Hrvatska stranka prava], and served as its secretary during the 1920s and as its sole elected deputy in the national parliament. Soon after King Aleksandar proclaimed a royal dictatorship in January 1929, Pavelić fled abroad, making contact with Bulgarian and Macedonian terrorists. In 1931, he co-founded the Ustaša [Rebel] organisation in Italy. Pavelić spent most of the subsequent years in Italy, enjoying the ambivalent hospitality of Italian dictator Benito Mussolini – for some of that time Pavelić and his associates were under de facto house arrest. In April 1941, after the Axis invasion of Yugoslavia, the Germans and Italians conceded Pavelić and his followers power in Croatia. Pavelić and his fellow Ustaše tried to claim the legacy of the Radić brothers and even that of the Croatian liberal, Ante Starčević – in the process effecting a falsification of history. Pavelić's regime also operated a network of concentration camps in which Serbs, Jews, Roma, and others whom the Ustaše considered undesirable were incarcerated and/or liquidated. Pavelić also endorsed the forcible conversion of Serbs to Catholicism, as a way of 'Croat-ising' them, and in the course of the years 1941–45, some 244,000 Serbs were re-baptised as Catholics. In April 1942, a Croatian Orthodox Church was established with Pavelić's blessing, to create an alternate route by which Serbs could become Croats. In May 1945, as the Axis powers went down to defeat, Pavelić fled to Austria, later making his way to Rome and eventually to Argentina. After surviving an assassination attempt in April 1957, Pavelić fled to Spain, where he died in Madrid in 1959.

Šarić, Ivan (1871–1960) was archbishop of Sarajevo during the Second World War and an outspoken supporter of the NDH. Born in Dolac, near Travnik, he entered the seminary in Travnik and was ordained in 1894. Four years later, he was awarded a doctorate by the Seminary Faculty in Zagreb. In 1908, he was named bishop-adjutor of Vrhbosna (Sarajevo) and in 1922 was elevated to archbishop and metropolitan of Vrhbosna. Šarić played an active role in organising the lay movement Catholic Action in his archdiocese. Also in 1922, Šarić launched the weekly newspaper *Nedjelja*, later renamed *Katolički tjednik* [*Catholic Weekly*]. The war forced clergy to take a stand on the politics of the day, and Šarić, having been pro-independence even before the war, chose to identify himself with the Ustaše, not only in the early months but also later. After the war, Šarić fled abroad, settling in Madrid, where he translated the New Testament into Croatian. He died in 1960 in Madrid, and his body was buried in the Church of St. Joseph in Sarajevo.

Stepinac, Alojzije (1898–1960) was archbishop of Zagreb from 1937 to 1960 and during the war years repeatedly protested against the atrocities being perpetrated by the Ustaše. Born in the village of Brezarić in the parish of Krašić, he was drafted into the Austro-Hungarian Army during the First World War and sent to the Italian front. Later, he volunteered for the Yugoslav Legion and served briefly in Salonika. Because of his service in the Yugoslav Legion, he was later given the Star of Karadjordje, an award for heroism. In 1924, he enrolled in the seminary and was ordained in 1930. Four years later he was named coadjutor, with Anton Bauer, of the see of Zagreb, succeeding Bauer as archbishop of Zagreb in 1937, upon the latter's death. When the NDH was first proclaimed, Stepinac welcomed the creation of the new state, and met with Slavko Kvaternik even before the Yugoslav Army had surrendered – for which he was later criticised. During the war, Stepinac welcomed the NDH's proscription of cursing but was revolted by the NDH's persecution and liquidation of Serbs and others, and protested both publicly and privately. On 26 October 1941, for example, Stepinac delivered a public sermon in which he criticised the Ustaša regime for poisoning people's minds and spreading hatred. He also was actively involved in saving Jews during the war. The issue of forced conversions proved a vexing problem. The Ustaša regime wanted to force Serbs to convert to Catholicism, in the belief that the Roman Catholic religion would help to turn Serbs into Croats. Stepinac initially did not want to allow conversions which were not driven by genuine faith in the Catholic religion. But after Serbs implored the archbishop to allow them to convert as the only chance to escape being slaughtered, Stepinac relented and allowed the conversions, but insisted that canonical rules for conversion be respected. After the war, communists throughout Eastern Europe tried to persuade local Catholic prelates to break with the Vatican and set up local 'national' churches which would work with communist authorities. None of them agreed. As a result, Stepinac, along with Archbishops Stefan Wyszyński (in Poland), Josef Beran (in Czechoslovakia), and József Mindszenty (in Hungary), was tried on trumped-up charges and imprisoned. After serving less than five years in prison Stepinac was released and confined to the parish of Krašić, where he died in 1960. In 1998, he was beatified by Pope John Paul II, in recognition of his moral courage in standing up to both the Ustaše and the communists.

von Horstenau, Edmund Glaise (1882–1946) was general-plenipotentiary representing the *Wehrmacht* in the NDH. A former Austrian imperial general staff officer, he later served as director of the Austrian War Archives (1925–38). During 1936–38, he also served as Minister of the Interior in the cabinet of Kurt Schuschnigg. After the *Anschluss*, he joined the German army. During his term in Croatia, he repeatedly criticised the atrocities being perpetrated by the Ustaše. He recorded his impressions of the NDH in his memoirs, which were published as a three-volume set. He died at Langwasser military camp near Nuremberg, Germany.

Bibliography

COMPILED BY SABRINA P. RAMET

Barić, Nikica. *Ustroj kopnene vojske domobranstva Nezavisne Države Hrvatske 1941–1945*. Zagreb: Hrvatski institut za povijest, 2003.
Basta, Milan. *Agonija i slom Nezavisne Države Hrvatske*. Belgrade: Rad, 1971.
Benigar, O. Aleksa. *Alojzije Stepinac, Hrvatski Kardinal*. Rome: Ziral, 1974.
Biondich, Mark. 'Religion and Nation in Wartime Croatia: Reflections on the Ustaša Policy of Forced Religious Conversions, 1941–42', in *Slavonic and East European Review*, Vol.83, No.1 (January 2005): 71–116.
Budak, Mile. *Hrvatski narod u borbi za samostalnu i nezavisnu Hrvatsku državu*. Philadelphia: Izdanje Hrvatskog kola u Sjedinjenim Državama i Kanadi, n.d. (1934?).
Bzik, Mijo. *Ustaška pobjeda. U danima ustanka i oslobođenja*. Zagreb: n.p., 1942.
———. *Ustaški pogledi (1928–1941–1944*. Zagreb: Naklada i izdanje Ustaške tiskare u Zagrebu, 1944.
Čolić, Mladen. *Takozvana Nezavisna Država Hrvatska 1941*. Belgrade: Delta pres, 1973.
Čulinović, Ferdo. *Okupatorska podjela Jugoslavije*. Belgrade: Vojnoizdavački zavod, 1970.
———. *Slom stare Jugoslavije*. Zagreb: Školska knjiga, 1958.
Djurić, Veljko Dj. *Ustaše i pravoslavna crkva*. Novi Beograd: Beletra, 1989.
Giron, Antun and Petar Strčić, *Poglavnikom vojnom uredu. Treći Reich, NDH, Sušak – Rijeka i izvješće dr. Oskara Turine 1943*. Rijeka: Povijesno društvo Rijeka, 1993.
Goldstein, Ivo with Slavko Goldstein. *Holokaust u Zagrebu*. Zagreb: Novi Liber & Židovska općina, 2001.
Goldstein, Ivo et al. *Antisemitizam, holokaust, antifasizam*. Zagreb: Židovska općina, 1996.
Horvat, Rudolf. *Hrvatska na mučilištu*. Zagreb: Hrvatstki Rodoljub, 1942.
Hory, Ladislaus and Martin Broszat. *Der kroatische Ustascha-Staat 1941–1945*. Stuttgart: Deutsche Verlags-Anstalt, 1964.
Jareb, Jere (ed.). *Državno gospodarstveno povjerenstvo Nezavisne Države Hrvatske od kolovoza 1941. do travnja 1945*. Zagreb: Hrvatski institut za povijest, Hrvatski državni arhiv, Dom i svijet, 2001.
Jareb, Mario. 'Njemačka promidžba u Nezavisnoj Državi Hrvatskoj od 1941. do 1945. godine', in Renata Trišler and Nikola Mak (eds.), *Godišnjak Njemačke narodnosne zajednice – VDG Jahrbuch 2001*. Osijek: Njemačka narodna zajednica & Zemaljska udruga Podunavskih Švaba u Hrvatskoj, 2001: 171–97.
———. 'Njemačko novinstvo i periodika u Nezavisnoj Državi Hrvatskoj (1941.–1945.)', in Renata Trišler and Nikola Mak (eds.), *Godišnjak Njemačke narodnosne zajednice – VDG Jahrbuch 2000*. Osijek: Njemačka narodna zajednica & Zemaljska udruga Podunavskih Švaba u Hrvatskoj, 2000: 139–72.

———. 'Odjek zločina u Katynskoj šumi u tisku Nezavisne Države Hrvatske od travnja do lipnja 1943. godine', in *Časopis za suvremenu povijest* (Zagreb), Vol.30, No.1 (1998): 117–30.

———. 'Odnos dr. Ante Pavelića i Ustaško-domobranskog pokreta s Bugarima i Bugarskom od kraja dvadesetih godina do uspostave NDH u travnju 1941', in Josip Bratulić (ed.), *Hrvatsko-bugarski odnosi u 19. i 20. stoljeću*. Zagreb: Hrvatsko-bugarsko društvo, 2005: 125–54.

———. 'Planovi i koncepcije ustaško-domobranskog pokreta od početka tridesetih godina do travnja 1941. o opsegu i granicama buduće nezavisne hrvatske države', in Alexander Buczynski, Milan Kruhek and Stjepan Matković (eds.). *Hereditas rervm Croaticarvm ad honorem Mirko Valentić*, Zagreb : Hrvatski institut za povijest, 2003: 302–14.

———. 'Problematika Nezavisne Države Hrvatske u povijesnoj literaturi od 1990. do 1995. godine', in *Časopis za suvremenu povijest*, Vol.28, No.1–2 (1996): 199–215.

———. 'Ustaški pukovnik i general Tomislav Sertić', in *Časopis za suvremenu povijest*, Vol.32, No.1 (2000): 271–315.

———. *Ustaško-domobranski pokret od nastanka do travnja 1941. godine*. Zagreb: Školska knjiga and Hrvatski institut za povijest, 2005 [2006].

Jelić, Ivan. *Hrvatska u ratu i revoluciji, 1941–1945*. Zagreb: Školska knjiga, 1978.

Jelić-Butić, Fikreta. *Četnici u Hrvatskoj, 1941–1945*. Zagreb: Globus, 1986.

———. 'Noviji prilozi proučavanju ustaškog pokreta i 'Nezavisne Države Hrvatske' u razdoblju 1941–1945. u našoj historiografiji', in *Časopis za suvremenu povijest*, Vol.2 (1970): 195–200.

———. 'Prilog proučavanju djelatnosti ustaša do 1941', in *Časopis za suvremenu povijest*, Vol.1 (1969): 55–92.

———. *Ustaše i NDH*. Zagreb: S.N. Liber & Školska knjiga, 1977.

———. 'Ustaški pokret i hrvatsko nacionalno pitanje', in *Jugoslovenski istorijski časopis* (1969): 185–90.

Kazimirović, Vasa. *NDH u svetlu nemačkih dokumenata i dnevnika Gleza fon Horstenau, 1941–1944*. Belgrade: Nova knjiga, 1987.

Kisić Kolanović, Nada. *NDH i Italija. Političke veze i diplomatski odnosi*. Zagreb: Naklada Ljevak, 2001.

———. *Poslanstvo NDH u Sofiji. Diplomatski izvještaji 1941–1945*, 2 vols. Zagreb: Hrvatski državni arhiv, 2003.

———. 'Podržavljenje imovine Židova u NDH', in *Časopis za suvremenu povijest*, Vol.30, No.1 (1998): 429–53.

———. 'Povijest NDH kao predmet istrazivanja', in *Časopis za suvremenu povijest*, Vol.34, No.3 (2002): 679–712.

———. *Zagreb-Sofija. Prijateljstvo po mjeri ratnog vremena 1941–1945*. Zagreb: Hrvatski državni arhiv i Dom i svijet, 2003.

——— (ed.). *Vojskovodja i politika. Sjećanja Slavka Kvaternika*, Zagreb: Golden Marketing, 1997.

Krišto, Jure. 'Crkva i država: Slučaj vjerskih prijelaza u Nezavisnoj Državi Hrvatskoj', in Hans-Georg Fleck and Igor Graovac (eds.), *Dijalog povjesničara-istoričara I*. Zagreb: Naklada Friedrich-Naumann, 2000.

———. *Katolička crkva i Nezavisna Država Hrvatska, 1941–1945*, 2 vols. Zagreb: Hrvatski institut za povijest, 1998.

———. *Sukob simbola. Politika, vjere i ideologije u Nezavisnoj Državi Hrvatskoj*. Zagreb: Globus, 2001.

Krizman, Bogdan. *Ante Pavelić i Ustaše*. Zagreb: Globus, 1978.

———. *Pavelić izmedju Hitlera i Mussolinija*. Zagreb: Globus, 1980.

———. *Pavelić u bjekstvu*. Zagreb: Globus, 1986.

———. *Ustaše i Treći Reich*, 2 vols. Zagreb: Globus, 1982.

Kudumija, Mato. *Petnaest hiljada vagona smrti. Zapisi o ustaškim zatvorima i logorima Jasenovca i Stare Gradiške*. Pakrac: Ogranak Matice hrvatske, 1966.

Kvaternik, Eugen Dido. *Sjećanja i zapazanja, 1925–1945. Prilozi za hrvatsku povijest*. Zagreb: Starčević, 1995.

Loker, Zvi. 'The Testimony of Dr. Edo Neufeld: The Italians and Jews of Croatia', in *Holocaust and Genocide Studies*, Vol.7, No.1 (Spring 1993): 67–76.

Mataušić, Nataša. *Jasenovac 1941–1945: Logor smrti i radni logor*. Jasenovac and Zagreb: Javna ustanova Spomen-područje Jasenovac, 2003.

Matić, Igor Phillip. *Edmund Veesenmeyer. Agent und Diplomat der nationalsozialistischen Expansionspolitik*. Munich: R. Oldenbourg Verlag, 2002.

Matković, Hrvoje. *Povijest Nezavisne Državne Hrvatske*, 2nd expanded ed. Zagreb: Naklada P.I.P. Pavičić, 2002.

Mužić, Ivan. *Pavelić i Stepinac*. Split: Logos, 1991.

——— (ed.). *Maček u Luburićevu zatočeništvu*. Split: Laus, 1999.

Pattee, Richard. *The Case of Cardinal Aloysius Stepinac*. Milwaukee: Bruce Publishing, 1953.

Pavelić, Ante. *Djela*, 4 vols. Buenos Aires: Domovina, 1968–77.

———. *Die Kroatische Frage*. Berlin: Privatdruck des Instituts für Grenz- und Auslandstudien, 1941.

Pečarić, Josip. *Serbian myth about Jasenovac*, trans. from Croatian by Ivana Pečarić. Zagreb: Stih, 2001.

Petrinović, Ivo. *Mile Budak – portret jednog političara*. Split: Književni krug, 2002.

Popović, Jovo. *Sudjenje Andriji Artukoviću i što nije rečeno*. Zagreb: Stvarnost/Jugoart, 1982.

Požar, Peter. *Hrvatska pravoslavna crkva u prošlosti i budućnosti*. Zagreb: Naklada P.I.P. Pavičić, 1996.

——— (comp.). *Ustaša. Dokumenti o ustaškom pokretu*. Zagreb: Zagrebačka stvarnost, 1995.

Ramet, Sabrina P. *The Three Yugoslavias: State-Building and Legitimation, 1918–2005*. Bloomington, Ind./Washington D.C.: Indiana University Press and The Wilson Center Press, 2006.

Redzić, Enver. *Bosnia and Hercegovina in the Second World War*. New York: Frank Cass, 2005.

Rojnica, Ivo. *Susreti i doživljaji 1938–1945*. Munich: Knjižnica Hrvatske revije, 1969.

Rusinović, Nikola. *Moja sjećanja na Hrvatsku*. Zagreb: Puljko, 1996.

Sadkovich, James J. 'La composizione degli ustascia: una valutazione preliminare', in *Storia contemporanea* (Milano), Vol.11, No.6 (1980): 989–1002.

———. *Italian Support for Croatian Separatism, 1927–1937*. New York/London: Garland, 1987.

———. 'Opportunismo esitante: la decisione italiana di appoggiare il separatismo croato, 1927–1929', in *Storia contemporanea*, Vol.16, No.3 (1985): 401–26.

Samardžija, Marko. *Hrvatski jezik u Nezavisnoj Državi Hrvatskoj*. Zagreb: Hrvatska sveučilišna naklada, 1993.

Steinberg, Jonathan. *All or Nothing: The Axis and the Holocaust, 1941–1943*. London/New York: Routledge, 1990.

Stuparić, Darko (ed.). *Tko je tko u NDH: Hrvatska 1941–1945*. Zagreb: Minerva, 1997.

Sundhaussen, Holm. 'Der Ustascha-Staat: Anatomie eines Herrschaftssystems', in *Österreichische Osthefte*, Vol.37, No.2 (1995): 497–533.

———. 'Zur Geschichte der Waffen-SS in Kroatien 1941–1945', in *Südost-Forschungen* (Munich), Vol.30 (1971): 176–96.

———. *Wirtschaftsgeschichte Kroatiens im nationalsozialistischen Grossraum 1941–1945: Das Scheitern einer Ausbeutungsstrategie*. Stuttgart: Deutsche Verlags-Anstalt, 1983.

Tomasevich, Jozo. *War and Revolution in Yugoslavia, 1941–1945: Occupation and Collaboration*. Stanford, Calif.: Stanford University Press, 2001.

Vojinović, Aleksandar. *Ante Pavelić*. Zagreb: Centar za informacije i publicitet, 1988.

———. *NDH u Beogradu*. Zagreb: P.I.P. Pavičić, 1995.

von Horstenau, Edmund Glaise. *Ein General im Zwielicht. Die Erinnerungen Edmund Glaise von Horstenau*, 3 vols. Peter Brouck (ed.). Vienna, 1980–1998.

Vrancić, Vjekoslav. *Branili smo državu. Uspomene, osvrti, doživljaji*, 2 vols. Barcelona/Munich: Knjižnica Hrvatske revije, 1985.

Žerjavić, Vladimir. *Population losses in Yugoslavia 1941–1945*. Zagreb: Dom & Svijet, 1997.

Anonymous (ed.). *The Third Reich and Yugoslavia, 1933–1945*. Belgrade: Institute for Contemporary History, 1977.

Index

abortion 14, 51
Adana 86
Adriatic 63, 67, 76
Africa 15, 81, 84, 89
agriculture 16, 24, 76
Akšamović, A. 36, 48, 50
albanisation 76
Aleksandar, King 17, 38, 96–9
Alexander III, Tsar 21
Alexander, S. 37, 44, 53
Alliance of State Organisations 65
Allies 3, 52, 65, 67, 81–2, 84–6, 96–7
Americans 81, 84–5, 88
anarchy 28
Anglo-Americans 84–5, 88, 90
Ankara 81–3, 91
Anti-Comintern Pact 75
anti-Semitism 8, 20, 25–6, 40
Antonescu, M. 14, 77–9
Aras, D. 4
Arendt, H. 32
Argentina 95, 97, 99
Arrow Cross 11
Artuković, A. 3, 26–7, 42, 49, 95
Aryans 5–6
Asia 81, 86
Asia Minor 81
atheism 40
Austria 34, 65, 97, 99
Austrians 100
Austro-Hungary 76, 81, 97, 99
Axis 1, 5, 7–8, 15
   Catholic Church 31–2, 39, 41, 50, 52
   foreign relations 78–9, 81, 83–4, 86, 89, 91
   personalities 98–9

Bačka 35
Balkans 8, 12, 14, 16–17
   Agreement 76
   Catholic Church 38
   foreign relations 78–82, 84–91
Banija 22

Banja Luka 5, 22, 32
Banovina 61–2, 98
Basher 85
Bauer, E. 36, 40
Beckerle, A. 78–9, 81, 87
Belgrade 3, 8, 21, 26
   Catholic Church 37, 41, 44, 50
   foreign relations 61
   personalities 98
Benzon, B. 77, 79–80, 84, 88
Berker, A.S. 82, 84
Berlek, T. 26
Berlin 1, 3, 7–8, 76, 86–9, 91, 95–6
Bern 84, 87
Biograd 63
Biondich, M. 6–7, 31–55
Bjeljina 20
Bjelovar 22, 61
Black Legion 96
black market 25
Blagaj 23
Bohemia-Moravia 65
Boka Kotorska 63, 65
Bolsheviks 38, 77, 80, 82–4
Bonefačić 3, 48
Bosanska krajina 22
Bosnia 5, 20, 24–5, 27–8
   Catholic Church 35, 47–8
   foreign relations 64, 83
   personalities 96
Bosnia-Herzegovina 4, 7, 21, 31–2, 34, 37
Bosnian Muslims 4, 32, 34–5, 37, 46, 53
Bosnians 44
bourgeoisie 38
Bozanić, J. 3
Bratislava 78
Brekalo, Z. 48
Brestovac Hospital 26
Brestovac-Sljeme Army Station 26
Britain 76, 81, 86, 89–90, 98
British 50, 83–4, 86, 89, 97–8

Bucharest 8, 77–80, 84, 88–9
Buchenau, K. 7
Budak, M. 19–20, 27, 87, 95
Budapest 78
Buenos Aires 3
Bulgaria 8, 16–17, 75–8, 81–4, 87–91
Bulgarian language 88
Bulgarians 78, 99
Bunjevi 35
Burić 48
Butorac 48

Cairo 50
Cambodia 15
Cape Bona 81
capitalism 12, 38–9
Caranfil 77, 79
Carinthia 67
Catholic Action 36, 99
Catholic Church 2–3, 5–7
   controversies 31–55
   Old 36
   personalities 95, 97, 99–100
   role 12–14, 21, 23–4, 28
Čečene, H. 83
censorship 83
Central Europe 15, 75, 78, 81–6, 91
centralism 33, 35–6
Chetniks 1, 7, 15, 24–5
   foreign relations 53, 64–5, 80
   personalities 96
   role 27–8
China 86, 88
Christians 13–14, 26, 39, 43
Ciano, G. 43, 46, 62
Čiovo 63
Civic Protection 62
civil war 12, 15–16
class 25–6, 36, 38, 51, 65
clericalists 34–5, 37
Codreanu 12
Comintern 15
commerce 82–3
communists 2, 5, 7–8, 12–16
   Catholic Church 32–3, 38–41, 44, 51–3
   foreign relations 62, 64–5, 80, 83–4, 90
   personalities 97–8, 100
   role 22, 27

concentration camps 1–2, 4, 23, 64, 95, 98–9
concentration phase 21
Concordat 36–7, 41
conservatives 34–5, 81, 85
Constantinople 82–3, 85
constitutions 36
conversions 2–3, 6–7, 14, 21, 23–4, 33, 42–50, 99–100
Cornwell, John 31
corporatism 15, 38
Croat People's Party (HPS) 35–7, 47
Croat Union 35
Croatdom 38
Croatian Catholic Bishops' Conference 46
Croatian Catholic Congress 35
Croatian Democratic Union (HDZ) 4
Croatian Domobran Association 4
Croatian language 5, 95, 99
Croatisation 99
Crusaders 36, 47
Čule 48
customs 63
Cyrillic alphabet 5
Czechoslovakia 11, 100
Czechs 4, 34

Dakovo 36
Dalmatia 8, 25–6, 35, 37
   Catholic Church 39, 48, 50
   foreign relations 63–4, 77, 80, 89, 91
Danube 85
decentralisation 36
democracy 17, 36–7, 39–40, 90–1
demography 1
Denmark 75
deportation 21–3, 26, 43, 49
Deutsche Volksgruppe in Kroatien 65
dictatorship 14, 33, 36–8, 40–1, 98–9
Dinara Chetnik Division 64–5
discrimination 42, 52, 98
Djilas, A. 47
Dnjestra 84
Dobrudža 8, 77–8, 87
Dominican Order 3
Draganović, K. 38, 40, 95–6
Dual Monarchy 36
Dubrovnik 42
Đujić, M. 64–5

Dvor na Uni 23

East Asia 86
Eastern Europe 15, 75, 100
Eastern Front 83–4, 88–9
Eastern-rite Catholics 7
economics 2, 12, 15–16, 24–5
   Catholic Church 40
   foreign relations 63, 65, 67, 76, 81
   role 28
education 34
Egypt 81
ekavian 95
Ekremov, M.S. 82
elections 13, 40, 98
emigration 24
England 40
English 81, 88
English language 5, 31
Enlightenment 6
Erdelj 77
espionage 85
ethnic cleansing 32
ethnicity 21, 24–5
European Union 3
evictions 22
excommunication 21
extermination 1, 4, 6, 15, 21

Falconi, C. 32, 54
famine 14
Far East 86
fascists 3–6, 8, 11–12, 15–17
   Catholic Church 13–14, 31, 38–40, 52
   foreign relations 63–5, 75, 90
   role 19, 23, 27
federalism 33, 36
Filipović, T. 48
Filipović-Majstorović, M. 96
Final Solution 31
Finland 75
First World War 15–16, 97–9
foreign relations 7
France 34, 39, 81
Francetić, J. 96, 98
Franciscan Order 19, 27, 32, 35,
   45–8, 95–6
Franco, F. 14
Frangeš, O. 26
Frankists 34–5

freemasons 40–1, 51
French language 82
Freundt, A. 7
Friedlander, S. 32

Gaj, L. 34
Gauleiter 67
gender 5
genocide 4–5, 7, 14–15, 21–2
   catastrophe 24, 26, 28
   Catholic Church 33, 47, 54
German Army 6, 100
German language 20
Germans 1–2, 4–8, 11, 14
   Catholic Church 32, 34, 39, 43, 49,
   51, 53
   foreign relations 61–2, 76, 78–81,
   85–90
   personalities 97–9
   role 19–20, 22–8
Germany 2, 7–8, 11–16, 20
   Catholic Church 39–40
   foreign relations 61–7, 75–6,
   78–81, 83–6, 88–91
   personalities 98, 100
   role 27
Gestapo 65
Glavaš, R. 48
Glina 22–3, 27, 42–3
gold 2
Goldhagen, D.J. 31
Goldstein, I. 6, 8, 19–28, 41
Goldstein, S. 8
Goths 6, 12
Gotovina, A. 3
graffiti 3
Great Depression 37–8, 41
Great Powers 62, 76, 79, 89
Greece 15–17, 76, 81, 88
Greeks 35, 45–7, 77
Gregorian Institute 95
Guberina, I. 38–40, 48
Gudovac 6, 22–3
Gutić, V. 22, 27
Gypsies 21

Habsburgs 33–4, 36, 42
Haeffner 26
hegemony 16, 81–6, 89–90, 98
Herzegovina 23, 25, 35, 37

foreign relations 64
personalities 95, 98–9
role 45, 48
historicism 37
historiography 31–3, 36, 46–7, 53, 75
Hitler, A. 11–12, 14, 16, 39–40, 43, 75, 81, 86, 88–9, 91
Hlinka movement 47
Hochhuth, R. 32
Home Guard Army 67
Home Guard Assembly 27
Hungarians 4, 77–9
Hungary 8, 11, 16–17, 24
Catholic Church 33
foreign relations 76–9, 84, 87
personalities 96–8, 100
Hvar 42

ideology 5–6, 11–12, 15, 19
Catholic Church 33–5, 37–8, 40
foreign relations 64, 75, 80
role 21, 28
Illyrianist movement 34
Imperial Council 88
imperialism 38
individualism 39
institutions 15, 23–4, 35, 38, 63, 65
insurgent movements 80
intelligence services 78, 80, 83, 86–91
intelligentsia 16, 37–8, 45
Internal Macedonian Revolutionary Organisation (IMRO) 6, 12
Iran 81
Islam 7, 14, 46–7, 82
Italian language 20, 65
Italianisation 63
Italians 2, 4–8, 11, 20, 24–6
Catholic Church 49
foreign relations 61, 63, 76, 80–1, 86–7, 89–90
personalities 99
role 28, 34–6
Italy 7–8, 11–13, 15–16, 20
Catholic Church 34, 38–42
foreign relations 61–7, 75–6, 78–9, 81, 84, 86–91
personalities 95, 99
role 23–5, 27
Iv čić, Z. 26

Jamaji, A. 87
Janka Puszta camp 96–7
Japan 7–8, 75, 78, 80, 86–91
Japanese-Soviet Non-Aggression Pact 90
Jareb, J. 3
Jareb, M. 7, 61–7, 95
Jasenovac camp 2, 4, 23, 48–50, 96, 98
Jegow, D. 78
Jelić-Butić, F. 3
Jerusalem 44
Jesuits 48
Jews 1–4, 6, 14, 19–28
Catholic Church 32, 40, 42, 45, 49–51
personalities 95, 99–100
role 64
John Paul II, Pope 32, 54, 100
Juretić, A. 47
Juričev, D. 46–8

Kahnic 36
Kamber, D. 42, 44
Karlovac 75
Kasche, S. 65, 78, 96
Kaštela 63
Katolički list 2
Khmer Rouge 15
Killinger, M. 78–9
Kisić Kolanović, N. 3, 7–8, 75–91
Knin 25, 27, 64–5
Komar, S. 27
Konavle 63
Korčula 63
Kordun 22, 64
Košarić, H. 83
Kostajnica 23
Košutić, A. 83, 98
Kotor 42
Kovalevski, N. 80
Kporivnica 23
Krajina 3
Krizman, B. 3
Krk 34, 36, 42, 63, 66
Kulenović, D. 96–7
Kulenović, O. 96–7
Kulmer, M. 35
Kus-Nikolajev, M. 38
Kvaternik, E.D. 2, 24, 26–7, 50, 97
Kvaternik, S. 42, 50, 61–2, 97, 100

labour 38
languages
 Bulgarian 88
 Croatian 5, 8, 95, 99
 English 5, 31
 French 82
 German 20
 Italian 20, 65
 Polish 88
 Russian 88
 Serbian 5, 95
Lasić, V. 3
Laval, P. 39
Laxa, V. 24
League of Communists of Yugoslavia 33
Lewy, G. 32
liberals 3, 5–6, 34–6, 38, 77
Lika 23, 37, 64
Ljubliana 35
London 44, 81, 85
Lorković, M. 27, 51, 67, 79, 87, 90, 97
Luburić, V.M. 24, 27, 97–8
Ludin, H. 78
Lutheran Church 7, 46–7

Macedonia 87
Macedonians 99
Maček, V. 7, 19, 61–2, 67, 98–9
Madrid 3, 99
Magdić, M. 38, 40
Maglione, L. 43, 51, 54
Magyars 34
Mahnič, A. 34
Majer, L. 26
Makanec, J. 51
Malletke, W. 7
malnutrition 25
Manchukuo 75
Maribor 83
Marx, K. 39
Marxism-Leninism 13
Marxists 3, 21, 39
materialism 39
Mažuranić, Z. 26
media 19–20
Mediterranean Sea 89
Medjimurje 8, 76–9, 97
Menemencioglu, N. 85
Mentes, V. 84

Mesić, S. 3–4
mesocracy 16
Metaxas 17
Middle East 81
mimetics 12
minerals 2
Ministry for Foreign Affairs 83, 97
Ministry of the Interior 4, 97
Ministry of Justice and Religion 7, 45, 48
Mišić, A. 45, 48, 50
missionaries 45
Miura, K. 87
Mljet 63
monetary union 63
monks 14
monopolies 38
Montenegrins 22
Montenegro 22
Moscow 81, 87–8, 90
Mosner, S. 83
mosques 82
Mostar 48, 50
Mujagić, M. 83
Muslims 6–7, 64, 82–3, 85
 Bosnian 4, 32, 34–5, 37, 46, 53
 personalities 96–7
 role 28
Mussolini, B. 6, 12, 16, 75, 98

Naderizović, N. 83
National Council of Slovenes, Croats and Serbs 97
National Party 34
National Socialism *see* Nazis
nationalists 2, 7, 12, 14–16
 Catholic Church 33–42, 48
 foreign relations 64, 80, 91
 personalities 98
Natural Law 5
navy 63
Nazi Party 65, 96
Nazis 4, 6–8, 12, 14
 Catholic Church 32, 38–40, 55
 foreign relations 62, 64, 67, 78, 86
 role 16, 19, 21–2, 27
Nazor, V. 27
Near East 81, 88
Nedić, M. 1–2, 11
Neubacher, H. 21

New European Order 39, 64, 76–81, 86, 88, 91
Nezavisna Dtržava Hrvatska (NDH)
   Catholic Church 31–55
   comparative perspective 11–17
   introduction 1–8
   Italy/Germany relations 61–7
   personalities 95–100
   road to catastrophe 19–28
   SE Europe/Turkey/Japan relations 75–91
Nikolić, V. 3
Northern Africa 81, 84
Norway 11
nostalgic-apologetics 3
Nova Hrvatska Desnica (NHD) 3

Office for Public Order and Security 4
oil 2
one-party rule 6, 13, 15
Operation Barbarossa 81
Orozović, E. 48
Oršanić, I. 38, 40
Orthodox Church 6, 14, 24, 26–7
   Catholics 32–8, 40–1, 44–7
   foreign relations 64
   personalities 96, 99
Oshima, H. 89
Ottomans 37, 47

Pacific 88
Pact of Non-Agression and Friendship 81
Pan-Slavism 87
Papal Institute of Saint Jerome 95
Papal Oriental Institute 95
Paraguay 95
Paris 86
Partisans 1–3, 5, 7, 13–16
   Catholic Church 32, 48–9, 53
   foreign relations 64–5, 80, 83
   personalities 95–6
   role 24, 27–8
Party of Right 34–5, 37, 95, 99
Pavelic, A. 1, 3–4, 7, 12, 16, 19–24, 27–8, 39, 42–3, 45–50, 54, 61–3, 67, 76, 81, 85, 89–90, 95, 97–9
Pavelić, V. 4
Payne, S.G. 5–6, 11–17

Peasant Party (HSS) 17, 19, 33, 35–9, 41, 52, 61–2, 67, 83, 97–8
peasants 12, 16–17, 21–2, 25, 38, 80, 95
People's Peasant Party (HPSS) 34
Perić, V. 82
Pétain, H-P. 6, 39
Petrov, S.C. 77
Pilar, I. 38
Pius XI, Pope 40
Pius XII, Pope 31–2, 46, 51, 53–4
Plenipotentary General 65
Plesioianua 81
Pobedonostev, C.P. 21
Poglavnik 4, 45–6, 51, 62, 85, 96, 99
pogroms 21
Poland 16, 39, 100
Poles 34
Polish language 88
Polyak, S. 79
Popular Front 15
populism 12
pornography 14, 51
Prašek, V. 26
Progressive Party 34
Progressive Youth 34
propaganda 5, 8, 20, 40
   Catholic Church 48, 52
   foreign relations 62–3, 77–8, 80, 85
   personalities 96
Protestantism 41
Public Order and Security Directorate 24
public silence 49–54
Puc, R. 26
Puk 27

Quisling, V. 11

Rab 63
Race Laws 42, 49
racialism 6, 12, 15, 27, 64
racism 2, 4, 8, 32
   Catholic Church 39, 49, 51, 54
   role 67, 90
Rački, F. 34, 36
Radev, S. 77
Radić, S. 5, 34–5, 37, 98–9
Radio Station Zagreb 62
Rainer, F.A. 67
Ramet, S.P. 1–8, 95, 101

Index

Rapotec, S. 50–1
rationalism 6
rationing 25
ratlines 95
Red Cross 50
refugees 50
religion 5, 8, 12–14, 25–6
   Catholic Church 33–5, 37–8, 47–8
   foreign relations 64, 83
Religious Section (VO) 46–8
resistance 15, 25, 33, 83, 89, 91
Rittig, S. 49
Roma 1, 6, 8, 19
   Catholic Church 32, 42
   personalities 95, 99
   role 21, 25
Roman Catholic Church 7, 24, 46, 100
Roman Treaties 63, 67, 75
Romania 8, 12–14, 16–17, 75–9, 81, 84, 88
Romanian Legion of the Archangel Michael 13
Romanians 77–81
Rome 7, 36, 50–1, 54, 86, 91, 95, 99
Rome Agreement 23, 25
Rosenberg, A. 7
rural areas 35, 38, 64
Rušinović, N. 50–1, 54, 85, 87
Russia 12, 15–16, 21, 82–3, 85, 89–90
Russian language 88
Russians 89

Sadkovich, J.J. 95
Šahinović Ekremov, M. 82
Salazar, A. 14
Saracoglu, S. 85
Sarajevo 25, 27, 34, 36
   Catholic Church 50, 52
   foreign relations 82
   personalities 95–6, 99
Šarić, I. 36, 48–50, 52, 95, 99
schisms 36, 41
Second Italian Army 76, 89
Second World War 1–3, 15, 28, 31–3, 40, 91, 96–7, 99
secret services 83, 88, 98
Senj 42
Serbdom 38
Serbia 1–3, 5, 11, 16
   Catholic Church 38, 50
   foreign relations 77, 90
   personalities 97
   role 22
Serbian language 5, 95
Serbs 1–7, 15, 19–28, 31–5
   Catholic Church 37, 40–7, 49–51
   foreign relations 64–5, 77, 84–5
   personalities 95, 97–100
Servatzy, V. 96, 98
sheriat 83
Šibenik 42, 63
Siberia 88
Šibl, I. 27
Simović, D. 44
Šimrak, J. 35
Slavinje 23
Slavs 6, 12, 34, 36, 38, 77, 87, 90
Slovakia 11, 14, 40, 47, 75–9, 97
Slovaks 4–6, 34, 77, 79–80
Slovene People's Party 35–7
Slovenes 4–5, 22–3, 34–5, 43, 49–50, 67
Slovenia 5, 35, 37, 43, 65, 97
socialists 4–5, 38
Sofia 8, 75–80, 82–9, 91
Šolta 63
South Slav Question 38
Southeast Europe 7–8, 75–91
Soviet Union 22–3, 40, 52, 81–91
Spaho, M. 96
Spain 3, 8, 13–14, 16, 75, 98–9
Spalatin, K. 38–9
Split 42, 63
Sporazum 37, 98
Stadler, J. 34–5
Stalin, J. 15
Stamboliski, A. 16
Starčević, A. 5, 34, 37, 99
starvation 25
Steigmann-Gall, R. 13
Stepinac, A. 2–3, 7, 23, 32–3, 40–6, 48–54, 99–100
Stolac 23–4
Strossmayer, J.J. 34–6
Suez Canal 81
Sufflay, M. 5
Sušak-Čabar 63, 66
Swiss 50
Switzerland 87
synagogues 49
syndicalism 38

Syria 97
Szalasi, F. 11–12

Tanriörf, S. 84
terrorists 12–13
Third Reich 5–6, 15, 19, 32
   Catholic Church 39, 41, 50, 52
   foreign relations 61, 64–5
   personalities 95
third way 12
Third World War 90
thirds formula 21, 23
Thompson, M.P. 4
Tisó 6
Tito, J.B. 3, 53, 64, 95
Tokyo 87–8, 90
Tomic 27
trade 82–3
Transylvania 77–9
Travnik 83, 95, 99
treason 41–4
Tripartite Pact 75–6, 78, 86
Trogir 63
Troll-Oberfell, H. 1
Tudjman, F. 2–4, 33
Tunis 81
Turkey 7–8, 75, 81–6, 88–91
Turks 50, 82

Übermensch 40
Ukraine 80, 87, 89, 91
Ukrainians 4
Umeda, R. 80, 86–90
Uniate Church 35, 45–7
unitarists 36
United States 3, 86, 88–90
urban areas 35, 38
USSR *see* Soviet Union
Ustaša Surveillance Service (UNS) 4
Ustaša 1–2, 4–8, 11–16, 19–28
   Catholic Church 31–3, 36–40, 42–7, 49
   clergy 47–9, 54
   Control 24
   Defense 4
   foreign relations 61–2, 64–5, 67, 76, 80, 83, 91
   Militia 96
   Movement 62
   Party 1, 6–7, 33, 46, 48

   personalities 95–100
   public silence 49–52
   Youth 40
usury 20

Vatican 14, 31, 36, 41
   personalities 100
   role 43, 46, 50–1, 53–4
Veljun 22
Vichy France 6, 11, 84
Vidovdan 22, 36
Vienna 62, 87
Vienna Resolution 35
violence 5–6, 15, 19, 43, 45, 49, 51–3, 89
Vladivostock 88
Vokić, A. 67, 97
Volksdeutsche 4, 65
von Horstenau, E.G. 1, 26, 51, 65, 100
von Papen, F. 85
von Ribbentrop, J. 62
von Veesenmayer, E. 61–2
Vukovac, S. 27

war crimes 2–3, 32, 54, 64, 95
War of Yugoslav Succession 3, 5
Warsaw 87
Wehrmacht 1, 100
Western Europe 15
Weygand, M. 39
women 5–6, 15

xenophobia 4

Yalta conference 86
Young Croats 34
youth organisations 6, 15
Yugoslav Army 50, 62, 100
Yugoslav Catholic Bishops' Conference 40
Yugoslav Legion 99–100
Yugoslavia 1–3, 15–16, 19, 25–6
   Catholic Church 32–3, 35–42, 47, 50, 52–3
   foreign relations 61–2, 64, 75–6, 82, 85, 88
   personalities 95–9
Yugoslavism 36

Zadar 3–4, 63, 65

Zagreb 1–8, 19, 21–3, 25–6
    Catholic Church 32, 35–6, 41–5, 47–50, 52
    County District 26
    foreign relations 61–2, 64–5, 75–8, 82–3, 85–7, 89–91
    personalities 95–6, 98–100
    Points 98
    Police Directorate 22
    University 75, 95, 98
Žerjavić, V. 1, 4
Židovec, V. 20, 75, 78–90